P9-DXS-467

Dillard's Presents

Southern Living®

Christmas COOKBOOK

benefiting Ronald McDonald House Charities

Southern Living® Tree available at Dillard's

Merry Christmas

from all your friends at Dillard's.

We are proud to support the

Ronald McDonald House.

The purchase of this book helps families of seriously ill children have a comfortable haven near their child.

Thank you for your generosity.
May your family have a wonderful holiday season and a healthy and prosperous 2018.

Published by Oxmoor House, an imprint of
Time Inc. Books
225 Liberty Street, New York, NY 10281

ISBN-13: 978-0-8487-5485-3

Printed in the United States of America
First Printing 2017

Vice President, Licensing and Brand Development: Kristen Payne

Marketing Manager: Kathryn Lott

Marketing and Homes Fellow: Elizabeth Malinowski

Manager, New Business Development: Laura Ferguson

Senior Editor: Katherine Cobbs

Assistant Editor: April Smitherman Colburn

Project Editor: Melissa Brown

Designer: AnnaMaria Jacob

Recipe Developers and Testers: Time Inc Food Studios, Oxmoor House Test Kitchen, Southern Living Test Kitchen, Cynthia Graubart

Food Stylists: Time Inc Food Studios, Catherine Crowell Steele

Photographers: Time Inc Food Studios, Jean Allsop, Iain Bagwell, Peter Frank Edwards, Becky Luigart-Stayner, Alison Miksch, Helen Norman, Hector Manuel Sanchez

Prop Stylist: Lisa Bailey, Kay E. Clarke, Claire Spollen

Assistant Production Director: Sue Chodakiewicz

Assistant Production Manager: Diane Rose Keener

Copy Editors: Donna Baldone, Adrienne Davis

Indexer: Mary Ann Laurens

Christmas COOKBOOK

YEAR-ROUND *Celebrations*

Believe

HOLIDAY STYLE

For a showstopping tree, a merry mantel, a festive door, and more, look no further than these bright ideas and beautiful decorations from Dillard's to deck your halls with cheer.

1

2

When it comes to creating a festive, inviting space, don't be afraid to mix patterns, textures, and shapes. Layering and mixing keep things fun and fresh all season long.

❶ Classic Christmas motifs never go out of style. Incorporate Old Saint Nick as a nod to tradition and Christmases past. ❷ Neutral colors, such as cream, add softness to your decor and create a warm, inviting atmosphere. Juxtaposing lighter colors with rich reds and greens gives your tree depth and dimension. ❸ Use home accents that you already have, such as a tiered cake stand, to artfully display extra ornaments and ribbon for added texture. ❹ Layer unexpected colors and patterns to create a cheerful and interesting holiday dining experience. Add a fresh bouquet of white roses with red and green accents for the ultimate holiday look. *Products shown available at Dillard's.*

3

4

O, CHRISTMAS TREE

Keep Christmas cheerful year after year by mixing bright, exciting decor with the traditional holiday colors and imagery that loved ones anticipate.

A CLASSIC CHRISTMAS

Christmas traditions are taken very seriously in the South. Celebrate the timelessness of the Southern holiday season by decorating your home in a more customary manner.

Include stand-out ornaments on your tree and plenty of garland and ribbon—items that never go out of style—around your home. Adorn the top of your tree with a large red bow for the perfect finishing touch.

❶ Incorporate blue into your Christmas decor to complement your traditional reds and greens for a well-rounded holiday home. Maybe Elvis was onto something... ❷ Here at *Southern Living* we're having our cake and eating it, too! The traditional white cake is appearing not only in our magazine, but also on our trees this Christmas season. *Products shown available at Dillard's.*

Use natural pieces, such as pinecones, to instantly transform your space into a winter wonderland fit for a Christmas gathering. Nestle the prickly cones (or faux versions attached to sticks) into pine branches for a woodland mantel garland or wreath. Spraypaint mini pinecones and adorn your tree with them for a festive topper. You can also incorporate stalks of cotton into the garland, wreath, or tree to give the scene a decidedly Southern aire.

❶ Nothing says "celebration" like gold accents. Make your home party-ready with a white and gold table setting that includes wine glasses, Champagne flutes, plates and beyond. You'll be rocking around the Christmas tree in no time. *Products shown available at Dillard's.*

SNOW WHITE

Even in the South, snow on Christmas morning just seems right. Replace predictable red and green holiday trimmings with crisp white hues reminiscent of a winter's snow to instantly update and elevate your holiday style, not to mention to cast a peaceful vibe throughout your home.

WARM AND WELCOMING

Sometimes a simple, no-frills (okay, maybe a few frills) look is exactly what's in order to celebrate the season. Look no further than your own backyard for inspiration; pinecones and natural greenery turn your home into a charming holiday haven.

Outdoors or indoors, natural textures and tones give your home the warm and cozy feel that everyone longs for during the cold Christmas season.

1 Who said wreaths had to stay on the front door? Simply place an appropriately sized wreath on an indoor surface for a rustic yet classic Christmas look. 2 *"Sleighbells ring, are you listening?"* Incorporating nostalgic holiday favorites such as sleighs into your holiday decoration makes guests feel right at home in your festive abode. 3 Complement your door decor by adorning porch lights with texured and pattered ribbons, greenery and, yes, more pinecones. *Products shown available at Dillard's.*

A SWEET CELEBRATION

No one appreciates a sweet treat like a Southerner, and for that reason Christmas would be incomplete without a warm batch of gingerbread cookies.

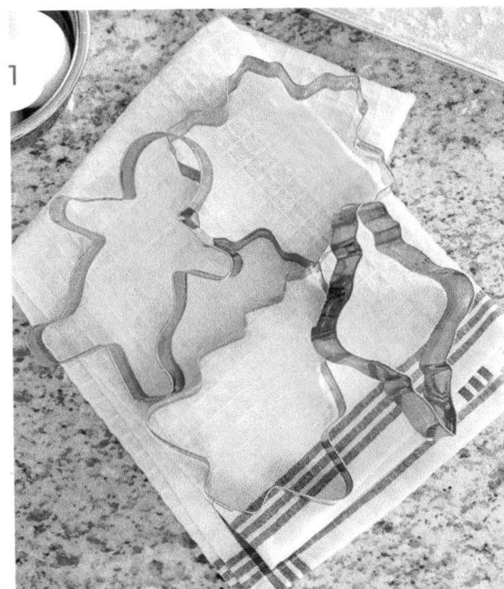

1

2

3

Whether you're indulging with friends or decorating with little ones, having these classic cookies at the ready is a holiday staple that need not be ignored.

❶ While the gingerbread man is a fan favorite, switch things up by using other cookie cutters in shapes such as a snowflake, Christmas tree, or tree ornament. Houseguests will love choosing their favorite sugary goody from among the festive selection. ❷ Nothing pairs better with cookie baking and decorating than a cup of hot cocoa (in a Santa Claus mug, of course!). ❸ As the center of the house, the kitchen should not be forgotten when decorating for the Christmas season. Be sure to spread Christmas cheer into the kitchen and beyond using decorative objects such as snow-white lanterns adorned with bells and bows and vintage-inspired art pieces that will encourage all to embrace the holiday spirit. *Products shown available at Dillard's.*

MERRY MORNINGS

Serve these breakfast goodies like Sausage and Roasted Tomato Ragoût ladled over Smoked Grits and warm Cinnamon-Apple-Bourbon Bread Pudding to early risers for a morning full of warmth, cheer, and satisfaction.

SPICY BLOODY MARYS

Bloody Marys are a classic brunch favorite. Make these easy by setting up your bar with homemade Bloody Mary mix and premium vodka so guests can mix their own. We suggest using Zing Zang Bloody Mary mix for the best results.

SERVES 4 to 6 • **HANDS-ON** 10 minutes • **TOTAL** 10 minutes

1 (32-ounce) bottle Bloody Mary mix
Zest and juice of 1 lime
2 tablespoons prepared horseradish
1 tablespoon Worcestershire sauce
1/4 teaspoon celery salt
4 to 6 ounces vodka
Garnishes: pickled green beans, celery sticks, olives, lime wedges, and whole pickled okra

Stir together the Bloody Mary mix, lime zest and juice, prepared horseradish, Worcestershire sauce, and celery salt in a large pitcher. Serve over ice with a shot of vodka in tall glasses. Garnish, if desired.

GINGER MANGOMOSAS

Try this twist on the traditional mimosa featuring spicy ginger and sweet, rich mango flavors cut with your favorite bottle of bubbly. If you want a sweeter drink, use Moscato instead of Champagne.

SERVES 6 • **HANDS-ON** 5 minutes • **TOTAL** 5 minutes

4 cups orange-mango juice
4 tablespoons ginger juice
Crystallized ginger, cut into 18 small pieces
Sparkling wine

Stir together the orange-mango juice and ginger juice in a large pitcher. Place 3 pieces of crystallized ginger in 6 Champagne flutes, and fill each with equal amounts of the sparkling wine (or Champagne) and juice mixture.

NOTE: We tested with Naked brand orange-mango juice and Ginger People ginger juice.

SMOKED GRITS

Smoky-flavored, creamy grits are a fantastic way to delight your guests at brunch. The smoking process is much easier than you might think. Simply use your stove to impart rich flavor into plain grits, making them a seemingly luxurious ingredient.

SERVES 6 • **HANDS-ON** 20 minutes • **TOTAL** 1 hour, 10 minutes

- 1 cup hickory wood chips
- 1 cup uncooked stone-ground grits
- 3½ cups water
- 2 cups milk
- 1½ teaspoons kosher salt
- 1 cup (4 ounces) shredded Parmesan cheese
- ¼ cup butter

1. Pierce 10 holes in the bottom of a 13- x 9-inch disposable aluminum pan. Arrange the wood chips over the holes. Place the grits on the opposite side of the pan.
2. Place the pan on the stove-top burner with the holes over burner; heat the burner to medium-high until the wood chips begin to smoke. Reduce the heat to medium; cover the pan with aluminum foil, and seal tightly. Cook 2 minutes. Remove from the heat, and uncover; set the foil aside.
3. Remove the wood chips, using tongs, and place on the foil to cool. Transfer the smoked grits to a bowl. (Be careful to not include any wood fragments.)
4. Bring 3½ cups water, milk, and salt to a boil in a medium saucepan over medium-high. Gradually whisk in the grits. Reduce the heat, and simmer, stirring often, 50 minutes or until thickened and tender. Stir in the cheese and butter until melted. Serve immediately.

NOTE: You can also use regular (not stone-ground) grits for this recipe; just reduce the water to 2 cups. We tested with McEwen & Sons stone-ground grits.

SAUSAGE AND ROASTED TOMATO RAGOÛT

Roasting tomatoes and shallots brings out their natural sweetness and amplifies the savory aspects of them as well. To save yourself some valuable time, make this mixture a day or two ahead of time, and store in a container in the refrigerator, as the flavors will deepen over a few days. Serve over Smoked Grits, if desired.

SERVES 6 • **HANDS-ON** 30 minutes • **TOTAL** 55 minutes

- 2 pints cherry tomatoes
- 6 shallots, cut into ¼-inch slices (about 2 cups)
- 2 large fresh thyme sprigs
- ¼ cup olive oil
- Table salt
- Black pepper
- 1 pound smoked hickory sausage, cut into ¼-inch slices
- 1 cup diced sweet onion
- 1 tablespoon chopped fresh thyme
- 2 tablespoons all-purpose flour
- 1½ cups chicken broth
- ¼ cup chopped fresh flat-leaf parsley
- Garnishes: fresh flat-leaf parsley, fresh thyme

1. Preheat the oven to 400°F. Place the first 4 ingredients in a medium bowl; season generously with table salt and pepper to taste, and toss to coat. Pour onto a jelly-roll pan, and spread in an even layer.
2. Bake at 400°F for 25 to 30 minutes or until the tomatoes are very tender and most of the liquid has thickened. Remove from the oven, and cool slightly.
3. Discard the thyme sprigs, and transfer the tomato mixture to a medium bowl, scraping the oil and browned bits from the pan into the bowl.
4. Cook the sausage in a large skillet over medium-high heat 6 minutes or until browned. Transfer to a paper towel-lined plate, reserving 2 tablespoons of the drippings in the skillet.
5. Add the onion and chopped thyme to the hot drippings, and sauté 4 to 5 minutes. Sprinkle with the flour, and cook, stirring constantly, 1 minute. Add the broth, stirring to loosen the browned bits from the bottom of the skillet. Cook until the mixture thickens. Stir in the sausage, tomato mixture, and any accumulated juices from the tomatoes. Reduce the heat to low, and simmer 5 minutes. Season with table salt and pepper to taste. Stir in the parsley. Garnish, if desired.

NOTE: We tested with Conecuh Original Smoked Sausage.

BAKED EGGS IN GARLIC-CREAMED KALE

Individual portions of baked eggs in a ramekin of creamy roasted garlic and baby kale are easy to make ahead and pop in the oven the morning of your brunch. To make this ahead, after Step 2, cool the mixture completely and store in an airtight container in the refrigerator overnight. In the morning, stir the mixture, pick up at Step 3, and add a couple more minutes to the cooking time.

SERVES 6 · **HANDS-ON** 40 minutes · **TOTAL** 55 minutes

1 cup heavy cream
6 garlic cloves, peeled and crushed
Dash of freshly ground nutmeg
1/4 teaspoon table salt
1/4 teaspoon freshly ground black pepper
2 tablespoons olive oil
1 (11-ounce) package baby kale
1/2 cup grated Parmesan cheese
6 large eggs
1 cup panko (Japanese breadcrumbs)
2 tablespoons chopped fresh parsley
1 teaspoon lemon zest

1. Preheat the oven to 400°F. Combine the cream and garlic in a medium saucepan over medium. Bring to a low simmer, reduce the heat, and cook 15 minutes or until the garlic is very tender. Whisk in the nutmeg, salt, and pepper. Remove from the heat.
2. Heat 1 tablespoon of the oil in a large skillet over medium-high. Gradually add the kale, stirring between batches, until the kale is wilted. Cook 4 minutes or until most of liquid has evaporated. Gently mash any whole garlic cloves into the cream mixture. Stir the cream mixture into the kale. Cook over medium heat 5 minutes or until thickened. Stir in 1/4 cup of the Parmesan cheese. Remove from the heat.
3. Coat 6 (10-ounce) ramekins with cooking spray. Place on a jelly-roll pan. Spoon 1/3 cup of the kale mixture into each ramekin. Crack 1 egg into center of each ramekin or mini skillet, and sprinkle with the desired amount of salt and pepper.
4. Bake at 400°F for 15 to 17 minutes or until the whites are set and the yolks are runny, rotating the pan halfway through baking (or as needed for even cooking).
5. Meanwhile, combine the panko, parsley, lemon zest, and the remaining 1 tablespoon oil and 1/4 cup Parmesan cheese in a small bowl.
6. Cook the panko mixture in a small skillet over medium-high, stirring often, 3 to 5 minutes or until the panko is golden and very crispy.
7. Remove the ramekins from the oven, and top with the toasted panko mixture before serving.

SWEET SRIRACHA BACON

Brown sugar and spicy Sriracha cloak crispy bacon slices to make your brunch guests crazy with delight. Do yourself a favor and double this recipe—you will need it! If, however, there are any leftovers, crumble them on a salad or mix into cornbread batter before baking.

SERVES 6 · **HANDS-ON** 15 minutes · **TOTAL** 55 minutes

12 thick-cut hickory-smoked bacon slices
1/2 cup packed brown sugar
3 tablespoons Sriracha chili sauce

1. Preheat the oven to 375°F. Arrange the bacon in a single layer on a lightly greased wire rack in an aluminum foil-lined broiler pan. Bake 10 minutes or just until the edges begin to curl.
2. Meanwhile, stir together the brown sugar and chili sauce in a small bowl until the sugar dissolves.
3. Remove the bacon from the oven, and place in a medium bowl. Add 2 tablespoons of the sugar mixture, tossing to coat. Return the bacon to the wire rack, and brush the tops of the slices with the sugar mixture.
4. Bake at 375°F for 20 minutes. Brush with the sugar mixture, and bake 10 to 15 more minutes or until the bacon is crisp and browned, rotating the pan if needed for even browning.
5. Cool on the wire rack 1 to 2 minutes. Transfer the bacon to a parchment paper-lined plate or pan, and cool 5 minutes (the bacon will crisp as it cools).

Grits and Greens Casserole

GRITS AND GREENS CASSEROLE

This rich and creamy grits casserole is as delicious alongside eggs and brunch dishes as it is with roasted meats and vegetables at your holiday dinner. Serve with your favorite hot sauce or pepper vinegar for authentic Southern flavor.

SERVES 10 to 12 • **HANDS-ON** 25 minutes • **TOTAL** 1 hour

- 10 ounces country ham slices, chopped (about 2 cups chopped)
- 2 tablespoons olive oil
- 1 tablespoon chopped garlic
- 6 cups chicken broth
- 2 cups half-and-half
- 2 cups uncooked stone-ground grits
- 1/2 cup unsalted butter
- 1 cup (4 ounces) shredded sharp white Cheddar cheese
- 1 (11-ounce) package baby kale, lightly chopped
- 1 1/2 cups panko (Japanese breadcrumbs)
- 1/2 cup grated Parmesan cheese
- 1/2 teaspoon freshly ground black pepper

1. Preheat the oven to 350°F. Cook the ham in hot oil in a Dutch oven over medium, stirring often, 10 to 12 minutes or until lightly browned (reduce the heat, if needed). Add the garlic, and cook, stirring often, 1 minute. Add the broth, and stir, scraping the bottom of the Dutch oven to remove the browned bits.

2. Increase the heat to medium-high, add the half-and-half, and bring to a low boil. Stir in the grits. Cook over medium, stirring often, 20 minutes or until the grits are tender and creamy. Add 6 tablespoons of the butter. Stir in the Cheddar cheese and kale, stirring until the cheese and butter are melted and the kale is wilted.

3. Coat a 13- x 9-inch baking dish with cooking spray. Spoon the grits mixture into the prepared dish.

4. Melt the remaining 2 tablespoons butter in a bowl. Add the panko, Parmesan cheese, and pepper, and toss to coat. Sprinkle over the grits mixture.

5. Bake at 350°F for 15 to 20 minutes or until thoroughly heated and the topping is golden brown. Serve immediately.

NOTE: We tested with McEwen & Sons stone-ground grits.

BRIE-AND-SAUSAGE BREAKFAST CASSEROLE

This delicious breakfast casserole features Brie cheese, hot pork sausage, and Parmesan cheese. Serve it at your next brunch or family breakfast for a nice twist on traditional breakfast casseroles.

SERVES 8 to 10 • **HANDS-ON** 17 minutes • **TOTAL** 9 hours, 7 minutes, includes chilling

- 1 (8-ounce) round Brie*
- 1 pound ground hot pork sausage
- 6 white bread slices
- 1 cup grated Parmesan cheese
- 7 large eggs
- 3 cups whipping cream
- 2 cups fat-free milk
- 1 tablespoon chopped fresh or 1 teaspoon dried rubbed sage
- 1 teaspoon seasoned salt
- 1 teaspoon dry mustard
- Garnish: chopped scallions

1. Trim and discard the rind from the top of the Brie. Cut the cheese into cubes; set aside.

2. Cook the sausage in a large skillet over medium-high, stirring until crumbled and no longer pink; drain well.

3. Cut the crusts from the bread slices, and place the crusts evenly in the bottom of a lightly greased 13- x 9-inch baking dish. Layer evenly with the bread slices, sausage, Brie, and grated Parmesan cheese.

4. Whisk together 5 of the eggs, 2 cups of the whipping cream, and the next 4 ingredients; pour evenly over the cheeses. Cover and chill 8 hours.

5. Preheat the oven to 350°F. Whisk together the remaining 2 eggs and 1 cup whipping cream; pour evenly over the chilled mixture.

6. Bake at 350°F for 50 minutes or until set. Garnish, if desired.

*Substitute 2 cups (8 ounces) shredded Swiss cheese, if desired.

WINTER CITRUS SALAD

The fresh, bright flavors of winter citrus temper fennel's sweetness and marry beautifully with the peppery bite of arugula and radishes. You can make the vinaigrette and slice the radishes, fennel, and grapefruit up to one day ahead. Keep chilled.

SERVES 6 • **HANDS-ON** 20 minutes • **TOTAL** 20 minutes

- 8 medium radishes, trimmed
- 1 medium fennel bulb, halved and cored
- 2 Ruby Red grapefruit
- 2 tablespoons minced shallots
- 1 tablespoon chopped fennel fronds
- 2 tablespoons sherry vinegar
- 1 tablespoon Dijon mustard
- 1 teaspoon honey
- ½ teaspoon kosher salt
- ⅛ teaspoon freshly ground black pepper
- ½ cup olive oil
- 1 (5-ounce) package baby arugula

1. Cut the radishes and fennel into very thin slices (about ⅛ inch thick), using a mandoline. Place in a medium bowl.
2. Grate the zest from 1 grapefruit to equal 1 teaspoon. Remove the peel and pith from both grapefruits; cut crosswise into ¼-inch slices.
3. Whisk together the grapefruit zest, shallots, and next 6 ingredients in a small bowl. Gradually add the oil, whisking constantly until blended.
4. Toss the arugula with 3 tablespoons of the vinaigrette; place on a large serving platter. Toss the fennel mixture with 2 tablespoons of the vinaigrette; place on top of the arugula. Arrange the grapefruit slices around the arugula; drizzle with the additional vinaigrette. Serve immediately.

LEMON-ROSEMARY DROP BISCUITS

Bright lemon and rosemary complement the richness of these classic drop biscuits and pair well with a number of toppings, such as sweet, creamy butter or raspberry preserves.

MAKES 14 biscuits • **HANDS-ON** 10 minutes • **TOTAL** 25 minutes

- 3½ cups self-rising soft-wheat flour
- 2¼ teaspoons baking powder
- 3 tablespoons sugar
- 1 tablespoon finely chopped fresh rosemary
- ½ cup cold butter, cut into pieces
- 1 cup cold buttermilk
- ½ cup cold heavy cream
- 1 teaspoon lemon zest
- 1 tablespoon butter, melted

1. Preheat the oven to 500°F. Whisk together the flour, baking powder, 2 tablespoons of the sugar, and rosemary in a large bowl. Cut in the cold butter with a pastry blender or fork until the mixture forms a coarse meal.
2. Whisk together the buttermilk, cream, and lemon zest; add to the flour mixture, and stir with a fork just until the dry ingredients are moistened.
3. Drop dough by ¼ cupfuls 2 inches apart onto parchment paper-lined baking sheets; brush with the melted butter, and sprinkle with the remaining 1 tablespoon sugar.
4. Bake at 500°F for 12 to 15 minutes or until golden brown.

NOTE: We tested with White Lily self-rising flour.

CINNAMON-APPLE-BOURBON BREAD PUDDING

This ooey-gooey decadent bread pudding is a snap to put together and will delight children and adults alike. Using frozen cinnamon rolls makes your job much easier, and your breakfast will still be delightfully homemade in appearance and flavor. If you have leftover cinnamon rolls from a day or two ago, use those and save the extra step of baking frozen rolls for the recipe. The bourbon adds a bit of special flavor but can be omitted, if desired.

SERVES 6 • **HANDS-ON** 15 minutes • **TOTAL** 1 hour, 20 minutes

- **1 (16-ounce) package frozen cinnamon rolls, thawed**
- **2 tablespoons butter**
- **1 large Fuji apple, diced (about 1½ cups)**
- **¼ cup packed brown sugar**
- **½ teaspoon ground cinnamon**
- **¼ teaspoon table salt**
- **3 tablespoons bourbon**
- **2 large eggs**
- **¾ cup half-and-half**
- **1 teaspoon vanilla extract**
- **¾ cup chopped pecans**
- **Garnishes: whipped cream, ground cinnamon**

1. Preheat the oven to 375°F. Break the cinnamon rolls apart, and place 1 to 2 inches apart on a parchment paper-lined baking sheet; reserve the icing packet.

2. Bake at 375°F for 12 to 15 minutes or until browned. Cool 10 minutes; tear into 1½-inch pieces.

3. Melt 1 tablespoon of the butter in a large skillet over medium-high. Add the apple, and sauté 3 minutes or just until beginning to brown. Add 2 tablespoons of the brown sugar, cinnamon, and salt; cook 1 minute, stirring constantly. Remove from the heat, and stir in the bourbon. Cool 10 minutes.

4. Whisk together the eggs, half-and-half, and vanilla in a large bowl; stir in the apple mixture and cinnamon roll pieces. Spoon the mixture into a lightly greased 8-inch square (2-quart) baking dish.

5. Microwave the remaining 1 tablespoon butter in a small microwave-safe bowl at HIGH 30 seconds or until melted; stir in the pecans and remaining 2 tablespoons brown sugar. Sprinkle over the mixture in the baking dish. Place the baking dish in a 13- x 9-inch pan; fill the pan with hot water to reach halfway up the sides of the baking dish.

6. Bake at 375°F for 35 minutes or until golden brown and set (a knife inserted in the center should come out clean). Drizzle the reserved icing over the bread pudding. Garnish, if desired.

NOTE: We tested with Sister Schubert's Bake & Serve Cinnamon Rolls.

BASIC BISCUIT, PANCAKE, AND WAFFLE MIX

This mix can be used to make flaky buttermilk biscuits, fluffy pancakes, and your new favorite waffles.

MAKES about 8 cups • **HANDS-ON** 5 minutes • **TOTAL** 5 minutes

- 6 cups all-purpose flour
- 1½ cups powdered buttermilk
- ¼ cup granulated sugar
- 2 tablespoons baking powder
- 1 tablespoon baking soda
- 1½ teaspoons table salt

Whisk together all the ingredients in a large bowl. Store in an airtight container up to 6 months.

NOTE: We tested with Saco Cultured Buttermilk Blend.

HOMEMADE BISCUITS

These light, fluffy biscuits are tailor-made for slathering with butter or smothering with sausage cream gravy.

MAKES 6 (2½-inch) biscuits • **HANDS-ON** 20 minutes • **TOTAL** 35 minutes

Preheat the oven to 450°F. Cut 5 tablespoons cold butter, cut into cubes, into 2⅔ cups Basic Biscuit, Pancake, and Waffle Mix using a pastry blender. Add ½ to ¾ cup ice-cold water, ¼ cup at a time, stirring with a wooden spoon after each addition (dough will be shaggy and sticky). Turn the dough out onto a lightly floured surface, and knead 3 or 4 times; pat into a ¾-inch-thick rectangle. Cut the dough into rounds, using a 2½-inch round cutter. Place on a parchment paper-lined baking sheet, and bake at 450°F for 15 minutes or until golden brown.

HOMEMADE PANCAKES

For a twist, whisk in 1 cup berries or ½ cup chopped nuts after whisking the mix into the wet ingredients.

MAKES 18 (4-inch) pancakes • **HANDS-ON** 20 minutes • **TOTAL** 25 minutes

Whisk together 1½ cups water, 2 large eggs, and 3 tablespoons canola or vegetable oil (or melted butter). Gently whisk in 2⅔ cups Basic Biscuit, Pancake, and Waffle Mix just until blended (do not overmix), and let stand 5 minutes. Pour about ¼ cup batter for each pancake onto a hot, lightly greased griddle or large nonstick skillet. Cook the pancakes over medium 1 to 2 minutes or until the tops are covered with bubbles and the edges look dry and cooked; turn and cook the other side. Serve with maple syrup.

HOMEMADE WAFFLES

Crisp outside, tender inside, waffles topped with syrup or whipped cream and berries make mornings great.

MAKES 12 (4-inch) Belgian waffles • **HANDS-ON** 20 minutes • **TOTAL** 25 minutes

Whisk 1½ cups water and ½ cup vegetable oil (or melted butter) with 2 large egg yolks. Beat 2 large egg whites at high speed with an electric mixer until stiff (2 minutes). Gently whisk 2⅔ cups Basic Biscuit, Pancake, and Waffle Mix into the oil mixture, and fold in the beaten egg whites. Coat a preheated waffle iron with cooking spray; add ½ cup of the batter to the waffle iron. Cook 2 to 3 minutes or until golden. Serve with maple syrup.

PARTY STARTERS

Get houseguests in the holiday spirit with these vibrant cocktails and delectable small bites such as Fig-Rosemary Rye Smash, Pistachio-Crusted Goat Cheese Log, and Horseradish and Roast Beef Crostini that are guaranteed to amp up any soirée of the season.

TAMARI-ROSEMARY COCKTAIL MIX

Tamari and rosemary add a delightfully different flavor element to the traditional holiday snack mix.

SERVES 15 • **HANDS-ON** 10 minutes • **TOTAL** 1 hour

3 cups roasted, salted whole cashews
3 cups rice cereal squares
3 cups wheat cereal squares
2 cups corn cereal squares
2 cups spicy Asian rice snack mix
2 cups sesame stick snacks
½ cup unsalted butter, cut into pieces
¼ cup tamari
¼ cup finely chopped fresh rosemary

1. Preheat the oven to 350°F. Toss together the cashews, rice cereal squares, wheat cereal squares, corn cereal squares, rice snack mix, and sesame stick snacks in a large bowl.
2. Microwave the butter, tamari, and rosemary at HIGH 30 seconds or until the butter melts, stirring after 15 seconds. Pour over the cereal mixture, tossing until blended.
3. Divide the mixture between 2 lightly greased jelly-roll pans, and spread into an even layer.
4. Bake at 350°F for 8 minutes. Then stir and rotate the baking sheets. Bake 8 more minutes or until golden and crispy. Cool completely on the baking sheets, about 30 minutes.

NOTE: We tested with Rice, Wheat, and Corn Chex Cereals.

BLOOD ORANGE-ROSEMARY FIZZ

At their seasonal peak, blood oranges lend a happy holiday hue to this refreshing cocktail.

SERVES 1 • **HANDS-ON** 5 minutes • **TOTAL** 5 minutes

2 teaspoons fresh rosemary leaves
⅓ cup vodka
1 to 1¼ cups blood orange soda
Garnishes: blood orange slices, fresh rosemary sprigs

Muddle the rosemary and 1 teaspoon of the vodka in a cup. Add the remaining 5 tablespoons vodka, and swirl to combine. Strain into glasses filled with ice, and top with the blood orange soda. Serve immediately. Garnish, if desired.

SPICED ROSEMARY DARK AND STORMY

Inspired by the classic Dark and Stormy, this easy cocktail has a holiday spin with notes of allspice, ginger, and rosemary. The longer the rum is infused with rosemary, the stronger the flavor.

SERVES 8 • **HANDS-ON** 10 minutes • **TOTAL** 8 hours, 10 minutes, includes standing

2 cups spiced rum
3 fresh rosemary sprigs
2 tablespoons Italian spiced liqueur, allspice dram, or other spiced liqueur
1/4 cup fresh lime juice
4 cups ginger beer

1. Combine the rum and rosemary in a 1-pint Mason jar. Seal the jar; let stand 8 hours or up to 1 week.
2. Discard the rosemary from infused rum. Combine the infused rum, spiced liqueur, and lime juice.
3. Divide the rum mixture among 8 tall glasses filled with ice. Top each evenly with the ginger beer. Serve immediately.

NOTE: We tested with Tuaca Italian spiced liqueur.

ELDERFLOWER-POMEGRANATE FIZZ

Look for St-Germain Elderflower liqueur for this recipe.

SERVES 8 • **HANDS-ON** 5 minutes • **TOTAL** 5 minutes

1/4 cup pomegranate liqueur
1/4 cup elderflower liqueur
1/4 cup lemon juice
1/4 cup pomegranate juice
Dry sparkling wine or Champagne, chilled

Stir together the pomegranate liqueur, elderflower liqueur, lemon juice, and pomegranate juice in a small pitcher. Divide among 8 chilled Champagne flutes. Top with the chilled dry sparkling wine or Champagne. Serve immediately

SPARKLING POMEGRANATE PUNCH

There's no better time to break out the punch bowl, and this fizzy, fruity cocktail will help everyone get into the holiday spirit.

MAKES 12 cups • **HANDS-ON** 20 minutes • **TOTAL** 5 hours, 20 minutes, includes freezing

POMEGRANATE ICE RING
3 cups pomegranate arils (seeds)
8 cups ice-cold distilled water

SIMPLE SYRUP
1 cup granulated sugar
1 cup water

PUNCH
3 cups cranberry juice, chilled
1 cup pomegranate juice, chilled
1 (750-milliliter) bottle prosecco, chilled
2 cups vodka
1 1/2 cups chilled ginger ale

1. Make the Pomegranate Ice Ring: Spread the pomegranate arils in an even layer in the bottom of a 12-cup Bundt pan. Pour 1 cup of the ice-cold distilled water over the arils. Place the Bundt pan in the freezer in a level position; freeze until frozen, about 1 hour. Add the remaining 7 cups ice-cold distilled water; freeze until set, about 4 hours. Let stand at room temperature 10 minutes before removing the ice ring from the Bundt pan.
2. Make the Simple Syrup: Bring the granulated sugar and water to a boil in a small saucepan over medium, stirring occasionally. Boil until the sugar dissolves, about 1 minute. Remove from the heat, and cool 30 minutes. Refrigerate in an airtight container up to 2 weeks.
3. Make the Punch: Stir together the cranberry juice and pomegranate juice in a large serving bowl. Stir in the prosecco, vodka, ginger ale, and 1/4 cup of the Simple Syrup. Gently place the ice ring in center; serve immediately.

SOUTHERN RUSSIAN PUNCH

Try Cathead Hoodoo Chicory Liqueur from Jackson, Mississippi, to boost the bold chicory flavor. If you can't find chicory coffee, use any strong brewed coffee to makethis riff on a White Russian. For a festive rim to your cup, dip it in corn syrup and dip again in turbinado sugar before ladling in the punch.

MAKES about 5 quarts • **HANDS-ON** 10 minutes • **TOTAL** 20 minutes

1 cup packed dark brown sugar
1 cup water
12 cups hot strong brewed chicory coffee
6 cups half-and-half
2 cups vodka
1 cup chicory liqueur
1 tablespoon vanilla extract

Stir together the brown sugar and water in a saucepan. Bring to a boil over high. Remove from the heat, and cool 10 minutes. Stir together the coffee, half-and-half, vodka, liqueur, vanilla, and 1/2 cup of the brown sugar syrup in a punch bowl. (Reserve the remaining brown sugar syrup for another use.) Serve warm.

FIG-ROSEMARY RYE SMASH

Sweet-and-savory with a spike of spirit and an herbal syrup infusion, this cocktail is equally delicious with bourbon in place of the rye.

SERVES 2 • **HANDS-ON** 10 minutes • **TOTAL** 1 hour, 5 minutes, includes syrup

- 1/2 cup rye whiskey
- 1 1/2 tablespoons fresh lemon juice
- 2 dashes of lemon bitters
- Garnishes: reserved fig pieces from Fig-Rosemary Honey Syrup, fresh rosemary sprigs, lemon zest strips

FIG-ROSEMARY HONEY SYRUP

- 1/2 cup chopped Mission figs
- 1/2 cup honey
- 1 fresh rosemary sprig
- 2/3 cup water

1. Make the Fig-Rosemary Honey Syrup: Bring all the ingredients to a boil over medium-high in a small saucepan, stirring constantly. Boil until the honey dissolves. Remove from the heat, and let stand 15 minutes. Pour through a strainer into a bowl. Reserve the figs for garnishing the drinks, if desired. Cool the syrup completely, about 30 minutes. Store in the refrigerator up to 1 week. Makes 3/4 cup.

2. Combine the rye whiskey, 1/4 cup of the Fig-Rosemary Honey Syrup, lemon juice, and lemon bitters in a cocktail shaker with ice. Cover with the lid, and shake vigorously until thoroughly chilled, about 30 seconds. Strain into 2 (8-ounce) rocks glasses filled with ice. Garnish, if desired. Serve immediately.

NOTE: We tested with Bulleit rye whiskey and Fee Brothers lemon bitters.

BRUSSELS SPROUT CROSTINI WITH PUMPKIN BUTTER AND HAZELNUTS

This recipe calls for store-bought crostini to help save time, but making your own will always impress your guests.

SERVES 6 to 8 • **HANDS-ON** 20 minutes • **TOTAL** 20 minutes

- 1 pound Brussels sprouts, thinly shaved
- 2 tablespoons olive oil
- 4 garlic cloves, minced
- 1 teaspoon ground coriander
- 1/2 teaspoon kosher salt
- 1/4 teaspoon ancho chili powder
- 1/4 teaspoon ground cumin
- 1 tablespoon sherry vinegar
- 2 tablespoons minced fresh chives
- 1 teaspoon lime or lemon zest
- 3/4 cup homemade or store-bought pumpkin butter
- 30 homemade or store-bought crostini
- 1/2 cup blanched hazelnuts, toasted and coarsely chopped

1. Cook the Brussels sprouts in the hot oil in a large skillet over medium-high, stirring occasionally, until bright green. Cover, reduce the heat, and cook 5 minutes or until just tender.

2. Add the garlic, coriander, salt, ancho chili powder, and cumin. Cook, stirring constantly, 1 minute or until fragrant. Add the vinegar, stirring to loosen the browned bits from the bottom of the skillet. Remove from the heat, and stir in the chives and lime zest.

3. Spread about 1 teaspoon of the pumpkin butter on each crostini. Top with the Brussels sprouts mixture and hazelnuts. Serve warm or at room temperature.

NOTE: We tested with McCutcheon's pumpkin butter.

CALVADOS-BOURBON TODDY

This is a warm and comforting drink with a pleasant aroma and flavor. Warm your mugs before adding the cocktail by filling them with boiling water while you mix the drink together. Empty the mugs when you're ready to fill them with the cocktail.

SERVES 4 • **HANDS-ON** 5 minutes • **TOTAL** 5 minutes

1 cup bourbon
1 cup apple cider, warmed
1 cup boiling water
½ cup Calvados (French apple-flavored brandy)
2 tablespoons fresh lemon juice
2 tablespoons raw wildflower honey
4 cinnamon sticks
Garnishes: lemon zest strips, cinnamon sticks

Combine the first 7 ingredients in a heatproof measuring cup, and pour through a wire-mesh strainer into 4 mugs. Garnish, if desired.

MINI BISCUITS WITH HAM, WHITE CHEDDAR, AND SWEET SHALLOT RELISH

These two-bite appetizers will disappear fast!

SERVES 12 • **HANDS-ON** 40 minutes • **TOTAL** 2 hours, 10 minutes

2 tablespoons butter
1½ cups finely chopped shallots
2 tablespoons brown sugar
3 tablespoons apple cider vinegar
2 tablespoons water
1 tablespoon whole-grain mustard
Table salt
Freshly ground black pepper
3 cups self-rising flour
½ teaspoon baking powder
¼ teaspoon table salt
¼ cup cold shortening, cut into pieces
¼ cup cold butter, cut into pieces
1 cup cold buttermilk
¼ cup butter, softened
8 ounces thinly sliced ham, torn into 2-inch pieces
5 ounces sharp white Cheddar cheese, cut into 24 (⅛-inch-thick) squares

1. Melt the butter in a medium skillet over medium. Add the shallots, and cook, stirring often, 15 minutes or until beginning to caramelize. Add the brown sugar, and cook 1 minute or until the sugar is melted. Stir in the vinegar and water.
2. Bring to a simmer; cook 2 minutes or until reduced and syrupy. Remove from the heat; stir in the mustard, and season with table salt and freshly ground pepper to taste. Cool completely, about 1 hour.
3. Preheat the oven to 475°F. Combine the flour, baking powder, and salt in a large bowl. Cut in the shortening and cold butter with a pastry blender until the mixture forms a coarse meal. Add the buttermilk; stir with a fork until the dry ingredients are moistened.
4. Turn the dough out onto a lightly floured surface, and gently knead 3 or 4 times. Pat the dough to ¾-inch thickness. Cut into 24 rounds, using a 1¾-inch round cutter, rerolling the scraps once. Place the dough rounds ½ inch apart on a parchment paper-lined baking sheet.
5. Bake at 475°F for 11 to 13 minutes or until golden brown. Transfer to a wire rack, and cool completely, about 15 minutes.
6. Cut the biscuits in half horizontally; spread the cut sides with the softened butter. Top the bottom halves of the biscuits with the ham, cheese, and shallot relish. Cover with the biscuit tops.

CHILLED GAZPACHO SHOOTERS

Roasted tomatoes add lots of flavor to this refreshing appetizer. The recipe yields enough for two (1-ounce) shooters each.

SERVES 12 • **HANDS-ON** 20 minutes • **TOTAL** 1 hour, 30 minutes, plus chilling time

4 large vine-ripened tomatoes, halved and cored
2 tablespoons olive oil
1/2 teaspoon table salt, plus more to taste
1/2 teaspoon black pepper, plus more to taste
1 ounce rustic day-old bread, crusts removed
1 cup water
1/2 hothouse cucumber, peeled, seeded, and chopped
1/2 red bell pepper, chopped
1/4 small white onion, chopped
2 garlic cloves, chopped
2 tablespoons fresh basil leaves
2 tablespoons high-quality sherry vinegar
Garnishes: olive oil, micro basil (or other microgreens), smoked paprika, chopped cucumber, chopped red bell pepper

1. Preheat the oven to 425°F. Toss together the tomatoes, 1 tablespoon of the oil, salt, and pepper in a bowl. Transfer to a baking sheet. Bake 30 minutes. Remove from the oven, and cool to room temperature, about 30 minutes.
2. Peel the tomatoes, and discard the skins.
3. Combine the bread and water in a large bowl; let stand 10 minutes.
4. Add the tomatoes and any accumulated juices, cucumber, bell pepper, white onion, garlic, basil leaves, and sherry vinegar to the bread mixture. Season with table salt and pepper to taste.
5. Process the mixture, in batches, in a blender until smooth. Transfer to a bowl. Whisk in the remaining 1 tablespoon oil, and season with table salt and pepper to taste. Chill until ready to serve. Serve chilled in tall shot glasses. Garnish, if desired.

STUFFED ENDIVE WITH HERBED GOAT CHEESE

If desired, include red Belgian endive leaves along with the green, to make this look more Christmasy.

SERVES 12 • **HANDS-ON** 15 minutes • **TOTAL** 15 minutes

1 ounce goat cheese, crumbled
2 ounces cream cheese, softened
1 teaspoon lemon zest plus 1 tablespoon fresh juice
1/4 teaspoon kosher salt
1/4 teaspoon black pepper
2 1/2 tablespoons finely sliced fresh chives
1 1/2 tablespoons finely chopped fresh flat-leaf parsley
2 1/2 teaspoons finely chopped fresh tarragon
24 green Belgian endive leaves

1. Stir together the goat cheese, cream cheese, zest, juice, salt, pepper, 2 tablespoons of the chives, 1 tablespoon of the parsley, and 2 teaspoons of the tarragon in a bowl. Spoon the mixture evenly into the bottom halves of the endive leaves.
2. Combine the remaining 1/2 tablespoon each chives and parsley and 1/2 teaspoon tarragon. Sprinkle evenly over the stuffed leaves. Serve immediately.

Chilled Gazpacho
Shooters

PEPPER JELLY PALMIERS

Leftover puff pastry? Combine it with that beloved Southern pantry staple, pepper jelly, for an addictive holiday party nibble: sweet-and-savory palmiers (the French word for "palm tree").

MAKES about 4 dozen • **HANDS ON** 20 minutes • **TOTAL** 2 hours, 10 minutes

1 (17.3-ounce) package frozen puff pastry sheets, thawed
1 cup finely shredded Parmesan cheese, plus 2 tablespoons
6 tablespoons chopped fresh chives
1/2 teaspoon kosher salt
1/2 teaspoon freshly ground black pepper
1/2 cup hot pepper jelly

1. Roll 1 pastry sheet into a 12- x 10-inch rectangle on lightly floured parchment paper. Sprinkle with half of the cheese, 3 tablespoons of the chives, and 1/4 teaspoon each of the salt and pepper. Roll up the pastry, jelly-roll fashion, starting with each short side and ending at the middle of the pastry sheet. Wrap the pastry tightly with the parchment paper. Repeat the procedure with the remaining pastry sheet, cheese, chives, and remaining salt and pepper. Freeze 1 to 24 hours.
2. Preheat the oven to 375°F. Remove the pastries from the freezer, and let stand at room temperature 10 minutes. Cut each roll into 1/4-inch-thick slices, and place on parchment paper-lined baking sheets.
3. Bake, in batches, at 375°F for 20 minutes or until golden.
4. Microwave the pepper jelly in a microwave-safe bowl at HIGH 1 minute. Spread 1/2 teaspoon of the pepper jelly onto each palmier. Serve immediately.

CRAB AND ENDIVE SPEARS WITH SALMON ROE

These stylish appetizers come together quickly without using the stove. Feel free to prep the crab salad ahead of time, refrigerate, and assemble before guests arrive.

SERVES 10 • **HANDS-ON** 25 minutes • **TOTAL** 25 minutes

1 pound fresh lump crabmeat
1/3 cup crème fraîche
1/4 cup finely chopped fennel
1/4 cup finely chopped shallots
2 tablespoons finely chopped fresh chives
2 tablespoons finely chopped fresh flat-leaf parsley
1 1/2 tablespoons lemon zest
3 tablespoons lemon juice
1/2 teaspoon table salt
1/2 teaspoon freshly ground black pepper
4 large heads Belgian endive
2 ounces fresh salmon roe

1. Pick the crabmeat, removing any bits of the shell.
2. Stir together the crème fraîche, fennel, shallots, chives, parsley, lemon zest, lemon juice, salt, and pepper in a bowl. Gently fold in the crabmeat.
3. Trim the root ends from the endive, and separate into spears. Arrange the spears on a platter. Spoon the crabmeat salad onto the wide ends of the endive (about 2 tablespoons on each). Top with the salmon roe. Serve immediately or chilled.

BAKED BRIE BITES

This five-ingredient appetizer packs a lot of flavor and texture into one bite. For some holiday green, top red pepper jelly with fresh parsley.

MAKES 24 • **HANDS-ON** 10 minutes • **TOTAL** 18 minutes

24 frozen mini phyllo pastry shells, thawed
3 ounces Brie cheese, rind removed
2 tablespoons red pepper jelly
24 toasted pecan halves
1 teaspoon flaky sea salt
Garnish: fresh flat-leaf parsley

1. Preheat the oven to 350°F.
2. Arrange the pastry shells on a rimmed baking sheet. Cut the Brie into 24 small pieces. Spoon ¼ teaspoon of the jelly into each shell; top evenly with the Brie pieces and pecans.
3. Bake at 350°F until the cheese is melted, 7 to 8 minutes. Sprinkle with the salt; garnish, if desired. Serve immediately.

OYSTERS WITH MIGNONETTE TRIO

Oysters on the half shell are a chic and interesting cocktail-party treat. Serving with a variety of tart mignonette sauces makes them even better.

SERVES 12 • **HANDS-ON** 50 minutes, includes all mignonettes
TOTAL 2 hours, 20 minutes, plus shucking time, includes all mignonettes

3 dozen oysters in the shell, shucked

SPARKLING ROSÉ MIGNONETTE

1/4 cup Champagne vinegar
1 small shallot, finely minced
1/4 teaspoon kosher salt
1/4 teaspoon freshly ground black pepper
4 tablespoons sparkling rosé, chilled

CHILE-CUCUMBER MIGNONETTE

1/4 cup peeled, seeded, and finely chopped cucumber
1 red chile pepper, minced
1 shallot, finely minced
1/4 teaspoon kosher salt
1/4 teaspoon freshly ground black pepper
2 tablespoons apple cider vinegar
3 tablespoons Champagne vinegar

PICKLED FENNEL MIGNONETTE

1/4 cup minced fennel bulb
2 tablespoons chopped fennel fronds
1 small shallot, finely minced
1/4 teaspoon kosher salt
1/4 teaspoon freshly ground black pepper
1/2 cup Champagne vinegar

ADDITIONAL INGREDIENT

Lemon wedges

1. Make the Sparkling Rosé Mignonette: Whisk together the Champagne vinegar, shallot, salt, and pepper. Chill 30 minutes. Whisk in the rosé before serving. Makes 1/2 cup.
2. Make the Chile-Cucumber Mignonette: Stir together all the ingredients in a small bowl. Chill 30 minutes before serving. Serve chilled. Makes 1/2 cup.
3. Make the Pickled Fennel Mignonette: Stir together all the ingredients in a small bowl. Chill 30 minutes before serving. Serve chilled. Makes 3/4 cup.
4. Serve the oysters on ice with the mignonettes and lemon wedges.

HERBED FETA AND SUN-DRIED TOMATO DIP

Serve with crackers or crudités for an addictive dip—a perfect accompaniment with cocktails.

SERVES 10 • **HANDS-ON** 15 minutes • **TOTAL** 15 minutes

6 ounces crumbled feta cheese
6 ounces cream cheese, softened
1/2 cup sun-dried tomatoes in oil
1/3 cup mayonnaise
1/3 cup sour cream
1/4 cup firmly packed fresh basil leaves, coarsely chopped
1 tablespoon chopped fresh dill
1 teaspoon lemon zest
1 garlic clove, minced
1/4 teaspoon crushed red pepper
1/4 teaspoon freshly ground black pepper

Pulse all the ingredients in a food processor 10 to 15 seconds or until blended.

PISTACHIO-CRUSTED GOAT CHEESE LOG

Accented with dried apricots and thyme, this cheese log is savory with a hint of sweetness.

SERVES 12 to 16 • **HANDS-ON** 10 minutes • **TOTAL** 4 hours, 10 minutes, includes chilling

8 ounces cream cheese, softened
1 (8-ounce) log goat cheese, softened
1/2 cup finely chopped dried apricots
3 tablespoons chopped scallions
2 teaspoons chopped fresh thyme
1/2 teaspoon fine sea salt
1/4 teaspoon freshly ground black pepper
3/4 cup roasted, salted pistachios, chopped

1. Beat the cream cheese and goat cheese with an electric mixer at medium speed until smooth; beat in the apricots, scallions, thyme, salt, and pepper until well blended.
2. Turn the mixture out onto a large piece of plastic wrap; use the plastic wrap to shape the mixture into an 8- x 2-inch log. Wrap in the plastic wrap, and chill 4 hours or until firm.
3. Unwrap the cheese log; roll in the pistachios to coat. Serve immediately, or chill, wrapped in the plastic wrap, until ready to serve.

CHEESE AND ALMOND FIG BITES

Serve these bites on top of water crackers and garnish with fresh basil leaves, if desired.

SERVES 24 • **HANDS-ON** 10 minutes • **TOTAL** 10 minutes

24 dried Mission figs
1 (5.2-ounce) package spreadable cheese with black pepper
Marcona almonds
Wildflower honey (optional)
Garnish: fresh mint

Top each fig with about 1 teaspoon of the cheese and 2 or 3 almonds. Drizzle with the honey, if desired. Garnish, if desired.

NOTE: We tested with Orchard Choice Mission figs as well as Alouette spreadable cheese.

PROSCIUTTO-CAPRESE SKEWERS

White cheese, cherry red tomatoes, and green pesto combine for tasty Christmas-colored skewers.

SERVES 16 • **HANDS-ON** 15 minutes • **TOTAL** 15 minutes

- 1 (3/4-pound) package small mozzarella cheese balls (such as ciliegini)
- 1 (4-ounce) package thinly sliced prosciutto
- 1 (10.5-ounce) package cherry tomatoes
- 8 teaspoons basil pesto
- 2 teaspoons extra-virgin olive oil

Thread the cheese balls onto 3-inch skewers or wooden picks. Tear the prosciutto into 4 pieces each, and thread onto the skewers. Thread 1 cherry tomato onto each skewer. Stir together the basil pesto and extra-virgin olive oil, and drizzle over the skewers. Serve at room temperature.

MARINATED BURRATA

Burrata cheese is a hollowed out ball thinly lined with mozzarella that's filled with velvety cream. Here, the red chile pepper and lemon zest are the perfect balance to the rich, buttery filling.

SERVES 6 • **HANDS-ON** 10 minutes • **TOTAL** 8 hours, 10 minutes, includes chilling

- 1/4 cup olive oil
- 1 minced red chile pepper
- 2 tablespoons chopped fresh basil
- 1 teaspoon lemon zest
- 1 1/2 teaspoons table salt
- 1/2 teaspoon freshly ground black pepper
- 2 (8-ounce) balls burrata cheese
- Crackers

Whisk together the oil, chile pepper, chopped fresh basil, lemon zest, salt, and pepper in a bowl. Carefully place the burrata cheese balls in an 11- x 7-inch baking dish, and top with the olive oil mixture. Cover and chill at least 8 hours or up to 24 hours. Carefully transfer to a small platter, and serve with the crackers.

SMOKED SALMON SPREAD

This spread is excellent on bagels for Christmas brunch or with drinks for a predinner appetizer served with bagel chips or water crackers. We tested with Nova lox, which has a bright pink color.

MAKES 3 cups • **HANDS-ON** 15 minutes • **TOTAL** 15 minutes

12 ounces cream cheese, softened
8 ounces cold-smoked salmon, torn into pieces
1/2 cup sour cream
2 tablespoons finely diced red onion
1 tablespoon fresh lemon juice
1 tablespoon capers, drained
1 tablespoon chopped fresh dill
1/2 teaspoon freshly ground black pepper
Table salt

Puree the cream cheese, salmon, sour cream, 1 tablespoon of the red onion, lemon juice, capers, 1 teaspoon of the dill, and pepper in a food processor until a coarse puree forms. Season to taste with table salt. Transfer the spread to a small serving bowl. Sprinkle with the remaining 2 teaspoons fresh dill and 1 tablespoon red onion.

RADISH, OLIVE, AND HERB BUTTER TARTINES

A classic French snack of radishes and butter gets an upgrade with an herb-and-olive flavor infusion.

SERVES 10 • **HANDS-ON** 15 minutes • **TOTAL** 15 minutes

1/2 cup unsalted butter, softened
2 tablespoons chopped fresh parsley
2 tablespoons chopped fresh chives
1 tablespoon pitted kalamata olives, chopped
2 teaspoons chopped fresh dill
1 small garlic clove, chopped
1/2 teaspoon kosher salt
1/2 teaspoon freshly ground black pepper
1 French bread baguette, cut diagonally into 1/2-inch-thick slices
6 medium radishes, very thinly sliced
Garnishes: flaky sea salt, fresh herbs

Pulse the first 8 ingredients in a food processor until blended but not smooth (about 20 [1-second] pulses), scraping the sides of bowl as needed. Spread 1 to 1 1/2 teaspoons of the herb butter over 1 side of each bread slice, and top with the sliced radishes. Garnish, if desired.

SOPRESSATA, SMOKED GOUDA, AND APPLE CANAPÉS WITH BALSAMIC MUSTARD

This is a great dish for any friends who are gluten-free.

SERVES 20 • **HANDS-ON** 20 minutes • **TOTAL** 20 minutes

- 1/4 cup balsamic glaze
- 1 tablespoon whole-grain Dijon mustard
- 2 medium Granny Smith or Gala apples, cut crosswise into 10 (1/4-inch-thick) slices
- 1 medium lemon, halved
- 8 ounces smoked Gouda cheese, cut into 1/16-inch-thick slices
- 8 ounces thinly sliced Italian salami (such as sopressata)
- Garnish: fresh basil leaves

1. Stir together the balsamic glaze and mustard in a small bowl.

2. Rub the apple slices with the lemon halves. Top each apple slice with 1 slice of the cheese and 2 slices of the salami. Drizzle with the glaze mixture. Garnish, if desired.

NOTE: We tested with 2 (4-ounce) packages of Boar's Head sliced sopressata.

HORSERADISH AND ROAST BEEF CROSTINI

Make your own crostini, if desired, using a French baguette from the deli, or purchase store-bought crostini for a fast and easy option. You may need to cut the roast beef in half crosswise to fit, depending on the size of your crostini.

SERVES 15 • **HANDS-ON** 15 minutes • **TOTAL** 15 minutes

- 1/2 cup crème fraîche (or sour cream)
- 1 tablespoon prepared horseradish
- 1/8 teaspoon table salt
- 1/8 teaspoon freshly ground black pepper
- 30 store-bought or homemade crostini toasts
- 8 ounces premium thinly sliced deli-roasted roast beef
- 1 (2-ounce) package fresh watercress

1. Stir together the crème fraîche, horseradish, salt, and pepper.

2. Spread 1 side of each crostini with the crème fraîche mixture. Top with the roast beef and watercress.

HALIBUT CEVICHE WITH AVOCADO AND LIME

This ceviche is super refreshing thanks to fresh cilantro and lime. Serve with store-bought deep-fried wonton wrappers.

MAKES 2½ cups • **HANDS-ON** 10 minutes • **TOTAL** 30 minutes

- 1 pound very fresh halibut (or similar firm, white fish), cut into ½-inch pieces
- 1 avocado, diced
- 2 small shallots, cut into rings
- 7 tablespoons fresh lime juice
- ¼ cup coarsely chopped fresh cilantro
- 1 small jalapeño pepper, seeded and minced
- 1¼ teaspoons kosher salt

Combine all the ingredients in a bowl, and let stand at room temperature until the fish is opaque, about 20 to 30 minutes.

ZESTY MARINATED SHRIMP

This new-school spin on an old-school Southern favorite gets a bit of kick from crushed red pepper and brightness from lemon zest and fresh herbs. Most supermarkets sell cooked, peeled shrimp, but visit your local seafood market for the best quality.

SERVES 12 • **HANDS-ON** 10 minutes • **TOTAL** 8 hours, 10 minutes, includes chilling

- 1½ pounds peeled, medium-size cooked shrimp
- 1½ cups thinly sliced red onion
- ½ cup extra-virgin olive oil
- ⅓ cup red wine vinegar
- 2 tablespoons chopped fresh flat-leaf parsley
- 2 tablespoons chopped fresh dill
- 3 tablespoons drained capers
- 1 teaspoon lemon zest
- 3 tablespoons fresh lemon juice
- 1 teaspoon kosher salt
- ½ teaspoon crushed red pepper
- 2 garlic cloves, thinly sliced

Combine all the ingredients in a large ziplock plastic freezer bag. Seal and chill 8 to 24 hours, turning occasionally.

FESTIVE ENTRÉES

Crown your holiday table with a main dish that will have guests begging for the recipe. From Stuffed Beef Tenderloin to Short Rib and Stout Pies to Herb-Crusted Salmon and more, there's something here for everyone to enjoy.

SWEET TEA-BRINED TURKEY WITH CARAMELIZED ONION AND FENNEL GRAVY

Gone are the days of dry, flavorless turkey breasts and rubbery skin. With the succulently tender meat and unbelievably crispy skin, you won't want to make turkey any other way again. If your turkey is frozen, begin thawing in the refrigerator two to three days in advance. Serve with chutney, if desired.

SERVES 6 to 8 • **HANDS-ON** 1 hour, 40 minutes • **TOTAL** 7 hours, 20 minutes, plus 24 hours for brining

TURKEY

- 3/4 cup kosher salt
- 1 gallon brewed sweet tea
- 1/4 cup black peppercorns
- 3 tablespoons fennel seeds, crushed
- 3 tablespoons coriander seeds, crushed
- 10 garlic cloves, smashed
- 3 bay leaves
- 1 gallon water, plus 1/2 cup
- 1 (12- to 14-pound) whole turkey
- 1 large fennel bulb, trimmed and cut into 1-inch wedges
- 1 large Vidalia onion, cut into 1-inch wedges
- 3 fresh thyme sprigs
- 2 fresh oregano sprigs
- Kitchen string

HERB-CITRUS BUTTER

- 1 cup unsalted butter, softened
- 2 tablespoons finely chopped fresh oregano
- 2 1/2 teaspoons lemon zest
- 2 1/2 teaspoons orange zest
- 2 teaspoons ground coriander
- 1/2 teaspoon freshly ground black pepper
- 1 tablespoon Dijon mustard

CARAMELIZED ONION AND FENNEL GRAVY

- 1 medium parsnip, cut into 1-inch pieces
- 3 celery stalks with leaves, cut into 1-inch pieces
- 1/2 cup gin
- 1 (32-ounce) container chicken broth
- Table salt
- Freshly ground black pepper

1. Make the Turkey: Bring the first 7 ingredients and 1 gallon of the water to a boil in a large stockpot. Let cool to room temperature, about 1 hour. Remove the giblets and neck from the turkey. Place the turkey and brine in a very large food-safe container, and weight with plates, if necessary, to keep the turkey submerged. Chill 24 hours.

2. Preheat the oven to 325°F. Remove the turkey from the brine, and pat dry. Let stand at room temperature 1 hour.

3. Meanwhile, make the Herb-Citrus Butter: Stir together the butter and next 5 ingredients. Melt half of the butter mixture in a small saucepan over low heat.

4. Stir the Dijon mustard into the remaining half of the butter mixture. Starting from the neck, loosen and lift the skin from the turkey without completely detaching it. Spread the mustard mixture under the skin of the turkey thighs, breasts, and legs. Carefully replace the skin.

5. Place the fennel, onion, thyme, oregano, and remaining 1/2 cup water in a single layer in a large roasting pan. Place the turkey, breast side up, on a lightly greased roasting rack, and place on top of the vegetables in the pan. Tie the ends of the turkey legs together with the string; tuck the wing tips under.

6. Bake at 325°F for 3 hours and 15 minutes to 4 hours or until a meat thermometer inserted into the thickest portion of the thigh registers 165°F, basting every 30 minutes with the pan juices and melted herb butter. Shield with aluminum foil after 1 1/2 hours to prevent excessive browning, if necessary.

7. Remove the turkey from the oven, and let stand 30 minutes. Transfer the turkey to a serving platter. Pour the pan drippings through a wire-mesh strainer into a bowl. Discard all solids except the fennel and onion. (Do not wipe the pan clean.)

8. Make the Caramelized Onion and Fennel Gravy: Place the parsnip and celery in roasting pan. Cook over medium 8 minutes or until a deep golden brown. Add the fennel and onion; cook 2 minutes or until beginning to brown. Remove from the heat, and stir in the gin, scraping the bottom of the pan to loosen the browned bits.

9. Return to the heat, and cook 1 minute or until the liquid has almost evaporated. Add the broth, and bring to a boil. Reduce the heat, and simmer 10 minutes or until slightly thickened.

10. Process the gravy in a blender or food processor until pureed. Return to the pan, and stir in the reserved pan drippings. Season with table salt and pepper to taste, and serve with the turkey.

ROASTED HERB TURKEY AND GRAVY

For crisp, golden skin and juicy meat, we coated this beautiful bird with an aromatic infused butter, made with sage, thyme, and fennel seeds. And for the best gravy, we added onions, carrots, and celery to the roasting pan.

SERVES 8 • **HANDS-ON** 45 minutes • **TOTAL** 4 hours, includes gravy

3 tablespoons salted butter
2½ tablespoons kosher salt
1 tablespoon dried thyme
2 teaspoons dried sage
2 teaspoons freshly ground black pepper
1 teaspoon fennel seeds, lightly crushed
1 (12-pound) fresh whole turkey
2 tablespoons canola oil
Kitchen string
4 cups coarsely chopped yellow onions
3 cups coarsely chopped carrots
2 cups coarsely chopped celery
2 bay leaves
3 cups water

TURKEY GRAVY

Drippings and vegetables from Roasted Herb Turkey
4 cups chicken broth
¼ cup all-purpose flour

1. Melt the butter in a small skillet over medium. Add the salt, thyme, sage, pepper, and fennel seeds; cook, stirring often, until fragrant, about 1 minute. Remove from the pan, and cool completely, about 10 minutes. Reserve 1 tablespoon of the butter mixture.

2. Remove the giblets and neck from the turkey; reserve for another use. Pat the turkey dry, and remove the excess skin. Starting from the neck, loosen and lift the skin from the turkey without completely detaching it. Spread the butter mixture remaining in the bowl evenly under the skin. Carefully replace the skin. Drizzle the skin with the oil, and rub with the reserved 1 tablespoon butter mixture. Tie the ends of the legs together with kitchen string; tuck the wing tips under. Let stand at room temperature for 1 hour, or refrigerate 12 to 24 hours. (If refrigerated, let the turkey stand at room temperature 1 hour before cooking.)

3. Preheat the oven to 375°F. Place the onions, carrots, celery, and bay leaves in the bottom of a roasting pan; add a roasting rack. Coat the rack with cooking spray. Place the turkey on the rack, and transfer to the oven. Add the water to the pan. Bake at 375°F until a meat thermometer inserted in the thickest portion of the thigh registers 165°F, about 1 hour and 45 minutes, rotating the pan halfway (on the same rack) after 55 minutes. Remove the turkey from the oven, and let stand at least 30 minutes; reserve the pan drippings in pan for making Turkey Gravy.

4. Make the Turkey Gravy: Transfer the drippings and vegetables from the roasting pan from the cooked turkey in the Roasted Herb Turkey to a medium saucepan; add 3½ cups of the chicken broth. Bring to a boil over high. Reduce the heat to medium, and simmer 20 minutes. Pour the mixture through a wire-mesh strainer into a bowl, pressing on the vegetables to extract the juices. Discard the vegetables. Return the broth mixture to the saucepan. Whisk together the flour and the remaining ½ cup chicken broth in a small bowl; whisk into the broth mixture. Bring to a boil over high; boil until reduced to about 4 cups, about 20 minutes. Serve the turkey with 2 cups of the gravy, and reserve the remaining 2 cups gravy for another use.

PEPPERCORN-CRUSTED STANDING RIB ROAST WITH ROASTED VEGETABLES

Prepare for "oohs" and "ahhs" when you place this roast on your holiday table. Although it looks difficult, it's truly simple to prepare—slather it with our herb butter the night before; then let your oven do the work. Roasting the vegetables separately from the meat preserves their bright color and keeps them from getting mushy.

SERVES 10 • **HANDS-ON** 23 minutes • **TOTAL** 16 hours, 55 minutes, includes chilling

- ½ cup salted butter, softened
- 2 tablespoons kosher salt
- 2 tablespoons coarsely ground black pepper
- 1 tablespoon chopped fresh rosemary
- 1 tablespoon chopped fresh sage
- 1 tablespoon chopped fresh thyme
- 1 tablespoon extra-virgin olive oil
- 1 (8-pound) 4-rib prime rib roast, chine bone removed

ROASTED VEGETABLES

- 1 pound small carrots with tops, trimmed and peeled
- 1 pound parsnips, peeled and cut lengthwise into 3-inch pieces
- 8 ounces golden beets, peeled and cut into 1-inch wedges
- 8 ounces Chioggia beets (candy cane beets), peeled and cut into 1-inch wedges
- 2 tablespoons chopped fresh rosemary
- 2 tablespoons olive oil
- 2 teaspoons kosher salt
- 1 teaspoon freshly ground black pepper
- Garnish: fresh rosemary sprigs

1. Stir together the butter, salt, pepper, rosemary, sage, thyme, and oil in a small bowl. Spread evenly over the roast. Chill, uncovered, 12 hours or up to 24 hours.
2. Remove the roast from the refrigerator; let stand at room temperature 1 hour.
3. Preheat the oven to 450°F. Place the roast on a lightly greased rack in a roasting pan. Bake at 450°F on the lowest oven rack 45 minutes. Reduce the oven temperature to 350°F; bake until a meat thermometer inserted in the thickest portion registers 120° to 130°F for medium-rare or 130° to 135°F for medium, about 1 hour and 30 minutes.
4. Let stand 30 minutes. Transfer the roast to a serving platter, reserving ½ cup drippings for the gravy.
5. Meanwhile, make the Roasted Vegetables: Preheat the oven to 400°F. Toss together the first 8 ingredients in a large bowl. Spread in a single layer in a 17- x 11-inch rimmed baking pan. Bake at 400°F until tender, about 45 minutes, stirring every 15 minutes. Serve with the roast. Garnish, if desired.

STUFFED BEEF TENDERLOIN

Stuffed beef tenderloin pairs well with a classic Béarnaise sauce for the perfect sumptuous holiday meal.

SERVES 12 • **HANDS-ON** 30 minutes • **TOTAL** 1 hour, 15 minutes

BEEF

- 1 pound fresh Swiss chard, stemmed and chopped
- 2 tablespoons olive oil
- 2 garlic cloves, minced
- 1/2 teaspoon kosher salt
- 1/4 teaspoon freshly ground black pepper
- 1 tablespoon butter
- 2 (4-ounce) packages exotic blend mushrooms, chopped
- 1 (5-pound) beef tenderloin, trimmed
- Kitchen string

RUB

- 1 tablespoon kosher salt
- 1 tablespoon fennel seed, toasted and crushed
- 1 tablespoon chopped fresh rosemary
- 1 tablespoon freshly ground black pepper
- 5 garlic cloves, pressed
- 1 tablespoon olive oil

1. Make the Beef: Preheat the oven to 500°F. Cook the Swiss chard in the hot oil in a large nonstick skillet over medium-high, stirring constantly, until the chard begins to wilt. Cook 1 minute or until completely wilted. Add the minced garlic, 1/4 teaspoon of the salt, and 1/8 teaspoon of the pepper; sauté 1 minute. Transfer to a bowl; let stand until cool enough to handle.

2. Gently squeeze the excess moisture from the cooked chard.

3. Melt the butter in the skillet over medium-high. Add the mushrooms and remaining 1/4 teaspoon salt and 1/8 teaspoon pepper. Cook, stirring occasionally, 8 minutes or until browned. Stir into the chard.

4. Butterfly the beef by making a lengthwise cut in 1 side, but not through the opposite side (leave about 1/2 inch); unfold. Flatten to a uniform thickness (about 3/4 inch), using a rolling pin or flat side of a meat mallet. Sprinkle with salt and pepper. Spoon the chard mixture down the center of the beef, leaving a 1/4-inch border. Fold the beef over the chard, and tie with the string at 2-inch intervals. Place the beef, seam side down, on a lightly greased jelly-roll pan.

5. Make the Rub: Stir together the kosher salt and next 4 ingredients in a small bowl. Stir in the oil to form a paste. Rub the mixture over the beef.

6. Bake at 500°F for 10 minutes. Reduce the oven temperature to 350°F. Bake 20 to 25 minutes or until a meat thermometer inserted into the thickest portion of the tenderloin registers 130°F (rare). Let stand 15 minutes before slicing.

BÉARNAISE SAUCE

Classic Béarnaise sauce is emulsified in the blender for an easy yet elegant sauce to accompany roasted beef tenderloin. If your sauce is too thick, gradually whisk in very hot water, 1 teaspoon at a time, to reach desired consistency.

MAKES 1 1/4 cups • **HANDS-ON** 15 minutes • **TOTAL** 15 minutes

- 1/4 cup Champagne vinegar
- 1/4 cup dry white wine
- 2 tablespoons minced shallots
- 2 tablespoons chopped fresh tarragon
- 1 cup butter
- 3 large egg yolks
- 1/4 teaspoon table salt
- 1/4 teaspoon freshly ground black pepper
- 1 tablespoon hot water
- 1 teaspoon fresh lemon juice (optional)

1. Combine the first 3 ingredients and 1 tablespoon of the tarragon in a small saucepan. Bring to a simmer over medium-high, and cook 3 minutes or until reduced to 2 tablespoons. Pour through a fine wire-mesh strainer into a blender. Discard the solids. Let cool slightly.

2. Meanwhile, microwave the butter in a microwave-safe bowl at HIGH 1 minute or until melted.

3. Process the egg yolks in the blender with the vinegar mixture until smooth. With the blender running, add the hot butter in a slow, steady stream, processing until smooth. Add the salt, pepper, hot water, and, if desired, lemon juice. Process until blended.

4. Transfer to a bowl, and stir in the remaining 1 tablespoon tarragon. Store at room temperature until ready to use (up to 1 hour).

IRON SKILLET TAMALE PIE

Not to be confused with authentic Mexican tamales, this American invention is essentially thick chili topped with a cornbread crust. What could be more comforting than that? It's a perfect low-key family meal for a winter evening. You may want to place a baking sheet on the oven rack below the skillet to catch any drips. To save time, use a box of cornbread mix instead of making the homemade cornbread topping.

SERVES 8 to 10 • **HANDS-ON** 35 minutes • **TOTAL** 55 minutes

FILLING

1½ pounds ground chuck
1 medium onion, chopped
2 poblano peppers, chopped
3 garlic cloves, minced
2 tablespoons ancho chili powder
1 tablespoon ground cumin
1 teaspoon dried oregano
2 (14.5-ounce) cans fire-roasted diced tomatoes
1 (16-ounce) can red chili beans in medium sauce
1 cup beef broth
1 cup frozen whole kernel corn, thawed
3 tablespoons chopped fresh cilantro
Table salt
Black pepper

CORNBREAD TOPPING

1¼ cups stone-ground yellow cornmeal
1 cup (4 ounces) shredded extra-sharp Cheddar cheese
¾ cup all-purpose flour
1 teaspoon baking soda
1 teaspoon baking powder
1 teaspoon table salt
¼ teaspoon freshly ground black pepper
1¼ cups buttermilk
¼ cup butter, melted
2 large eggs

SERVE WITH

Sour cream
Sliced scallions

1. Make the Filling: Preheat the oven to 425°F. Cook the ground beef, onion, poblanos, and garlic in a 12-inch cast-iron skillet 8 to 10 minutes or until the meat crumbles and is no longer pink and the onions are tender. Stir in the ancho chili powder, cumin, and oregano; cook 2 minutes. Stir in the tomatoes and next 3 ingredients; bring to a simmer. Reduce the heat, and simmer 10 minutes or until slightly thickened. Stir in the cilantro and salt and pepper to taste.
2. Meanwhile, make the Cornbread Topping: Combine the cornmeal and next 6 ingredients in a large bowl. Whisk together the buttermilk, butter, and eggs; add to dry ingredients, stirring just until moistened. Dollop the batter over the mixture in the skillet; spread into an even layer.
3. Bake at 425°F for 20 minutes or until golden brown and a wooden pick inserted in center of the cornbread comes out clean. Serve with the sour cream and scallions.

SHORT RIB AND STOUT PIES

Complex flavors make these mini pies unforgettable. A layer of puff pastry cut into rounds, stars, or any shape you'd like covers ramekins of hearty stew and bakes until golden brown.

SERVES 6 • **HANDS-ON** 1 hour • **TOTAL** 4 hours, 50 minutes

- 6 pounds large short ribs
- 1 tablespoon table salt
- 2 teaspoons freshly ground black pepper
- 1/4 cup all-purpose flour
- 2 tablespoons extra virgin olive oil
- 4 celery ribs, chopped (about 3/4-inch pieces)
- 1 large onion, chopped (about 3/4-inch pieces)
- 4 carrots, chopped (about 3/4-inch pieces)
- 2 bay leaves (fresh or dried)
- 1 tablespoon chopped fresh thyme
- 1 tablespoon fresh rosemary leaves, chopped
- 1/4 teaspoon fennel seeds
- 1/4 teaspoon crushed red pepper
- 2 large garlic cloves, minced
- 1 (12-ounce) bottle extra-stout ale
- 3 cups beef broth
- 3 tablespoons brandy
- 1 tablespoon balsamic vinegar
- 1 teaspoon sugar
- 1 (17.3-ounce) package frozen puff pastry sheets, thawed
- 1 large egg, beaten
- 1 tablespoon water

1. Season the ribs with the salt and pepper, and let stand at room temperature 30 minutes. Toss the ribs in the flour, and shake off excess (reserve the excess flour).
2. Heat the oil in a large ovenproof Dutch oven over medium-high. Cook the ribs, in batches, in the hot oil until dark brown on all sides.
3. Preheat the oven to 300°F. Drain the oil from the Dutch oven, reserving 1 tablespoon of the oil in the Dutch oven. Reduce the heat to medium. Add the celery and next 8 ingredients, and cook, stirring occasionally, 10 minutes or until the onion is translucent. Add the reserved flour and any salt and pepper left after coating the ribs; cook 30 seconds.
4. Add the stout, stirring to loosen the browned bits from the bottom of the Dutch oven. Add the broth and next 3 ingredients, and return the ribs to the Dutch oven. Bring to a boil; cover with the lid.
5. Bake at 300°F, covered, for 2 hours. Uncover and bake 1 hour or until the ribs are very tender but retain their shape.
6. Remove the ribs from the stew, and cool slightly. Increase the oven temperature to 400°F.
7. Cook the liquid and vegetables in the Dutch oven over medium-high until the liquid is reduced to about 4 cups; remove the fat from the surface of the liquid as it cooks.
8. When cool enough to handle, coarsely shred the meat, discarding the bones. Stir the meat into the stew, and season with salt to taste. Ladle the stew into 6 (10- to 12-ounce) deep ovenproof soup bowls or large ramekins.
9. Roll out the puff pastry sheets on a flat surface; cut out 6 rounds or stars about 1/2 inch larger than the soup bowls. Arrange the pastry cutouts over the soup.
10. Whisk together the egg and water. Brush the pastry with the egg mixture. Arrange the soup bowls on an aluminum foil-lined baking sheet.
11. Bake at 400°F for 15 to 20 minutes or until the pastry is golden brown. Remove from the oven, and cool 5 minutes.

BLACK PEPPER-CRUSTED RACKS OF LAMB WITH HORSERADISH CRÈME FRAÎCHE

Feel free to prep the horseradish crème fraîche and panko coating ahead of time, freeing you up to spend time with guests. Cutting the racks into double chops makes for an impressive serving for a dinner party.

SERVES 4 • **HANDS-ON** 15 minutes • **TOTAL** 55 minutes

1 cup crème fraîche
2 tablespoons prepared horseradish
2 teaspoons table salt
2 tablespoons whole black peppercorns
½ cup panko (Japanese breadcrumbs)
1 tablespoon minced garlic
2 tablespoons unsalted butter, melted
2 teaspoons fresh rosemary leaves, chopped
1 teaspoon fresh thyme leaves, chopped
½ teaspoon lemon zest
2 (3-pound) frenched racks of lamb (8 ribs)
2 tablespoons Dijon mustard

1. Preheat the oven to 425°F. Stir together the crème fraîche, horseradish, and ½ teaspoon of the salt in a bowl. Chill until ready to serve.

2. Coarsely crush the peppercorns using a mortar and pestle. Transfer the crushed peppercorns to a bowl, and stir in the panko, next 5 ingredients, and remaining 1½ teaspoons salt.

3. Place the lamb, fat sides up, on an aluminum foil-lined baking sheet. Spread 1 tablespoon of the mustard over the fat side of each rack, and top with the panko mixture, pressing to adhere.

4. Bake at 425°F for 30 to 35 minutes or until a meat thermometer registers 132° to 135°F (medium-rare). Cover loosely with foil after 20 minutes, if necessary, to prevent excessive browning. Let stand 10 minutes before slicing. Cut the racks into double or single chops. Serve with the horseradish crème fraîche.

HERB-CRUSTED SALMON

Lots of herbs transform this salmon from special to extraordinary. Be sure that all of the pin bones are removed from the fish.

SERVES 4 to 6 • **HANDS-ON** 10 minutes • **TOTAL** 30 minutes

1 (2½-pound) salmon fillet, pin bones removed
1½ cups panko (Japanese breadcrumbs)
¼ cup loosely packed fresh flat-leaf parsley leaves, chopped
¼ cup loosely packed fresh dill, chopped
¼ cup loosely packed fresh basil leaves, chopped
2 garlic cloves, finely minced
6 tablespoons unsalted butter, melted
2 tablespoons honey mustard
2 teaspoons fresh thyme leaves, chopped
2 teaspoons lemon zest
2 tablespoons fresh lemon juice
2 teaspoons kosher salt
1 teaspoon freshly ground black pepper
Lemon wedges

1. Preheat the oven to 425°F. Rinse the salmon, and pat dry with paper towels. Place the salmon, skin side down, on a parchment paper-lined baking sheet.
2. Stir together the panko and next 11 ingredients in a bowl. Gently press the mixture onto the salmon to form a thick crust.
3. Bake at 425°F for 20 minutes or until the salmon is just cooked through and flakes easily with a fork. Serve immediately with the lemon wedges.

SQUASH GALETTE WITH FONTINA AND CARAMELIZED ONIONS

Caramelizing onions and making fresh dough require work, but it's worth it for this satisfying meatless dish in which tender veggies and cheese are wrapped in a buttermilk crust. The dough can be made up to 2 days ahead and stored in the refrigerator, making day-of meal prep easier. (Pictured on opposite page, on left side of image.)

SERVES 6 • **HANDS-ON** 15 minutes • **TOTAL** 2 hours, 25 minutes

- 2½ cups all-purpose flour
- 2 teaspoons table salt
- ½ teaspoon freshly ground black pepper
- 1 cup unsalted butter, chilled and cut into ½-inch cubes
- ¼ cup buttermilk
- ¼ cup ice-cold water
- 2 (1¼-pound) packages fresh cubed butternut squash
- 3 tablespoons olive oil
- 1 tablespoon unsalted butter
- 2 pounds Vidalia onions, thinly sliced
- 1½ teaspoons fresh thyme leaves, chopped
- ¼ teaspoon sugar
- 1 (8-ounce) wedge fontina cheese, coarsely shredded
- 1 large egg, beaten
- 2 tablespoons water

1. Pulse the flour, ½ teaspoon of the salt, and ¼ teaspoon of the pepper in a food processor until blended. Add 1 cup cubed butter, and pulse until mixture is the texture of coarse sand. Add the buttermilk and ice-cold water, and pulse just until a dough forms. Pat the dough into a disk, wrap in plastic wrap, and chill at least 1 hour or up to 2 days.
2. Preheat the oven to 400°F. Toss the squash with 1 tablespoon of the oil, ½ teaspoon of the salt, and the remaining ¼ teaspoon pepper. Spread in a single layer on a parchment paper-lined baking sheet.
3. Bake at 400°F for 30 minutes or until the squash is tender, stirring once halfway through baking.
4. Meanwhile, melt 1 tablespoon butter with the remaining 2 tablespoons oil in a heavy skillet over medium-low heat. Add the onion, thyme, sugar, and remaining 1 teaspoon salt, and cook, stirring occasionally, 25 to 30 minutes or until the onions are caramelized. Let cool.
5. Roll the dough into a 16-inch circle on a flat surface. Transfer to a parchment paper-lined pizza pan or baking sheet. Spread half of the onions onto the dough, leaving a 2-inch border. Top with half of the cheese. Top with the squash and remaining onions and cheese. Fold the border over the filling, pleating as needed, leaving the center open.
6. Whisk together the egg and 2 tablespoons water. Brush the outside of the dough with the egg mixture. Bake at 400°F for 40 to 50 minutes or until brown.

ROASTED BUTTERNUT SQUASH-APPLE SOUP

The Walnut-Chive Oil can be made 3 days ahead and refrigerated. Remember to bring it to room temperature before serving with the soup. This bright green oil is a great finishing touch to the Roasted Butternut Squash-Apple Soup. The soup itself can also be made ahead and will be great with lunch the next day.

SERVES 6 to 8 • **HANDS-ON** 45 minutes • **TOTAL** 1 hour, 55 minutes

2 1/2 pounds butternut squash, peeled and cut into 3/4-inch cubes
2 medium Gala apples, peeled and cut into 3/4-inch cubes
1 medium leek, cut into 1/2-inch half-moons
2 medium shallots, quartered
1 tablespoon finely chopped fresh thyme
1 tablespoon finely chopped fresh sage
2 tablespoons olive oil
1 teaspoon kosher salt
1 teaspoon smoked paprika
1/2 teaspoon freshly ground black pepper
5 cups chicken broth
1 bay leaf
1 cup heavy cream
Table salt
Black pepper

WALNUT-CHIVE OIL
1 cup water
1/2 (1-ounce) package fresh chives
1/3 cup olive oil
1/2 cup coarsely chopped walnuts
1/4 teaspoon lemon zest
1/4 teaspoon kosher salt

Garnish: toasted walnuts

1. Preheat the oven to 450°F. Toss together the first 10 ingredients in a large bowl; divide between 2 large jelly-roll pans.
2. Bake at 450°F for 30 to 35 minutes or until tender, rotating the pans and tossing the vegetables halfway through.
3. Meanwhile, make the Walnut-Chive Oil: Fill a large bowl with ice. Bring the water to a boil in a small skillet. Add the chives, and simmer 5 to 10 seconds or until the chives are bright green and tender. Immediately place the skillet in the ice. Remove the chives, and drain on paper towels, squeezing out the excess water. Wipe the skillet clean. Cook the oil and walnuts in the skillet over medium-low, stirring occasionally, 5 minutes or until the walnuts are toasted and fragrant. Pour the oil through a strainer into a bowl, reserving the toasted walnuts for another use. Let the oil cool 20 minutes. Process the cooled oil and chives in a blender until smooth. (If desired, pour the oil mixture through a cheesecloth-lined wire-mesh strainer into a bowl and discard the solids.) Stir in the lemon zest and salt.
4. Transfer the vegetables to a large saucepan, and add the broth and bay leaf. Bring to a boil, and reduce the heat. Simmer 15 minutes or until the liquid is reduced slightly. Discard bay leaf.
5. Puree the mixture, in batches, in a blender until smooth (or use a handheld immersion blender, if desired). Return each batch to the pan.
6. Stir in the cream and table salt and pepper to taste. Ladle the soup into bowls, and drizzle with the Walnut-Chive Oil. Garnish, if desired.

ALL THE TRIMMINGS

Round out your meal with these crowd-pleasing Southern side dishes. From Savory Sweet Potato Casserole to Sweet Corn and Poblano Pudding, you'll find well-loved standbys as well as classics with a new twist that are sure to become new favorites.

SAUTÉED MUSTARD GREENS WITH GARLIC AND LEMON

This dish is a fast take on the usual long-simmered greens. Swap out other hearty greens such as kale, collards, or turnip greens for the mustard greens, if you prefer.

SERVES 8 • **HANDS-ON** 10 minutes • **TOTAL** 20 minutes

- 2 tablespoons olive oil
- 4 garlic cloves, thinly sliced
- 3 pounds mustard greens, washed, trimmed, and chopped (about 24 cups)
- 2 tablespoons fresh lemon juice (from 1 lemon)
- 1/4 to 1/2 teaspoon crushed red pepper
- 3/4 teaspoon kosher salt
- 3/4 teaspoon freshly ground black pepper

1. Heat the oil in a Dutch oven over medium. Add the garlic; cook, stirring often, until the garlic is golden brown and crispy, about 1 minute.
2. Stir in the greens, in batches; cook until wilted, 1 to 2 minutes, before adding more greens. Cover and cook, stirring occasionally, until tender-crisp, about 10 to 12 minutes.
3. Stir in the lemon juice and 1/4 teaspoon of the crushed red pepper. Sprinkle with the salt and pepper. Stir in an additional 1/4 teaspoon crushed red pepper, if desired.

CORNMEAL POPOVERS

Don't peek at the popovers while they're baking—keeping the oven door closed will help them rise.

MAKES 12 popovers • **HANDS-ON** 12 minutes • **TOTAL** 30 minutes

- 1 1/2 cups all-purpose flour
- 1/2 cup fine white cornmeal
- 1 1/2 teaspoons kosher salt
- 1 3/4 cups whole milk
- 4 large eggs
- 1/4 cup salted butter, melted

1. Place a 12-cup muffin pan in the oven. Preheat the oven to 450°F. (Do not remove the pan.)
2. Whisk together the flour, cornmeal, and salt in a large bowl. Whisk together the milk and eggs in a medium bowl. Gradually whisk the milk mixture into the flour mixture until well blended.
3. Remove the muffin pan from the oven. Spoon 1 teaspoon of the melted butter into each cup of the hot pan; return the pan to the oven for 2 minutes.
4. Remove the muffin pan. Divide the batter among the prepared muffin cups. Bake until puffed and golden brown, 18 to 20 minutes. (The centers will be moist.) Serve immediately.

SEA SALT-POPPY SEED CLOVERLEAF ROLLS

There is nothing quite like freshly baked rolls, but if pushed for time, make these a day in advance and reheat just before serving. Wrap tightly in aluminum foil and store at room temperature.

MAKES 12 rolls • **HANDS-ON** 25 minutes • **TOTAL** 2 hours, 45 minutes

- 1 cup warm milk (100° to 110°F)
- 1 (1/4-ounce) envelope active dry yeast
- 2 tablespoons sugar
- 3 cups all-purpose flour
- 1 1/4 teaspoons table salt
- 6 tablespoons butter, melted
- 1 large egg, lightly beaten
- 1 1/2 teaspoons poppy seeds
- 1 1/2 teaspoons flaky sea salt

1. Stir together the milk, yeast, and 1 tablespoon of the sugar in a 2-cup glass measuring cup; let stand 5 minutes.
2. Combine the flour, table salt, and remaining 1 tablespoon sugar in the bowl of a heavy-duty electric stand mixer; let stand 5 minutes. Add 4 tablespoons of the melted butter, egg, and yeast mixture; beat at low speed, using the paddle attachment, 3 minutes or until blended and a soft, sticky dough forms. Increase the speed to medium, attach the dough hook, and beat 6 minutes or until the dough is smooth and elastic but still slightly sticky. Cover the bowl with plastic wrap, and let rise in a warm place (80° to 85°F), free from drafts, 1 hour or until doubled in bulk.
3. Punch the dough down. Turn out onto a lightly floured surface. Divide the dough into 12 equal portions (about 2 ounces each). Gently shape each portion into 3 (1/4-inch) balls; place 3 balls in each of 12 buttered muffin cups. Brush the tops of the dough with the remaining 2 tablespoons melted butter. Cover and let rise in a warm place (80° to 85°F), free from drafts, 30 to 45 minutes or until doubled in bulk.
4. Preheat the oven to 375°F. Sprinkle the rolls evenly with the poppy seeds and sea salt.
5. Bake at 375°F for 15 to 17 minutes or until golden brown. Transfer to a wire rack. Serve warm or cool completely, about 30 minutes.

ORANGE, RADISH, AND BUTTER LETTUCE SALAD

Combining bright and juicy winter citrus with a light vinaigrette and butter lettuce makes for an enticing start to your holiday meal.

SERVES 12 • **HANDS-ON** 20 minutes • **TOTAL** 20 minutes

6 navel oranges
1 tablespoon finely chopped shallots
1 tablespoon chopped fresh mint
2 teaspoons Dijon mustard
1 teaspoon honey
½ teaspoon orange zest
½ teaspoon kosher salt
¼ teaspoon freshly ground black pepper
2 tablespoons olive oil
2 tablespoons canola oil
6 cups frisée lettuce
2 medium-size heads butter lettuce, torn into bite-size pieces
2 bunches radishes, thinly sliced (about 3 cups)
½ cup chopped dry-roasted pistachios

1. Cut a ¼-inch-thick slice from each end of the oranges, using a sharp, thin-bladed knife. Place the fruit, cut sides down, on a cutting board. Peel the fruit; cut away the bitter white pith. Slice between the membranes, and gently remove the whole segments, holding the fruit over a bowl to collect the juices. Gently squeeze the membranes to release any juice. Discard the membranes. Reserve the segments and juice (about 2 cups segments and ¾ cup juice).
2. Whisk together 6 tablespoons of the reserved orange juice, shallots, and next 6 ingredients in a bowl until blended. Whisk in both the oils until well blended.
3. Add the frisée, butter lettuce, and radishes; toss gently to coat. Top the individual servings with the orange segments. Sprinkle with the pistachios.

RUSTIC WILD MUSHROOM-HERB DRESSING

A simple, traditional dressing gets an elegant upgrade with a rosemary-sea salt European-style crusty bread, meaty shiitake and oyster mushrooms, leeks, and dry sherry.

SERVES 8 • **HANDS-ON** 40 minutes • **TOTAL** 3 hours, 10 minutes

- 1 (1-pound) day-old rosemary-sea salt-olive oil bread loaf or round, torn or cut into 1-inch pieces (about 10 cups)
- 2 large leeks
- 1 cup butter
- 1½ cups chopped celery
- 8 ounces shiitake mushrooms, thinly sliced (about 5 cups sliced)
- 3 (3.5-ounce) packages oyster mushrooms, thinly sliced (about 2 cups sliced)
- 1½ teaspoons kosher salt
- 1 teaspoon freshly ground black pepper
- ⅓ cup dry sherry or dry white wine
- ⅓ cup chopped fresh flat-leaf parsley
- 1 tablespoon chopped fresh rosemary
- 1 tablespoon chopped fresh thyme
- 1 tablespoon chopped fresh sage
- 2½ cups chicken broth
- 2 large eggs, lightly beaten

1. Preheat the oven to 250°F. Place the bread in a single layer in a jelly-roll pan.
2. Bake at 250°F for 1 hour or until dried out, stirring occasionally. Cool completely, about 20 minutes. Transfer to a large bowl. Increase the oven temperature to 350°F.
3. Meanwhile, remove and discard the root ends and dark green tops of the leeks. Cut in half lengthwise, and rinse thoroughly under cold running water to remove the grit and sand. Drain; thinly slice.
4. Melt ½ cup of the butter in a large skillet over medium. Add the leeks and celery, and cook, stirring occasionally, 12 minutes or until softened and golden brown. Add to the bread.
5. Melt the remaining ½ cup butter in skillet over medium-high. Add all the mushrooms, ¾ teaspoon of the kosher salt, and ½ teaspoon of the pepper. Sauté 10 minutes or until golden brown. Stir in the sherry; cook 1 minute or until almost completely evaporated.
6. Add the mushroom mixture, parsley, next 3 ingredients, and remaining ¾ teaspoon salt and ½ teaspoon pepper to the bread mixture. Toss until blended.
7. Whisk together the broth and eggs. Pour over the bread mixture; toss gently until blended. Let stand 10 minutes, stirring once (for the bread to absorb the liquid). Spoon into a greased 13- x 9-inch baking dish. Cover with aluminum foil.
8. Bake at 350°F for 40 minutes. Then uncover and bake 20 minutes or until lightly browned.

TUSCAN KALE WITH CRISPY GARLIC AND PANCETTA

Colors of red and green will make you think "Christmas" as soon as this dish hits the table.

SERVES 6 • **HANDS-ON** 25 minutes • **TOTAL** 25 minutes

- 4 ounces thinly sliced pancetta, cut into thin strips
- 2 tablespoons olive oil
- 6 garlic cloves, thinly sliced
- 4 (½-pound) bunches Tuscan (lacinato) kale, stemmed and cut into bite-size pieces
- 2 tablespoons apple cider vinegar
- 1 teaspoon lemon zest
- Kosher salt
- Freshly ground black pepper

1. Cook the pancetta in the hot oil in a Dutch oven over medium-low 8 minutes or until the pancetta is crisp. Transfer the pancetta to a paper towel-lined plate, using a slotted spoon, reserving the drippings in the Dutch oven.
2. Increase the heat to medium, and add the garlic to the hot drippings; cook 3 minutes or until browned (do not burn). Transfer to a second paper towel-lined plate, using a slotted spoon.
3. Increase the heat to medium-high, and add the kale to the Dutch oven. Cook, tossing with tongs, until coated with the oil. Cover and cook, tossing occasionally, 3 minutes or until wilted and tender. Add the vinegar, and remove from the heat. Stir in the lemon zest, and season with the kosher salt and freshly ground pepper to taste. Top with the crispy pancetta and garlic, and serve immediately.

BABY KALE AND PEARS WITH ROASTED SHALLOT VINAIGRETTE

Tender baby kale leaves dressed in a savory, rich, roasted shallot vinaigrette are enhanced by the sweetness of fall pears in this festive side dish. Use a vegetable peeler to get pretty curls of cheese to garnish each plate of dressed salad.

SERVES 8 • **HANDS-ON** 15 minutes • **TOTAL** 45 minutes

- 4 large shallots, halved
- ½ cup olive oil
- 1 large fresh thyme sprig
- ¼ cup high-quality sherry vinegar
- 1 tablespoon chopped fresh thyme
- 1 tablespoon Dijon mustard
- 1 tablespoon honey
- 1 teaspoon kosher salt
- ¼ teaspoon freshly ground black pepper
- 4 medium-size, ripe Bosc pears, thinly sliced
- 2 (5-ounce) packages mixed greens with baby kale
- 1 cup toasted pecan halves
- 4 ounces Parmigiano-Reggiano cheese, shaved

1. Preheat the oven to 375°F. Place the shallots, oil, and thyme sprig in a small baking dish. Cover loosely with aluminum foil. Bake 30 minutes or until the shallots are light golden brown and very tender. Discard the thyme sprig.
2. Pulse the roasted shallot mixture, vinegar, chopped thyme, mustard, honey, ¾ teaspoon of the salt, and pepper in a blender until the shallots are mashed. Process until blended, scraping down the sides as needed.
3. Toss the pears with ¼ cup of the vinaigrette in a bowl.
4. Toss the mixed greens with ¼ cup vinaigrette in a large bowl, and sprinkle with the remaining ¼ teaspoon salt. Transfer the greens to a large platter, top with the pears, and sprinkle with the pecans and cheese.

NOTE: To make ahead, prepare the recipe as directed through Step 3 up to 1 hour ahead. Store the pears and vinaigrette in the refrigerator. Proceed with the recipe as directed in Step 4 when ready to serve.

CREAMY KABOCHA SQUASH-PARSNIP MASH

Also called Japanese pumpkin, kabocha squash's earthiness marries beautifully with the sweetness of parsnips and cream.

SERVES 8 • **HANDS-ON** 30 minutes • **TOTAL** 1 hour, 30 minutes

- 1 (6- to 8-pound) kabocha squash, halved and seeded
- 2 tablespoons unsalted butter, melted
- 1 tablespoon kosher salt
- 2 teaspoons freshly ground black pepper
- 1 pound parsnips, peeled and cut into 1-inch pieces
- 2 cups heavy cream
- ½ cup chicken broth
- 4 fresh thyme sprigs
- 3 garlic cloves, smashed
- 1 bay leaf
- Table salt
- Black pepper
- Garnish: freshly ground black pepper

1. Preheat the oven to 450°F. Brush the cut sides of the squash with the butter, and sprinkle with 2 teaspoons of the salt and 1 teaspoon of the pepper. Place the squash, cut sides down, on a large jelly-roll pan.
2. Bake at 450°F for 35 to 40 minutes or until tender when pierced with a fork and the pulp is easily scooped from the skin. Cool on the pan 15 minutes.
3. Scrape out the pulp from the squash into a bowl, and mash with a potato masher until smooth.
4. Bring the parsnips, next 5 ingredients, and remaining 1 teaspoon salt and 1 teaspoon pepper to a boil in a saucepan over medium. Reduce the heat, and simmer, covered, 15 to 20 minutes or until the parsnips are very tender. Pour through a strainer into a bowl, reserving the liquid; discard the thyme sprigs, garlic, and bay leaf.
5. Pulse the squash pulp and parsnips in a food processor, adding enough reserved liquid, 2 tablespoons at a time, to reach the desired consistency. Season with the salt and pepper to taste. Garnish, if desired.

SKILLET SQUASH BLOSSOM

The best part of this showstopping dish is the caramelized edges.

SERVES 8 • **HANDS-ON** 10 minutes • **TOTAL** 50 minutes

- 1 (1½-pound) butternut squash, peeled, halved lengthwise, seeds removed
- 3 center-cut bacon slices
- ½ cup diced yellow onion
- 2 tablespoons olive oil
- 1 tablespoon chopped fresh thyme
- 2 teaspoons kosher salt
- ½ teaspoon freshly ground black pepper
- 4 teaspoons pure maple syrup
- Garnish: fresh thyme

1. Preheat the oven to 400°F. Place the squash, cut side down, in an 8-inch square baking dish; fill with 1 inch of water. Cover with plastic wrap, and microwave on HIGH 5 minutes. Thinly slice the squash, and place in a large bowl.
2. Heat a 10-inch cast-iron skillet over medium. Cook the bacon 5 minutes. Increase the heat to medium-high, and cook until golden brown. Remove the bacon, reserving the drippings in the skillet. Crumble the bacon, and set aside. Reduce the heat to medium; add the onion to the skillet, and cook until translucent, about 2 minutes. Stir in the oil, thyme, salt, pepper, and 2 teaspoons of the maple syrup. Add the mixture to the squash slices; toss to combine.
3. Starting at the outer edge of the same skillet, arrange the squash slices in slightly overlapping concentric circles to form a flower shape. Bake at 400°F until the squash is tender and the edges begin to crisp, about 40 minutes. Drizzle with the remaining 2 teaspoons maple syrup. Top with the bacon. Garnish, if desired.

FENNEL-POTATO GRATIN

This gratin dish can be made one day ahead of time and reheated, covered with foil, in a 350°F oven for 30 minutes.

SERVES 12 • **HANDS-ON** 45 minutes • **TOTAL** 1 hour, 45 minutes

- 2 tablespoons butter
- 1 tablespoon olive oil
- 2 fennel bulbs (about 2¼ pounds), halved and thinly sliced crosswise (about ⅛ inch thick)
- 1 teaspoon kosher salt
- ½ teaspoon freshly ground black pepper
- ⅓ cup dry white wine
- 2½ pounds Yukon gold potatoes, peeled and cut into ⅛-inch-thick slices
- 3 garlic cloves, minced
- 3 cups heavy cream
- 2 cups (8 ounces) shredded Comté cheese

1. Preheat the oven to 350°F. Melt the butter with the oil in a large skillet over medium. Add the fennel, ½ teaspoon of the salt, and ¼ teaspoon of the pepper. Cook, stirring occasionally, 2 minutes. Add the wine; cover, reduce the heat to medium-low. Cook, stirring occasionally, 20 minutes or until the fennel is tender.
2. Increase the heat to medium-high, and cook, uncovered and stirring often, 7 to 8 minutes or until the fennel is lightly browned.
3. Bring the potatoes, garlic, cream, and remaining ½ teaspoon salt and ¼ teaspoon pepper to a low simmer in a Dutch oven over medium-high. Cover, reduce the heat to medium-low, and simmer 10 minutes or until the potatoes are almost tender.
4. Place one-third of the potatoes in an even layer in a lightly greased 3-quart baking dish, using a slotted spoon. Sprinkle with ⅔ cup of the cheese. Top with half of the fennel. Repeat the layers once. Top with the remaining potatoes and ⅔ cup cheese. Pour the remaining cream mixture over the top. Cover with aluminum foil.
5. Bake at 350°F for 20 minutes. Uncover and bake 30 to 35 minutes or until bubbly and golden brown. Let stand 10 minutes before serving.

WHIPPED CELERY ROOT-AND-POTATO GRATIN WITH ROSEMARY-GRUYÈRE CRUST

Half-and-half and butter go into puréed celery root and potatoes to make this dish super creamy. Assemble this ahead of time and bake right before serving.

SERVES 10 to 12 • **HANDS-ON** 45 minutes • **TOTAL** 1 hour, 20 minutes

- 3 medium-size celery roots (about 2½ pounds), peeled and cut into 1-inch pieces (about 8 cups)
- 1½ pounds baking potatoes, peeled and cut into 1-inch pieces (about 4 cups)
- 1½ pounds Yukon Gold potatoes, peeled and cut into 1-inch pieces (about 4½ cups)
- 8 garlic cloves, peeled and smashed
- 2 tablespoons kosher salt, plus 1 teaspoon
- ¾ cup half-and-half
- ½ cup unsalted butter
- ¾ teaspoon freshly ground black pepper
- 1¾ cups (6½ ounces) shredded Gruyère cheese
- 1 cup chopped pecans
- 1½ tablespoons finely chopped fresh rosemary

1. Preheat the oven to 425°F. Combine the first 4 ingredients and 2 tablespoons of the salt in large stockpot. Add cold water to cover by 1 inch, and bring to boil over medium-high. Reduce the heat to medium-low, and simmer, partially covered, 20 minutes or until the celery root and potatoes are tender.
2. Meanwhile, heat the half-and-half and butter in a small saucepan over medium-low until the butter melts.
3. Drain the potato mixture. Process, in batches, in a food processor until almost smooth. (If the mixture is too dry, add a few tablespoonfuls of the warm half-and-half to moisten.) Return the pureed potato mixture to the pot.
4. Stir in the half-and-half mixture, pepper, and remaining 1 teaspoon salt. Transfer the mixture to a 13- x 9-inch baking dish, and sprinkle with the cheese, pecans, and rosemary.
5. Bake at 425°F for 30 minutes or until the cheese is melted and slightly browned. Let cool 5 minutes before serving.

BABY HASSELBACK POTATOES WITH BLUE CHEESE AND BACON

Hasselback-style potatoes have thin, accordion-like slices that turn crisp in the oven. Blue cheese and bacon bring them over the top for the holidays.

SERVES 10 • **HANDS-ON** 35 minutes • **TOTAL** 1 hour, 25 minutes

- 10 (2½-ounce) small Yukon Gold potatoes
- ½ cup salted butter, melted
- 1½ tablespoons finely chopped fresh rosemary
- 1½ teaspoons kosher salt, divided
- 1 ounce blue cheese, crumbled (about ¼ cup)
- ½ cup crumbled cooked bacon (about 6 slices)
- ¼ cup chopped fresh chives

1. Preheat the oven to 425°F. Slice each potato crosswise at ⅛-inch intervals, cutting to within ¼ inch of the bottom of the potato. (Do not cut all the way through the potatoes.) Arrange the potatoes, cut side up, on a lightly greased baking sheet.
2. Combine the melted butter, rosemary, and 1 teaspoon of the salt in small bowl. Spoon ⅓ cup of the melted butter mixture evenly over the potatoes.
3. Bake at 425°F on the middle oven rack until tender, 45 to 50 minutes. Spoon the remaining butter mixture evenly over the potatoes. Sprinkle evenly with the blue cheese and remaining ½ teaspoon salt. Bake until the cheese is slightly melted and the potatoes are golden, about 5 minutes.
4. Sprinkle evenly with the bacon and chives, and serve immediately.

SAVORY SWEET POTATO CASSEROLE

This savory take on the classic super-sweet standard will be a welcome addition to your holiday menu. Use your time wisely and bake the sweet potatoes ahead. You can even put the casserole together a day or two ahead of time (wait to sprinkle the topping on just before baking).

SERVES 10 to 12 • **HANDS-ON** 15 minutes • **TOTAL** 1 hour, 40 minutes

- 4 pounds sweet potatoes
- 2 (5.2-ounce) packages garlic-and-herb spreadable cheese
- ½ teaspoon kosher salt
- ¼ teaspoon freshly ground black pepper
- 3 large eggs
- 2 tablespoons butter, melted
- ¾ cup chopped pecans
- ¾ cup panko (Japanese breadcrumbs)
- ¼ cup shaved Parmesan cheese
- 2 tablespoons chopped fresh parsley

1. Preheat the oven to 400°F. Place the sweet potatoes on a baking sheet. Bake 1 hour or until tender. Cool slightly, and peel.
2. Place the sweet potato flesh in a medium bowl. Beat together the sweet potato flesh, cheese, salt, and pepper until smooth, using a hand mixer with a whisk attachment. Beat in the eggs, 1 at a time, until blended. Spoon the sweet potato mixture into a 13- x 9-inch baking dish coated with cooking spray.
3. Stir together the butter, pecans, panko, Parmesan, and parsley in a bowl. Sprinkle the mixture over the sweet potato mixture.
4. Bake at 400°F for 20 minutes or until puffed and golden. Let stand 5 to 10 minutes before serving.

Baby Hasselback Potatoes
with Blue Cheese and Bacon

BUTTER BEAN GRATIN WITH HERBED CORNBREAD CRUST

Sometimes we Southerners have the presence of mind to store away the bounty of summer gardens and "put up" some butter beans in our freezers. The holidays are a perfect time to enjoy distant memories of fresh peas and beans, and this is a perfect way to present them, complete with a crust made of crunchy herbed cornbread.

SERVES 10 to 12 • **HANDS-ON** 30 minutes • **TOTAL** 2 hours, 10 minutes

BEANS

6 bacon slices
1 cup diced sweet onion
1 shallot, chopped
3 cups chicken broth
3 cups heavy cream
1 bay leaf
3 tablespoons chopped fresh chives
1 tablespoon chopped fresh thyme
1 teaspoon lemon zest
Table salt
Black pepper
6 cups fresh baby butter beans*

*5 (10-ounce) packages frozen baby limas, thawed, may be substituted.

TOPPING

1½ cups buttermilk
1 cup plain yellow cornmeal
½ cup all-purpose flour
½ cup (2 ounces) shredded Parmesan cheese
¼ cup canola oil
2 tablespoons chopped fresh parsley
1½ teaspoons baking powder
1 teaspoon baking soda
½ teaspoon table salt
1 large egg, lightly beaten

1. Prepare the Beans: Preheat the oven to 400°F. Cook the bacon in a large, deep skillet or Dutch oven over medium 6 to 8 minutes or until crisp. Drain the bacon on a paper towel-lined plate, reserving 2 tablespoons of the drippings in the skillet. Increase the heat to medium-high. Crumble or chop the bacon.
2. Sauté the onion and shallot in the hot drippings 4 to 5 minutes or until softened. Add the broth, cream, and bay leaf, and bring to a boil. Stir in 1 tablespoon of the chives, thyme, and lemon zest. Season with salt and pepper to taste, and remove from the heat.
3. Place the butter beans in a lightly greased 13- x 9-inch baking dish; pour the hot cream mixture over the beans. Place the baking dish on a jelly-roll pan.
4. Bake at 400°F for 1 hour and 20 minutes or until the sauce is thickened.
5. Meanwhile, prepare the Topping: Stir together the buttermilk, next 9 ingredients, reserved bacon, and remaining 2 tablespoons chives in a medium bowl until blended. (Prepare the topping just as the beans are finished baking.)
6. Spoon the cornmeal mixture over the bean mixture, smoothing to cover the entire surface evenly.
7. Bake at 400°F 20 minutes or until golden brown.

ROASTED HEIRLOOM ROOT VEGETABLES IN LEMON-HORSERADISH BUTTER

Roasting brings out the natural sweetness and earthiness of these beautiful root vegetables and is one of the easiest methods of cooking. Be sure your vegetables are uniform in size so they cook in the same amount of time. The compound butter makes enough to freeze for other uses, or even for holiday gift giving, such as with our Sea Salt-Poppy Seed Cloverleaf Rolls (page 82).

SERVES 12 • **HANDS-ON** 20 minutes • **TOTAL** 5 hours, 35 minutes, includes chilling

1 cup butter, softened
1 tablespoon chopped fresh thyme
1 tablespoon chopped fresh flat-leaf parsley
2 to 3 tablespoons freshly grated horseradish
1 teaspoon lemon zest
2 tablespoons fresh lemon juice
2 pounds Chioggia beets, trimmed (about 6 medium)
2 pounds golden beets, trimmed (about 5 medium)
3 (6-ounce) packages fresh baby rainbow carrots, cut into 1-inch pieces
1 pound parsnips, cut into 3/4-inch-thick slices
3 tablespoons extra-virgin olive oil
Kosher salt
Freshly ground black pepper

1. Mash together the first 6 ingredients in a medium bowl, using a fork.
2. Place the butter mixture on a large piece of parchment or wax paper. Bring 1 side of the paper over the mixture. Hold down the other end of the paper. Place the flat edge of a baking sheet or other sturdy flat object next to the butter on the paper. Using your other hand, hold the end of the baking sheet, and push the bottom of the baking sheet away from you into the base of the butter mixture, forming a 1 1/2-inch-wide log. Chill 4 hours.
3. Meanwhile, preheat the oven to 425°F. Cut all the beets into 3/4- to 1-inch wedges, if needed, for uniform pieces. Toss together the beets, carrots, and next 2 ingredients in a large bowl. Season lightly with the desired amount of kosher salt and freshly ground pepper, and toss. Place in a single layer on 2 large baking sheets, leaving space between the vegetables.
4. Bake at 425°F for 1 hour and 15 minutes to 1 1/2 hours or until vegetables are tender and golden brown, stirring every 20 minutes.
5. Transfer the roasted vegetables to a large bowl. Add 1/4 cup of the butter mixture. Toss until coated. Serve immediately with the remaining butter mixture.

ROOT VEGETABLE GRATIN

Assemble layers of veggies and bubbly cheese a day ahead to save on Christmas Day prep.

SERVES 8 • **HANDS-ON** 30 minutes • **TOTAL** 1 hour, 40 minutes

- 1 large rutabaga, peeled and cut into 1/8-inch-thick slices
- 2 large russet potatoes, peeled and cut into 1/8-inch-thick slices
- 3 large parsnips, peeled and cut into 1/8-inch-thick slices
- 1 1/2 teaspoons kosher salt
- 1 1/2 cups heavy cream
- 8 ounces Gruyère cheese, shredded (about 2 cups)
- Garnish: Chopped fresh parsley

1. Preheat the oven to 400°F. Toss together the rutabaga, potatoes, parsnips, salt, and 3/4 cup of the cream in a large bowl. Spread one-third of the mixture evenly in a lightly greased 11- x 7-inch baking dish; top with 3/4 cup of the Gruyère. Layer one-third of the rutabaga mixture, 3/4 cup of the Gruyère, and the remaining rutabaga mixture and 3/4 cup cream. Top with the remaining 1/2 cup Gruyère.

2. Cover loosely with aluminum foil. Bake at 400°F for 45 minutes. Uncover and bake until the vegetables are tender and the cheese is golden brown, 20 to 25 more minutes. Transfer to a wire rack; cool 5 minutes. Garnish, if desired.

LEMON-ROASTED TURNIPS WITH BACON AND THYME

The earthy flavor of roasted turnips and bacon is enhanced by the sweet-and-sour combination of ingredients in this dish. Served alongside your favorite holiday meats, this will surely delight your dinner guests. If you can't find sorghum, use honey, though sorghum is preferred.

SERVES 8 to 10 • **HANDS-ON** 20 minutes • **TOTAL** 1 hour

- 1/2 pound thick-cut bacon slices, chopped
- 3 pounds turnips, cut into 1/2-inch wedges
- 1 large sweet onion, sliced
- 2 tablespoons olive oil
- 1 tablespoon apple cider vinegar
- 1 tablespoon sorghum
- 2 teaspoons lemon zest
- 1 tablespoon chopped fresh thyme
- 1 teaspoon fresh lemon juice
- Table salt
- Black pepper
- Lemon wedges
- Garnish: fresh thyme

1. Preheat the oven to 475°F. Line 2 large jelly-roll pans with parchment paper.
2. Cook the bacon in a large skillet over medium-high 8 to 10 minutes or until crisp. Remove the bacon with a slotted spoon, and drain on paper towels, reserving 2 tablespoons of the drippings in a large bowl.
3. Stir the turnips and next 5 ingredients into the drippings in the bowl. Place in a single layer on the prepared pans.
4. Bake at 475°F for 40 to 45 minutes or until golden brown and tender, rotating and turning the baking sheets halfway through. Remove from the oven, and sprinkle with the thyme, lemon juice, and bacon. Season with the salt and pepper to taste. Serve immediately with the lemon wedges. Garnish, if desired.

CARAMELIZED CARROTS WITH HAZELNUT GREMOLATA

This colorful side is the perfect complement to roasted meats, providing sweetness and crunch. Toast the hazelnuts in a skillet over medium-low until fragrant.

SERVES 8 • **HANDS-ON** 15 minutes • **TOTAL** 25 minutes

- 1/4 cup hazelnuts, toasted and chopped
- 3 tablespoons fresh flat-leaf parsley leaves, chopped
- 1 teaspoon lemon zest
- 1 teaspoon fresh lemon juice
- 1 pound carrots, cut into 3- to 4-inch-long (1/2-inch-thick) pieces
- 1/2 cup water
- 2 tablespoons unsalted butter
- 1 tablespoon maple syrup
- 1 teaspoon kosher salt
- 1/2 teaspoon freshly ground black pepper

1. Stir together the first 4 ingredients in a small bowl.
2. Bring the carrots and water to a boil in a large saucepan, covered, over high. Boil 5 minutes. Uncover and cook until the liquid evaporates, about 1 minute. Decrease the heat to medium.
3. Add the butter, syrup, salt, and pepper. Cook, stirring occasionally, 4 minutes or until the edges of the carrots are caramelized and lightly browned. Transfer the carrots to a serving platter, and sprinkle with the hazelnut gremolata.

OVEN-ROASTED HARICOTS VERTS WITH BLISTERED TOMATOES AND OLIVES

Roasting transforms year-round ingredients into extraordinary accents.

SERVES 6 to 8 • **HANDS-ON** 10 minutes • **TOTAL** 35 minutes

- 2 pounds haricots verts (French green beans)
- 2 (10-ounce) containers grape or cherry tomatoes
- 3 large shallots, thinly sliced
- 1/4 cup olive oil
- 2 tablespoons chopped fresh thyme
- 1 1/2 tablespoons chopped fresh oregano
- 1 1/2 teaspoons kosher salt
- 1/2 teaspoon freshly ground black pepper
- 1/3 cup chopped pitted kalamata olives
- 1 tablespoon chopped fresh parsley

1. Preheat the oven to 425°F. Toss together the first 8 ingredients in a large bowl. Divide between 2 large jelly-roll pans.
2. Bake at 425°F for 25 to 30 minutes or until the beans are tender and the tomatoes burst, rotating the pans after 15 minutes.
3. Transfer to a serving platter, and top with the olives and parsley. Serve hot or at room temperature.

CHEESY HAM, CORN, AND GRITS BAKE

This impressive-looking casserole bakes up puffy and golden with pockets of fresh corn and savory ham. Think of it as a soufflé without the work.

SERVES 8 · **HANDS-ON** 35 minutes · **TOTAL** 1 hour, 40 minutes

- 2 tablespoons salted butter
- 1/4 cup finely chopped yellow onion
- 2 teaspoons minced garlic
- 4 1/2 cups water
- 1 teaspoon table salt
- 1 1/2 cups uncooked yellow stone-ground grits
- 2 (8-ounce) package cubed boneless ham, drained and patted dry with paper towels
- 1 (8-ounce) package shredded sharp Cheddar cheese
- 1 (8-ounce) package shredded extra-sharp Cheddar cheese
- 1 cup whole milk
- 1 cup frozen whole kernel corn, thawed
- 1 1/2 teaspoons chopped fresh thyme
- 1/4 teaspoon freshly ground black pepper
- 4 large eggs, lightly beaten

1. Preheat the oven to 350°F. Lightly grease a 3-quart baking dish.

2. Melt the butter in a Dutch oven over medium; stir in the onion and garlic, and cook, stirring constantly, 2 minutes. Stir in the water and salt, increase the heat to medium-high, and bring to a boil. Whisk in the grits, and stir in the ham; return to a boil. Reduce the heat to medium-low, and simmer, whisking occasionally, until thickened and the grits are almost tender, 15 to 20 minutes. Remove from the heat; add both cheeses, stirring until completely melted. Stir in the milk, corn, thyme, pepper, and eggs. Spoon the mixture into the prepared baking dish.

3. Bake at 350°F oven until golden and cooked through, 50 minutes to 1 hour. Let stand 15 minutes before serving.

BRUSSELS SPROUTS WITH CORNBREAD CROUTONS

Toasty brown-butter croutons make simple roasted Brussels sprouts holiday worthy.

SERVES 8 to 10 • **HANDS-ON** 5 minutes • **TOTAL** 40 minutes

- 2 pounds Brussels sprouts, trimmed and halved
- 1½ tablespoons olive oil
- 1 teaspoon kosher salt
- ¼ teaspoon black pepper
- 2 cups cubed day-old cornbread (½-inch cubes)
- ¼ cup salted butter
- 1 shallot, minced
- 1 tablespoon fresh thyme leaves

1. Preheat the oven to 425°F. Toss together the first 4 ingredients in a large bowl; divide evenly between 2 rimmed baking sheets. Bake in the 425°F oven until golden brown, about 20 minutes. Reduce the oven heat to 350°F.

2. Spread the cornbread cubes evenly on a baking sheet; bake at 350°F until browned and crispy, about 15 minutes.

3. Cook the butter, stirring constantly, in a medium skillet over medium until foaming. Add the shallot and thyme; cook, stirring often, 1 minute. Drizzle the butter mixture over the toasted cornbread. Arrange the Brussels sprouts in a serving dish; top with the cornbread mixture.

ROASTED BRUSSELS SPROUTS WITH LEMON BROWN BUTTER AND HAZELNUTS

Sumptuous brown butter with a touch of lemon cloaks tender roasted Brussels sprouts. Topped with crunchy, earthy, toasted hazelnuts, this side dish may steal the show.

SERVES 8 • **HANDS-ON** 20 minutes • **TOTAL** 45 minutes

- 2 pounds Brussels sprouts
- 2 tablespoons olive oil
- 3/4 teaspoon kosher salt
- 1/2 teaspoon freshly ground black pepper
- 6 tablespoons unsalted butter
- 1 teaspoon lemon zest
- 1/4 cup fresh lemon juice
- 1/2 cup chopped toasted hazelnuts

1. Preheat the oven to 400°F. Trim the ends of the Brussels sprouts, and remove the outer leaves. Cut any large Brussels sprouts in half lengthwise (through the stem and bottom ends). Place on a large jelly-roll pan; drizzle with the oil, and sprinkle with 1/2 teaspoon of the salt and pepper. Toss gently.
2. Bake at 400°F for 25 minutes or until tender and lightly browned, stirring after 10 minutes.
3. Meanwhile, cook the butter in a medium skillet over medium-high, whisking constantly, 5 minutes or until fragrant and deep golden brown (do not burn). Whisk in the lemon zest and juice.
4. Toss the Brussels sprouts with the browned butter mixture and the remaining 1/4 teaspoon salt in a large bowl. Sprinkle with the hazelnuts; serve immediately.

SWEET CORN AND POBLANO PUDDING

Most Southerners are bound to have "put up" corn from their summer gardens, and, by all means, use it in this casserole. However, frozen corn from the Piggly Wiggly will do just fine, too.

SERVES 10 to 12 • **HANDS-ON** 20 minutes • **TOTAL** 55 minutes

- 2 tablespoons butter
- 1 cup chopped sweet onion
- 1 cup chopped red bell pepper
- 1 cup chopped poblano pepper
- 4 cups frozen corn kernels, thawed
- 5 large eggs
- 1 cup heavy cream
- 3/4 cup half-and-half
- 1/4 cup chopped fresh parsley
- 1/4 cup chopped fresh cilantro
- 1 tablespoon hot sauce
- 1 tablespoon Worcestershire sauce
- 1/2 teaspoon ground cumin
- 2 cups (8 ounces) shredded white Cheddar cheese
- 1 cup crushed tortilla chips

1. Preheat the oven to 350°F. Melt the butter in a large skillet over medium-high. Add the onion and both peppers; cook 4 minutes or until softened. Add the corn, and cook 3 minutes. Remove from the heat, and cool slightly.
2. Whisk together the eggs and next 7 ingredients in a bowl until blended. Stir in the vegetables and cheese. Pour the mixture into a 13- x 9-inch baking dish coated with cooking spray.
3. Bake at 350°F for 30 to 35 minutes. Sprinkle with the chips, and bake 5 more minutes or until golden brown and set.

WHOLE ROASTED CAULIFLOWER WITH RICOTTA-PECORINO CRUST

This dish can be poached a full day ahead, then roasted at the last minute after your guests arrive.

SERVES 6 • **HANDS-ON** 30 minutes • **TOTAL** 1 hour

- 1 (750-milliliter) bottle dry white wine
- ½ cup kosher salt
- 1 large Vidalia onion, cut into wedges
- 3 bay leaves, halved
- 3 garlic cloves, smashed
- 2 fresh thyme sprigs
- 1 tablespoon crushed red pepper
- 3 medium lemons, zested and juiced
- 1 gallon water
- 2½ pounds fresh whole cauliflower, trimmed and outer leaves removed
- 1 cup whole-milk ricotta cheese
- ¼ cup plain Greek yogurt
- 2 ounces Pecorino Romano cheese, shredded
- 1 tablespoon extra-virgin olive oil
- Table salt
- Freshly ground black pepper
- ¼ cup panko (Japanese breadcrumbs)
- 1½ teaspoons chopped fresh parsley

1. Preheat the oven to 400°F. Combine the wine, salt, onion, bay leaves, garlic, thyme, red pepper, lemon juice and lemons, and water in a very large saucepan, and bring to a boil. Reduce the heat; simmer 5 minutes or until the onions are soft. Remove the solids using a slotted spoon.
2. Return the liquid to a simmer, and add the cauliflower; simmer 13 minutes or until a knife inserted into the center of the cauliflower is met with slight resistance. Carefully remove the cauliflower from the pan, and drain in a colander. Place on a parchment paper-lined jelly-roll pan.
3. Stir together the ricotta, yogurt, cheese, oil, and 1 teaspoon lemon zest until smooth. Season with table salt and pepper to taste.
4. Combine the panko, parsley, and ¼ teaspoon lemon zest. Coat the outside of the cauliflower with the ricotta mixture. Coat with the panko mixture.
5. Bake at 400°F for 20 minutes or until golden brown.

CLASSIC BREAD DRESSING

Though cornbread dressing reigns supreme in the South, we love this sourdough version too.

SERVES 8 • **HANDS-ON** 22 minutes • **TOTAL** 1 hour, 22 minutes

- 1 tablespoon olive oil
- 2 tablespoons unsalted butter
- 2 cups sliced celery
- 3 leeks, white parts only, thinly sliced
- 3 garlic cloves, chopped
- 1½ tablespoons chopped fresh thyme
- 1½ teaspoons kosher salt
- 1 teaspoon black pepper
- 2 cups reduced-sodium chicken broth
- 9 cups cubed sourdough bread (about 16 ounces), toasted
- ¼ cup melted unsalted butter
- 3 large eggs, lightly beaten
- 1 tablespoon chopped fresh flat-leaf parsley

1. Preheat the oven to 375°F. Heat the oil and butter in a large nonstick skillet over high until the butter melts. Stir in the celery and leeks; cook, stirring occasionally, until tender, about 5 minutes. Add the garlic; cook, stirring, 1 minute. Add the thyme, salt, pepper, and ½ cup of the broth; cook, stirring, 1 minute.
2. Combine the celery mixture and bread cubes in a large bowl. Add the melted butter, eggs, and remaining 1½ cups broth; stir to combine.
3. Spoon the mixture into a lightly greased 11- x 7-inch baking dish; let stand 15 minutes. Bake at 375°F until golden brown, 40 to 45 minutes. Sprinkle with the parsley.

Whole Roasted Cauliflower
with Ricotta-Pecorino Crust

WILTED CHARD WITH SALAMI CRUMBS

Feel free to swap out the salami for pancetta or bacon, and the chard for kale or collards. We tested with sopressata salami.

SERVES 6 • **HANDS-ON** 25 minutes • **TOTAL** 25 minutes

- 1 cup chopped Italian dried salami (about 4 ounces)
- 2 tablespoons extra-virgin olive oil
- 3 garlic cloves, minced
- 1/4 teaspoon crushed red pepper
- 1/2 cup panko (Japanese breadcrumbs)
- 1 3/4 pounds Swiss chard, coarsely chopped
- 1 tablespoon sherry vinegar
- 1 teaspoon kosher salt
- 1/2 teaspoon freshly ground black pepper

1. Sauté the salami in 1 tablespoon of the hot oil in a large skillet over medium until crisp, 6 to 8 minutes. Add the garlic and red pepper; sauté 1 minute. Add the panko, and cook 3 minutes or until just beginning to brown. Transfer to a bowl.
2. Heat the remaining 1 tablespoon oil in skillet over medium-high. Add the chard; cook 4 minutes or just until wilted, stirring with tongs. Drizzle with the vinegar, salt, and pepper, and transfer to a platter. Sprinkle with the breadcrumb mixture.

OYSTER CASSEROLE

Crumbled crackers often top this casserole, but we prefer homemade breadcrumbs because they soak up more butter.

SERVES 4 • **HANDS-ON** 20 minutes • **TOTAL** 30 minutes

- 5 tablespoons salted butter, divided
- 1/4 cup chopped yellow onion
- 1/4 cup chopped green bell pepper
- 1/4 cup chopped celery
- 2 scallions, thinly sliced
- 1 teaspoon minced garlic
- 2 (16-ounce) containers fresh oysters, drained well
- 4 ounces fresh mushrooms, sliced
- 2 tablespoons all-purpose flour
- 1/2 cup heavy cream
- 1 ounce Parmesan cheese, grated
- 3/4 teaspoon kosher salt
- 1/4 teaspoon freshly ground black pepper
- 1/4 teaspoon ground nutmeg
- 1 cup coarse fresh breadcrumbs (from 1/4 baguette)

1. Preheat the broiler. Melt 2 tablespoons of the butter in a skillet over medium-high. Add the onion, bell pepper, celery, scallions, and garlic. Cook, stirring, until the vegetables soften, 5 to 7 minutes. Add the oysters and mushrooms. Bring to a simmer, and cook, stirring often, 5 minutes. Set aside.
2. Melt 1 tablespoon of the butter in a small saucepan over medium. Whisk in the flour, and cook, whisking constantly, until smooth, 30 seconds to 1 minute. Add the cream, and cook, whisking constantly, until very thick and beginning to bubble. Add the Parmesan, and cook, whisking constantly, until the cheese is melted. Remove from the heat.
3. Using a fine wire-mesh strainer, strain the oyster mixture; discard the liquid. Add the oyster mixture to the cheese sauce; stir until fully incorporated. Stir in the salt, pepper, and nutmeg. Spread the mixture into a 11- x 7-inch baking dish lightly coated with cooking spray. Melt the remaining 2 tablespoons butter; toss the breadcrumbs with the melted butter. Sprinkle the breadcrumbs over the oyster mixture.
4. Broil on the middle rack of the oven until the breadcrumbs are deep golden brown and the mixture is bubbly, 4 to 5 minutes.

ULTIMATE MACARONI AND CHEESE

It seems that everyone at the holiday table loves mac and cheese. It's comfort food at its finest and is best when presented in a deep dish with a crispy, crunchy topping.

SERVES 10 to 12 • **HANDS-ON** 20 minutes • **TOTAL** 40 minutes

1 (16-ounce) box mini penne pasta
1/2 cup unsalted butter
1/2 cup all-purpose flour
1 quart milk
1 (8-ounce) block Havarti cheese, grated
1 (8-ounce) block sharp white Cheddar cheese, grated
1 (8-ounce) wedge Parmesan cheese, grated
1 teaspoon table salt
1/2 teaspoon freshly ground black pepper
Dash of freshly ground nutmeg
Dash of cayenne pepper
1/2 (12-ounce) day-old French bread baguette, slightly stale
1/4 cup salted butter
1/4 cup chopped fresh flat-leaf parsley
Table salt
Black pepper

1. Preheat the oven to 350°F. Prepare the pasta according to the package directions for al dente.
2. Melt the unsalted butter in a large saucepan over medium-high. Whisk in the flour, and cook, whisking constantly, 1 to 2 minutes. Gradually whisk in the milk until well blended. Reduce the heat to medium, and cook, stirring often, 5 minutes or until the sauce thickens enough to coat back of a spoon. Add the Havarti, Cheddar, and half of the Parmesan; stir well until smooth. Remove from the heat, and stir in the salt, pepper, nutmeg, and cayenne pepper.
3. Add the cheese sauce to the pasta, and stir to coat. Spoon the mixture into a lightly greased 13- x 9-inch baking dish.
4. Bake at 350°F for 10 minutes.
5. Meanwhile, pulse the bread in a food processor until coarsely crumbled. Melt the salted butter in a small microwave-safe bowl at HIGH 30 seconds or until melted. Add the breadcrumbs, parsley, remaining Parmesan cheese, and salt and pepper to taste, tossing to coat the breadcrumbs. Sprinkle the breadcrumb mixture over the top of the pasta mixture.
6. Bake at 350°F for 10 to 15 minutes or until the topping is crispy and golden.

SWEET ENDINGS

Indulge your wildest sugar cravings with these fantastical and decadent Christmas cakes! With frostings piled high to cookie embellishments, these recipes truly take the cake. Plus, here you'll also find recipes for pies and other goodies.

WHITE CHOCOLATE POINSETTIA CAKE

Here, the creamy sweetness of white chocolate is showcased in three ways—the cake, mousse, and buttercream.

SERVES 8 • **HANDS-ON** 52 minutes • **TOTAL** 2 hours, 37 minutes

POINSETTIA COOKIES

1 (16.5-ounce) package refrigerated sugar cookie dough

ROYAL ICING

16 ounces powdered sugar
2 teaspoons meringue powder
5 to 6 tablespoons warm water

COOKIE DECOR

Gold dragées (optional)
Edible ivory luster dust
Edible gold luster dust

CAKE LAYERS

1 (4-ounce) white chocolate baking bar, chopped
1 cup boiling water
1 3/4 cups granulated sugar
1 1/4 cups salted butter, softened
7 large egg whites, at room temperature, lightly beaten
3 1/2 cups bleached cake flour
4 teaspoons baking powder
1/4 teaspoon table salt
2 teaspoons vanilla bean paste
Shortening, for greasing pan

WHITE CHOCOLATE MOUSSE FILLING

1 cup white chocolate chips
1 1/4 cups heavy cream
1 tablespoon crème de cacao

FROSTING

1 (4-ounce) white chocolate baking bar, chopped
1/3 cup heavy cream
1 cup salted butter, softened
1 (32-ounce) package powdered sugar
1/4 cup heavy cream
1/8 teaspoon table salt
2 teaspoons vanilla extract

1. Make the Poinsettia Cookies: Preheat the oven to 350°F. Roll out the dough to 1/8-inch thickness. Cut the dough into 12 large petals with a 3-inch leaf cookie cutter. Cut 3 small petals from the dough, using a 2-inch leaf cookie cutter and the center of the poinsettia using a 1 1/2-inch flower cutter. Bake for 7 to 9 minutes.
2. Decorate the Cookies: To make Royal Icing, beat the powdered sugar, meringue powder, and warm water with an electric mixer on high speed, 5 minutes. Pipe the icing onto the cooled cookies. Top the center of the poinsettia cookie with the dragées, if desired. (Remove before eating.) Let the cookies dry. Use a paintbrush to paint the cookies with the edible dusts.
3. Make the Cake Layers: Place the white chocolate in a bowl. Pour the boiling water over the chocolate, and let stand 1 minute; stir until the chocolate is melted and smooth. Cool completely.
4. Preheat the oven to 350°F. Beat the granulated sugar and butter with a heavy-duty stand mixer on medium speed until fluffy, about 5 minutes. Gradually add the egg whites, a third at a time, beating well after each addition.
5. Sift together the flour, baking powder, and salt; add to the butter mixture alternately with the white chocolate mixture, beginning and ending with the flour mixture. Beat on low speed until blended after each addition. Add the vanilla bean paste. Pour into 3 greased and floured 9-inch round cake pans.
6. Bake at 350°F until a wooden pick inserted in the center comes out clean, 22 to 25 minutes. Cool in the pans on wire racks 10 minutes; remove from the pans to the wire racks, and cool completely.
7. Make the Mousse Filling: Microwave the white chocolate chips and 1/4 cup of the cream in a microwave-safe glass bowl on MEDIUM (50% power), 1 1/2 to 2 minutes or until melted and smooth, at 30-second intervals. Stir in the crème de cacao. Cool 5 minutes. Beat the remaining 1 cup cream with an electric mixer on medium speed until soft peaks form; fold into the white chocolate mixture. Chill.
8. Make the Frosting: Microwave the chopped chocolate and 1/3 cup heavy cream in a microwave-safe bowl on MEDIUM (50% power) until melted and smooth, 1 to 1 1/2 minutes, stirring every 30 seconds. Cool completely.
9. Beat the butter with an electric mixer on medium speed until creamy; gradually add the powdered sugar, beating on low speed until blended after each addition. Add 1/4 cup heavy cream, 1 tablespoon at a time, beating on low until blended after each addition. Add the salt and white chocolate mixture. Beat on low until combined. Increase the speed to high; beat until light and fluffy. Stir in the vanilla.
10. Assemble the Cake: Place 1 Cake Layer on a serving plate. Pipe a 1/2-inch-thick ring of Frosting around the edge of the Cake Layer. Spread half of the Mousse Filling inside the Frosting border; top with 1 Cake Layer. Pipe a 1/2-inch ring of the Frosting around the edge of the Cake Layer. Spread the remaining Filling inside the border. Place the remaining Cake Layer on the top; spread the top and sides of the cake with the remaining Frosting.
11. Pipe the Cake: Make another batch of Royal Icing. Spoon it into a ziplock plastic bag, and snip 1 corner of the bag. Pipe a column of 4 (1-inch) dots of frosting down the side of the frosted cake. (The dots should touch.) Place a 1-inch-wide spatula on the center of the first dot, and drag the frosting outward, creating a petal-like shape. Repeat with the remaining 3 dots, wiping the spatula clean. Pipe a second column of dots on top of the swiped edges, and drag the frosting outward. Repeat, covering the cake, ending with 1 column of dots. Arrange the cookies in a poinsettia flower shape on top of the frosted cake.

EGGNOG COCONUT CAKE

Two holiday classics—coconut cake and eggnog—come together in this dessert and the results couldn't be more delicious. The eggnog custard makes a great filling for tarts that have a gingersnap or graham cracker crust.

SERVES 12 to 16 • **HANDS-ON** 45 minutes • **TOTAL** 9 hours, 25 minutes; includes frosting, filling, and chilling

EGGNOG CUSTARD FILLING

1⅓ cups eggnog
⅓ cup milk
3 tablespoons granulated sugar
2 tablespoons cornstarch
¼ teaspoon freshly ground nutmeg
⅛ teaspoon table salt
3 large egg yolks
1 tablespoon dark rum

CAKE LAYERS

1 cup unsalted butter, softened
1½ cups granulated sugar
½ cup cream of coconut
1 teaspoon vanilla extract
4 large eggs
2¾ cups all-purpose flour
1 tablespoon baking powder
½ teaspoon table salt
1 cup unsweetened coconut milk

WHIPPED CREAM FROSTING

2 cups heavy cream
¼ cup powdered sugar
1½ tablespoons dark rum
½ teaspoon vanilla extract

1½ cups unsweetened flaked coconut, toasted
Garnishes: blood orange wedges, whole kumquats, rosemary sprigs

1. Make the Eggnog Custard Filling: Whisk together the first 7 ingredients in a heavy saucepan. Bring to a boil over medium, whisking constantly. Boil, whisking constantly, 1 minute or until thickened. Remove from the heat; whisk in the rum.
2. Pour the mixture into a bowl. Place heavy-duty plastic wrap directly on the warm custard (to prevent a film from forming); chill 2 to 8 hours. Makes 2 cups.
3. Make the Cake Layers: Preheat the oven to 350°F. Grease 2 (9-inch) round cake pans; line the bottoms with parchment paper. Grease the parchment; dust the pans lightly with flour.
4. Beat the butter and sugar with a heavy-duty electric stand mixer on medium speed until fluffy. Beat in the cream of coconut and vanilla. Add the eggs, one at a time, beating just until blended after each addition.
5. Whisk together the flour, baking powder, and salt; add to the butter mixture alternately with the coconut milk, beginning and ending with the flour mixture. Beat at low speed just until blended after each addition. Divide the batter between the prepared pans.
6. Bake at 350°F for 30 to 35 minutes or until a wooden pick inserted in the center comes out clean. Cool in the pans on wire racks 10 minutes; remove from the pans to the wire racks, and cool completely, about 1 hour.
7. Make the Whipped Cream Frosting: Beat the heavy cream, powdered sugar, dark rum, and vanilla at medium speed with an electric mixer until stiff peaks form. Makes about 4 cups.
8. Assemble the Cake: Cut the Cake Layers in half horizontally with a serrated knife. Place 1 Cake Layer half on a serving plate or cake stand; spread with about ⅔ cup of the Eggnog Custard Filling. Repeat the procedure twice; top with the remaining Cake Layer half. Spread the Whipped Cream Frosting on the top and sides of the cake. Sprinkle the toasted flaked coconut around the sides of the cake. Garnish, if desired. Cover and chill 4 to 24 hours. Let stand at room temperature at least 1 hour before serving.

NOTE: We tested with Coco Real for cream of coconut.

COCONUT CAKE WITH RUM FILLING AND COCONUT ERMINE FROSTING

Ermine frosting is creamy and spreadable like buttercream but with a lighter texture. (This recipe is also shown on the cover.)

SERVES 8 • **HANDS-ON** 1 hour, 22 minutes • **TOTAL** 3 hours, 51 minutes

CAKE LAYERS

1½ cups sweetened shredded coconut
1½ cups heavy cream
2 cups granulated sugar
1½ cups unsalted butter, softened
3 large egg yolks
2 teaspoons vanilla extract
4 cups unbleached cake flour
2 teaspoons baking powder
1 teaspoon baking soda
½ teaspoon table salt
4 large egg whites
Shortening, for greasing pans

FILLING

1½ cups half-and-half
¾ cup packed dark brown sugar
6 tablespoons cornstarch
3 large egg yolks
¼ cup unsalted butter
2 tablespoons dark rum

FROSTING

1 cup granulated sugar
1 cup whole milk
½ cup all-purpose flour
½ teaspoon table salt
2 cups unsalted butter, softened
1 tablespoon coconut extract
2 teaspoons vanilla extract

TREE COOKIES

1 (16.5-ounce) package refrigerated sugar cookie dough

ROYAL ICING

16 ounces powdered sugar
2 teaspoons meringue powder
5 to 6 tablespoons warm water

White coarse sanding sugar
White Disco Dust
½ cup shredded sweetened coconut flakes

1. Make the Cake Layers: Pulse the shredded coconut in a food processor until finely chopped, about 20 times. Transfer to a bowl. Heat the heavy cream in a small saucepan over medium just until warm and beginning to release steam, about 5 minutes. Pour the warmed cream over the coconut, and cool completely, about 30 minutes.

2. Preheat the oven to 350°F. Beat the granulated sugar and butter with a mixer on medium speed until light and fluffy, about 2 minutes. Add the egg yolks, 1 at a time, and beat until blended after each addition. Add the vanilla, and beat just until smooth. Whisk together the flour, baking powder, baking soda, and salt in a medium bowl. Add the flour mixture, in batches, alternately with the cream mixture, beginning and ending with the flour mixture. Beat on low speed until blended after each addition.

3. Beat the egg whites in a bowl with a mixer fitted with a whisk attachment on high speed until stiff peaks form. Stir about one-third of the egg whites into the batter; fold in the remaining egg whites. Pour the batter into 4 greased (with shortening) and floured 8-inch round cake pans.

4. Bake at 350°F until a wooden pick inserted in the center comes out clean, 25 to 30 minutes. Cool in the pans on wire racks 20 minutes; remove from the pans to the wire racks, and cool completely, about 30 minutes.

5. Make the Filling: Stir together the half-and-half and next 3 ingredients in a small saucepan. Cook over medium-high, whisking constantly, just until the mixture thickens and comes to a boil, 10 to 12 minutes. Remove from the heat, and whisk in the butter and rum until smooth. Transfer to a glass bowl, and place plastic wrap directly on the warm custard (to prevent a film from forming). Cool completely, about 30 minutes. Chill until ready to use.

6. Make the Frosting: Whisk together the granulated sugar, milk, flour, and salt in a medium saucepan. Cook over medium, whisking constantly, until the mixture thickens, about 10 minutes. Immediately pour the mixture into a medium-size metal bowl, and cool completely, about 30 minutes, stirring occasionally.

7. Beat the butter with an electric mixer on medium speed until smooth. Slowly add the cooled custard to the butter mixture, ¼ cup at a time; beat until smooth after each addition. Add the coconut extract and vanilla; beat until smooth. Spoon 1 cup of the Frosting into a ziplock plastic freezer bag, snip off 1 corner for piping.

8. Make the Tree Cookies: Roll out the dough to ⅛-inch thickness. Use 1¾-inch and 2¾-inch tree cookie cutters to create about 18 small cookies. Use 2¾-inch, 4-inch, and 5½-inch tree cookie cutters to make about 5 large cookies. Bake the cookies at 350°F for 7 to 9 minutes. Cool on a wire rack.

9. Make the Royal Icing: Beat the powdered sugar, meringue powder, and warm water with an electric mixer on high speed, 5 minutes. Pipe the icing onto the cooled cookies. Top with the sanding sugar and Disco Dust.

10. Assemble the Cake: Place 1 Cake Layer on a cake plate, and pipe a ½-inch-thick ring of Frosting around the outer edge of the layer. Spread about ⅔ cup of Filling over the layer. Repeat with the second and third Cake Layers. Place the final layer on top, and frost the top and sides with the remaining Frosting.

11. Embellish the Cake: Drag a 1-inch-wide spatula up and down the sides of the frosted cake to create ridges. Arrange the large tree cookies on top of the cake. Press the small Tree Cookies into the sides of the cake. Top with the coconut.

PEPPERMINT CAKE WITH SEVEN-MINUTE FROSTING

Cool peppermint-vanilla cake and fluffy pink buttercream make a merry combination. Finish with dollops of mint frosting. The cake layers and buttercream can be made ahead to save time. (This cake is also shown on the cover.)

SERVES 8 • **HANDS-ON** 1 hour, 20 minutes • **TOTAL** 2 hours, 40 minutes

CAKE LAYERS

2 cups granulated sugar
1¼ cups unsalted butter, softened
4 large eggs
2 tablespoons vanilla extract
4 cups unbleached cake flour
1 tablespoon baking powder
½ teaspoon baking soda
½ teaspoon table salt
1 cup whole milk
Shortening, for greasing pans

PEPPERMINT BUTTERCREAM

3 cups powdered sugar
1 cup unsalted butter, softened
½ cup finely crushed hard peppermint candies (about 20 candies)
1 teaspoon vanilla extract
½ teaspoon table salt
1 to 2 teaspoons whole milk
2 to 3 drops of red liquid food coloring

SEVEN-MINUTE FROSTING

12 large egg whites
3 cups granulated sugar
3 tablespoons corn syrup
1 teaspoon table salt
½ teaspoon peppermint extract

CANDY

1¼ cups hard peppermint candies
1½ teaspoons white Disco Dust

1. Make the Cake Layers: Preheat the oven to 350°F. Beat the granulated sugar and butter with a mixer on medium speed until light and fluffy, about 2 minutes. Add the eggs, 1 at a time, and beat just until combined after each addition. Add the vanilla, and beat just until combined. Whisk together the flour, baking powder, baking soda, and salt in a medium bowl. Add the flour mixture, in batches, alternately with the milk, beginning and ending with the flour mixture. Beat on low speed just until blended after each addition. Pour the batter into 2 greased (with shortening) and floured 9-inch round cake pans.
2. Bake at 350°F until a wooden pick inserted in the center comes out clean, 28 to 30 minutes. Cool in the pans on wire racks 20 minutes; remove from the pans to the wire racks, and cool completely, about 30 minutes.
3. Make the Peppermint Buttercream: Beat the powdered sugar and butter with a mixer on medium speed until smooth, about 2 minutes. Add the crushed peppermints, vanilla, and salt; beat until blended. Beat in 1 teaspoon of the milk. Beat in up to 1 more teaspoon of the milk, ¼ teaspoon at a time, until the desired consistency is reached. Beat in the food coloring, 1 drop at a time, until the desired color is reached.
4. Make the Seven-Minute Frosting: Pour water to a depth of 2 inches into the bottom of a saucepan or double boiler; bring to a simmer over medium. Stir together the egg whites, granulated sugar, corn syrup, and salt in a heatproof bowl or the top of the double boiler. Place the bowl over simmering water, and whisk constantly until the sugar dissolves and the mixture is hot, about 7 minutes. Remove from the heat, and beat with an electric mixer on medium-high until stiff peaks form and the mixture is completely cooled, about 10 minutes. Beat in the peppermint extract.
5. Assemble the Cake: Place 1 Cake Layer on a cake plate. Spread Peppermint Buttercream in an even layer, about ½ inch thick, to within ½ inch of cake edge. Top with the remaining Cake Layer.
6. Spread cooled Seven-Minute Frosting over the top and sides of the cake. Reserve the remaining Frosting for garnish.
7. Make the Candy: Roughly crush 1 cup of the candies into small pieces. Crush an additional ¼ cup of the candies into fine pieces and set aside. Add 1 teaspoon of the Disco Dust to the 1 cup crushed candy, and stir to combine.
8. Decorate the Cake: Spoon the remaining Seven-Minute Frosting into a ziplock plastic bag, and snip 1 corner of the bag. Pipe swirls of frosting on the top of the cake. Lightly press the Disco Dust-coated crushed candy into the sides of the frosted cake until the sides of the cake are coated. Sprinkle the piped swirls with the finely crushed candy and the remaining ½ teaspoon Disco Dust.

RED VELVET CHEESECAKE-VANILLA CAKE WITH CREAM CHEESE FROSTING

Don't skip the crumb coat of frosting, which keeps the red velvet layer from showing through the frosting.

SERVES 8 • **HANDS-ON** 1 hour, 6 minutes • **TOTAL** 13 hours, 24 minutes, including chilling

CHEESECAKE LAYERS

4½ (8-ounce) packages cream cheese, softened
2¼ cups granulated sugar
6 large eggs, lightly beaten
1½ cups sour cream
¾ cup whole buttermilk
4½ tablespoons unsweetened cocoa
2 (1-ounce) bottles red liquid food coloring
1 tablespoon vanilla extract
1½ teaspoons distilled white vinegar

VANILLA CAKE LAYER

½ cup salted butter, softened
1 cup granulated sugar
1½ cups bleached cake flour
2 teaspoons baking powder
¼ teaspoon table salt
⅔ cup whole milk
1½ teaspoons vanilla extract
3 large egg whites
Shortening, for greasing pan

CREAM CHEESE FROSTING

2 (8-ounce) packages cream cheese, softened
½ cup salted butter, softened
1 (32-ounce) package powdered sugar
2 teaspoons vanilla extract

8-ounce bar of white chocolate

1. Make the Cheesecake Layers: Preheat the oven to 325°F. Line the bottom and sides of 2 (9-inch) round pans with aluminum foil, allowing 2 to 3 inches to extend over sides; lightly grease the foil. Beat the cream cheese and granulated sugar with an electric mixer on medium speed just until completely combined, about 1 minute. Add the eggs, sour cream, buttermilk, cocoa, red food coloring, vanilla, and vinegar, beating on low speed just until fully combined, about 4 minutes. (Do not overbeat.) Pour the batter into the prepared pans.

2. Bake at 325°F for 10 minutes; reduce the heat to 300°F, and bake until the center is slightly jiggly, about 1 hour and 5 minutes. Turn the oven off. Let the cheesecake layers stand in the oven 30 minutes. Remove the cheesecake layers from the oven; cool in the pans on wire racks 1 hour. Cover and chill 8 hours.

3. Make the Vanilla Cake Layer: Preheat the oven to 325°F. Beat the butter with a heavy-duty stand mixer on medium speed until creamy; gradually add the granulated sugar, beating until light and fluffy, about 5 minutes.

4. Stir together the flour, baking powder, and salt in a bowl; add to the butter mixture alternately with the milk, beginning and ending with the flour mixture. Beat on low speed just until blended after each addition. Stir in the vanilla.

5. Beat the egg whites in a clean bowl with an electric mixer fitted with a whisk attachment on high speed until stiff peaks form; fold about one-third of the egg whites into the batter. Gradually fold in the remaining egg whites. Pour the batter into 1 greased (with shortening) and floured 9-inch round cake pan.

6. Bake at 325°F until a wooden pick inserted in the center comes out clean, 33 to 36 minutes. Cool in the pan on a wire rack 10 minutes. Remove from the pan to the wire rack; cool completely, about 30 minutes.

7. Make the Cream Cheese Frosting: Beat the cream cheese and butter with a mixer on medium speed until creamy, about 5 minutes. Gradually add the powdered sugar, beating at low speed until blended after each addition; stir in the vanilla. Increase the speed to medium, and beat until light and fluffy.

8. Assemble the Cake: Lift the Cheesecake Layers from the pans, using the foil sides as handles. Place 1 Cheesecake Layer, bottom side up, on a cake plate. Place the Vanilla Cake Layer on the Cheesecake Layer. (This layer will be slightly taller than the Cheesecake Layers; trim the top of the layer, if desired). Top the Vanilla Cake Layer with the remaining Cheesecake Layer, bottom side up. Spread a thin layer of Cream Cheese Frosting over the top and sides of the cake to seal in the crumbs. Chill the cake 20 minutes. Spread the remaining frosting over the top and sides of the cake.

9. Decorate the cake: To curl the white chocolate, slightly soften it by heating it in the microwave at 50% power for 10 seconds. Shave the chocolate into large curls using a vegetable peeler. Pile the curls on top of the frosted cake.

CHERRY-ALMOND CRUMB CAKE

Fragrant and sweet, this is destined to be a holiday classic.

SERVES 10 to 12 • **HANDS-ON** 20 minutes • **TOTAL** 2 hours

STREUSEL

- 1/2 cup all-purpose flour
- 1/2 cup packed brown sugar
- 1/2 teaspoon ground cinnamon
- 1/4 cup butter, cut into pieces
- 1/2 cup sliced almonds

CAKE

- 2 cups water
- 1 (5-ounce) package dried tart cherries (about 1 cup)
- 2 1/2 cups all-purpose flour
- 1 teaspoon baking powder
- 1/2 teaspoon baking soda
- 1/2 teaspoon ground cardamom
- 1/2 teaspoon ground cinnamon
- 1/4 teaspoon table salt
- 3/4 cup butter, softened
- 1 1/4 cups granulated sugar
- 3 large eggs
- 1 teaspoon vanilla extract
- 1 1/4 cups sour cream

GLAZE

- 1/2 cup powdered sugar
- 1/4 cup sour cream
- 1/4 teaspoon vanilla extract

1. Make the Streusel: Combine the first 3 ingredients; cut in the butter with a pastry blender until it resembles small peas. Stir in the almonds. Cover and chill until ready to use.
2. Make the Cake: Preheat the oven to 350°F. Bring the water to a simmer in a small saucepan; add the cherries. Remove from the heat; let stand 5 minutes or until the cherries soften. Drain.
3. Whisk together the flour with the next 5 ingredients in a bowl. Toss the cherries with 1 tablespoon of the flour mixture.
4. Beat 3/4 cup butter with an electric mixer on medium speed until creamy. Add the granulated sugar; beat until light and fluffy. Add the eggs, 1 at a time, beating after each addition. Beat in the vanilla. Add the flour mixture to the butter mixture alternately with the sour cream. Beat at low speed just until blended after each addition. Fold in the cherries. Spoon the batter into a greased and floured 10-inch (12-cup) tube pan; sprinkle with the Streusel.
5. Bake at 350°F for 50 minutes or until a wooden pick inserted in the center comes out clean. Cool in the pan on a wire rack 15 minutes; remove from the pan to the wire rack to cool completely.
6. Make the Glaze: Combine all the ingredients; drizzle over the cake.

AMARETTI-CHOCOLATE TART

Crispy Italian amaretti cookies add lovely contrast to the creamy almond frangipane filling. (Pictured on opposite page, on right side of image.)

SERVES 8 • **HANDS-ON** 15 minutes • **TOTAL** 4 hours, 40 minutes, includes chilling and cooling

CRUST

1¼ cups all-purpose flour
1½ tablespoons sugar
½ cup cold butter, cut into pieces
2 tablespoons ice-cold water
1 large egg yolk

FILLING

1 (4-ounce) bittersweet chocolate baking bar, chopped
½ cup butter, softened
½ cup sugar
1 large egg
2 tablespoons brandy
1 teaspoon vanilla extract
1 cup finely ground blanched almonds (almond meal/flour)
1 tablespoon all-purpose flour
12 amaretti cookies, coarsely crushed (¾ cup)
⅓ cup sliced almonds

1. Make the Crust: Combine the flour and sugar in a medium bowl; cut in the butter with a pastry blender until the mixture resembles fine meal. Whisk the water with the egg yolk; gradually add to the flour mixture, stirring with a fork until the dry ingredients are moistened. Gather into a ball, shape into a disk, and wrap in plastic wrap. Chill 1 hour until firm.

2. Preheat the oven to 375°F. Roll the dough into a 12-inch round (about ⅛-inch thick) on a floured surface. Fit into a 9-inch tart pan with removable bottom; trim the edges. Line the dough with foil; fill with dried beans or pie weights.

3. Bake at 375°F until the edges are lightly browned, about 15 minutes. Remove the foil and pie weights; bake 10 minutes. Cool on a wire rack, about 30 minutes.

4. Make the Filling: Microwave the chocolate in a small microwave-safe bowl at HIGH 1 to 1½ minutes or until melted and smooth, stirring at 30-second intervals. Cool 5 minutes.

5. Beat the butter and sugar with a mixer on medium speed until light and fluffy; beat in the egg, brandy, and vanilla until well blended. Beat in the ground almonds and all-purpose flour at low speed until blended. Gradually add the melted chocolate, beating at low speed just until blended. Spread the mixture in an even layer in the tart shell. Sprinkle with the amaretti cookies and sliced almonds.

6. Bake at 375°F for 25 minutes or until puffed, lightly browned, and set. Cool completely on a wire rack, about 2 hours.

BITTERSWEET CHOCOLATE-CHESTNUT TORTE

Look for high-quality French sweetened chestnut puree at specialty markets and online. You'll need one 17.6-ounce can to prepare the torte and the accompanying cream.

SERVES 8 • **HANDS-ON** 25 minutes, includes cream • **TOTAL** 2 hours, 40 minutes

4 tablespoons unsweetened cocoa
6 ounces bittersweet chocolate baking bar, chopped
1/2 cup unsalted butter, softened
1/2 cup sugar
5 large eggs, separated
1 cup sweetened chestnut puree
1/4 cup all-purpose flour
1/4 teaspoon table salt
Chocolate shavings
Pomegranate arils
Garnishes: rosemary sprig, powdered sugar

CHESTNUT BOURBON CREAM
1 cup heavy cream
1/3 cup sweetened chestnut puree
1 tablespoon bourbon

1. Preheat the oven to 350°F. Grease a 9-inch springform pan; line the bottom with parchment paper, and grease the parchment. Dust lightly with 1 tablespoon of the cocoa.
2. Microwave the bittersweet chocolate in a small microwave-safe bowl at HIGH 1 minute or until melted and smooth, stirring at 30-second intervals. Let cool 5 minutes.
3. Beat the butter and 1/4 cup of the sugar with a mixer on medium speed until light and fluffy. Add the egg yolks, 1 at a time, beating until blended. Gradually beat in the chestnut puree and melted chocolate until well blended. Combine the flour, remaining 3 tablespoons cocoa, and salt; gradually add to the butter mixture, beating just until blended.
4. Beat the egg whites with a mixer on high speed until foamy. Gradually add the remaining 1/4 cup sugar, 1 tablespoon at a time, beating until stiff peaks form. Fold one-fourth of the egg whites into the chocolate mixture; gently fold in the remaining egg whites. Pour into the prepared pan, and smooth the top of the batter.
5. Bake at 350°F for 40 to 45 minutes or until a wooden pick inserted in the center comes out with a few moist crumbs. Cool completely in the pan on a wire rack, about 1 1/2 hours.
6. Meanwhile, make the Chestnut Bourbon Cream: Beat together all the ingredients with a mixer on medium speed until well blended; beat at high speed until soft peaks form. Makes about 2 1/2 cups.
7. Decorate the Cake: Run a sharp knife or offset spatula around the sides of the pan. Remove the sides of pan. Transfer the torte to a serving platter; top with Chestnut Bourbon Cream, chocolate shavings, and pomegranate arils. Garnish, if desired.

NOTE: We tested with Ghirardelli Bittersweet Chocolate Baking Bar and Roland Chestnut Cream for the sweetened chestnut puree.

BUTTER TOFFEE-PECAN LAYER CAKE

This buttery vanilla layer cake is swathed in a creamy toffee frosting made extra luscious with the addition of browned butter and lots of toasted pecans.

SERVES 8 • **HANDS-ON** 1 hour • **TOTAL** 2 hours, 55 minutes

BROWN BUTTER TOFFEE FROSTING

1 cup unsalted butter
2 cups packed dark brown sugar
1¼ cups heavy cream
2 tablespoons golden cane syrup (such as Lyle's Golden Syrup) or light corn syrup
¼ teaspoon kosher salt
1 tablespoon bourbon, dark rum, or cognac (optional)
3 cups powdered sugar
1 teaspoon vanilla extract

CAKE LAYERS

2 cups all-purpose flour
2 teaspoons baking powder
¾ teaspoon kosher salt
2 cups granulated sugar
1 cup unsalted butter, softened
3 large eggs
1 teaspoon vanilla extract
1 cup whole buttermilk
1 cup finely chopped toasted pecans
½ cup toffee bits (such as Heath Bits 'O Brickle Toffee Bits)

½ cup toasted pecan halves
¼ teaspoon flaky sea salt (such as Maldon), optional

1. Make the Frosting: Melt ¾ cup of the butter in a deep, heavy saucepan over low. Increase the heat to medium-high, and bring the butter to a boil, stirring constantly. Cook, stirring constantly, until the butter is fragrant and the milk solids start to brown, about 5 minutes.
2. Remove the pan from the heat, and stir in the brown sugar, cream, syrup, salt, and, if desired, bourbon. Return the pan to medium, and cook, stirring occasionally, until the sugar dissolves. Increase the heat to medium-high, and bring to a boil. Boil, stirring constantly, exactly 2 minutes. Remove the mixture from the heat, and pour into the bowl of a heavy-duty electric stand mixer fitted with a paddle attachment. Beat on low speed until the mixture is lukewarm, about 8 to 10 minutes. Gradually add the powdered sugar and vanilla, and beat on low speed until combined after each addition. Beat until the frosting is completely cool and consistency is thick, creamy, and spreadable, 6 to 10 minutes. Add the remaining 4 tablespoons butter, 1 tablespoon at a time, and beat on medium speed until fully incorporated after each addition. Cover the frosting, and let stand at room temperature until ready to use.
3. Make the Cake Layers: Preheat the oven to 350°F. Lightly coat 2 (9- x 2-inch) round cake pans with cooking spray, and line the bottoms with parchment paper. Sift together the flour, baking powder, and salt in a medium bowl. Set aside.
4. Beat the sugar and butter in a large bowl with a mixer on medium-high speed until thick and creamy, 4 to 5 minutes. Add the eggs, 1 at a time, and beat on medium speed until well blended after each addition. Beat in the vanilla. Add the flour mixture, one-third at a time, to the butter mixture alternately with the buttermilk, beginning and ending with the flour mixture. Beat on low just until smooth after each addition. (Do not overbeat or the cake will be tough.) Fold in the chopped pecans and toffee bits. Divide the batter evenly between cake pans, smoothing the surface.
5. Bake at 350°F until a wooden pick or cake tester inserted into the center of the cake comes out clean, 30 to 35 minutes. Cool in the pans on a wire rack 10 minutes. Invert the layers onto the wire rack, and peel off the parchment paper. Cool completely, about 1 hour.
6. Place 1 Cake Layer on a serving plate; spread evenly with 1 heaping cup of the frosting. Chill 15 minutes. Top with the remaining Cake Layer, and frost the top and sides of the cake with the remaining frosting. Place the pecan halves in a ring around the top edge of the cake. If desired, crush the sea salt with your fingers, and sprinkle over the pecans. Serve immediately, or store, covered, at room temperature for 3 to 5 days.

CARAMEL APPLE PIE WITH BROWNED BUTTER CRUST

Browning the butter for the crust provides an extra hint of nuttiness but is not essential. Feel free to use cold butter instead and skip Step 1. Make both the crust and caramel sauce up to two days in advance to save time.

SERVES 10 • **HANDS-ON** 45 minutes • **TOTAL** 8 hours, 15 minutes, includes chilling and cooling

CRUST
1 cup unsalted butter
2½ cups all-purpose flour
2 tablespoons granulated sugar
1 teaspoon table salt
½ cup plus 1 tablespoon cold buttermilk

CARAMEL
1 cup granulated sugar
¼ cup water
½ cup salted butter, cut into pieces
1 cup heavy cream

FILLING
½ cup packed brown sugar
3 tablespoons cornstarch
½ teaspoon ground cinnamon
¼ teaspoon freshly grated nutmeg
2 pounds Granny Smith apples, peeled and cut into ¾-inch slices
2 pounds Honeycrisp apples, peeled and cut into ¾-inch slices
1 tablespoon fresh lemon juice
1 large egg, lightly beaten
Garnish: white coarse sanding sugar

1. Make the Crust: Cook the butter in a heavy saucepan over medium, stirring constantly, 7 minutes or until the butter begins to turn golden brown. Remove the pan immediately from the heat, and pour the butter into a small bowl. Cover and chill 3 hours or until the butter is cold and solidified.
2. Pulse the flour, sugar, and salt in a food processor until blended. Cut the browned butter into small pieces; add to the processor, and pulse until the mixture resembles coarse meal. Gradually add ½ cup of the buttermilk, pulsing until the dough is moistened and just begins to come together, adding an additional 1 tablespoon of the buttermilk, if needed. Turn the dough out onto a flat surface; divide in half. Gently gather each half into a ball; press into a flat disk, and wrap in plastic wrap. Chill 1 hour or until firm.
3. Make the Caramel: Combine the sugar and water in a medium saucepan over medium-high. Bring to a boil, brushing the sides of the pan with a wet pastry brush to prevent crystals from forming. Cook until amber colored, 8 minutes. Remove from the heat; whisk in the butter and cream (the mixture will bubble vigorously). Cook over medium-low, whisking constantly until smooth, 2 to 3 minutes.
4. Make the Filling: Preheat the oven to 350°F. Combine the brown sugar and next 3 ingredients in a large bowl; add the apples, lemon juice, and ½ cup of the caramel sauce, and toss until blended.
5. Roll each dough round into a 13-inch circle on a lightly floured surface. Fit 1 dough round into a 9½-inch deep-dish pie plate; spoon the apple mixture into the dish. Top with the remaining dough round; seal the edges, and crimp. Brush the dough with the egg. Cut several slits in the dough to allow the steam to escape.
6. Bake at 350°F for 1 hour and 30 minutes or until the crust is deep golden brown, apples are tender, and filling is bubbly, shielding with aluminum foil, if needed. (Place a baking sheet on the oven rack below the pie while baking.) Cool the pie on a wire rack 2 hours. Serve with the remaining caramel sauce. Garnish, if desired.

COOKIE SWAP

This year gather all your friends and neighbors to exchange cookies and mingle around the tree! These homemade drop cookies, cutouts, sandwich cookies, and more are the perfect treats to bake, bag, and swap.

CRANBERRY-OATMEAL COOKIE BARK

This stir-together cookie dough couldn't be easier. There's no need to portion the dough or bake several batches. For an adult cookie swap, sprinkle the cookie bark with chopped pistachios or walnuts after drizzling with chocolate. Baking on the lower end of the bake time will produce a chewier bark, while baking longer will produce bark that is crispy throughout.

MAKES 2 dozen cookies • **HANDS-ON** 10 minutes • **TOTAL** 1 hour, 30 minutes

3/4 cup butter, melted
1/2 cup firmly packed brown sugar
1/2 cup granulated sugar
1 teaspoon orange zest
1 teaspoon vanilla extract
1 1/4 cups all-purpose flour
1/2 teaspoon baking soda
1/4 teaspoon table salt
3/4 cup uncooked quick-cooking oats
3/4 cup sweetened dried cranberries
1/2 (4-ounce) bittersweet chocolate baking bar, chopped

1. Preheat the oven to 350°F. Stir together the first 5 ingredients in a large bowl until well blended. Combine the flour, baking soda, and salt; stir into the butter mixture. Stir in the oats and cranberries (the dough will be slightly crumbly).
2. Press the dough into a 12- x 10-inch rectangle (about 1/4-inch thick) on a parchment paper-lined baking sheet.
3. Bake at 350°F for 25 to 30 minutes or until golden brown and firm. Cool on the baking sheet on a wire rack 10 minutes; slide the cookie, with the parchment paper, onto a wire rack, and cool completely, about 30 minutes. Break into pieces.
4. Arrange the cookie pieces on a baking sheet lined with clean parchment paper. Microwave the chocolate in a small microwave-safe bowl at HIGH 1 minute or until melted and smooth, stirring at 30-second intervals. Drizzle the chocolate over the cookie pieces; chill 15 minutes or until chocolate is set.

DARK CHOCOLATE CRINKLES

These rich, chewy, brownie-like cookies will have the perfect crackled top if well coated in powdered sugar.

MAKES 2 1/2 dozen cookies • **HANDS-ON** 15 minutes • **TOTAL** 1 hour, 30 minutes

1 (4-ounce) bittersweet chocolate baking bar, chopped
1/3 cup granulated sugar
1/3 cup packed dark brown sugar
1/4 cup butter, softened
1 large egg
1/2 cup all-purpose flour
1/4 cup unsweetened Dutch-process cocoa
1 teaspoon baking powder
1/8 teaspoon table salt
1 tablespoon coffee liqueur
1 cup powdered sugar

1. Microwave the chopped chocolate in a small microwave-safe bowl at HIGH 1 to 1 1/2 minutes or until melted and smooth, stirring at 30-second intervals. Cool 5 minutes.
2. Beat together the granulated sugar and next 2 ingredients at medium speed with a mixer until light and fluffy; add the egg, beating well. Beat in the melted chocolate. Combine the flour and next 3 ingredients; gradually add to the sugar mixture, beating at low speed just until blended. Beat in the coffee liqueur. Cover and chill the dough 30 minutes.
3. Preheat the oven to 350°F. Roll the dough into 1-inch balls; roll the balls in the powdered sugar twice, letting the balls stand 1 to 2 minutes in the sugar between coatings. Place 2 inches apart on parchment paper-lined baking sheets.
4. Bake at 350°F for 12 to 14 minutes or until crackled and set. Cool on the baking sheets 2 minutes; transfer to wire racks, and cool completely, about 20 minutes.

Cranberry-Oatmeal Cookie Bark

RASPBERRY JAM THUMBPRINTS

You can make the dough for the cookies one day ahead; store in the refrigerator.
(Pictured on page 133)

MAKES 4 dozen cookies • **HANDS-ON** 40 minutes • **TOTAL** 1 hour, 40 minutes

- 1 cup unsalted butter, softened
- 3/4 cup powdered sugar
- 1/4 cup packed light brown sugar
- 1 large egg yolk
- 1 teaspoon vanilla extract
- 3 cups all-purpose flour
- 1/2 teaspoon kosher salt
- 1/2 teaspoon baking powder
- 1/3 cup seedless raspberry jam
- 4 ounces white chocolate baking bar, chopped
- 1/4 cup heavy cream

1. Preheat the oven to 375°F with the oven racks in the top third and bottom third of the oven. Beat the butter and both sugars with a mixer on medium speed until smooth, about 1 minute. Add the egg yolk and vanilla, and beat on low speed just until incorporated. Whisk together the flour, salt, and baking powder in a small bowl, and gradually add to the butter mixture, beating on low speed just until incorporated after each addition.
2. Drop the dough by tablespoonfuls 1 inch apart onto parchment paper-lined baking sheets. Press your thumb or the end of a wooden spoon into each ball, forming an indentation.
3. Bake at 375°F until the cookies are set and beginning to brown, about 12 minutes, switching the pans top rack to bottom rack halfway through baking. Cool on the pans on wire racks 5 minutes; remove the cookies to the wire racks, and cool completely, about 30 minutes.
4. Fill each indentation with about 1/2 teaspoon of the jam, and let stand at room temperature 15 minutes.
5. Combine the white chocolate and cream in a small heatproof bowl. Bring a small saucepan filled with 1 inch of water to a simmer over medium, and place the bowl with the chocolate mixture over the simmering water. Cook, stirring often, until the chocolate is melted and smooth, about 2 minutes. Cool 10 minutes. Spoon the chocolate mixture into a ziplock plastic freezer bag with 1 corner snipped or a piping bag, and pipe the mixture over the cookies.

AMBROSIA MACAROONS

For a sweeter, more decadent cookie, dip the bottoms in melted white chocolate, or drizzle it over the top.

MAKES 4 dozen cookies • **HANDS-ON** 15 minutes • **TOTAL** 1 hour, 10 minutes

- 1 (14-ounce) package sweetened flaked coconut
- 1 (14-ounce) can sweetened condensed milk
- 1/2 cup chopped dried pineapple
- 1 teaspoon vanilla extract
- 1 teaspoon orange zest
- 1 teaspoon grapefruit zest
- 2 large egg whites
- 1/4 teaspoon table salt

1. Preheat the oven to 350°F. Combine the first 6 ingredients in a large bowl. Beat the egg whites and salt with a mixer on medium speed until stiff peaks form; fold into the coconut mixture. Scoop the mixture by level tablespoons 1 inch apart on parchment paper-lined baking sheets.
2. Bake at 350°F for 18 to 20 minutes or until golden brown. Cool completely on a wire rack, about 20 minutes.

COCONUT THUMBPRINTS WITH DULCE DE LECHE

Finish these cookies with a pinch of flaky salt—it balances the sweet caramel filling and toasted coconut. *(Pictured on page 133)*

MAKES 4 dozen cookies • **HANDS-ON** 30 minutes • **TOTAL** 1 hour

1 cup sweetened shredded coconut
1 cup unsalted butter, softened
3/4 cup powdered sugar
1/4 cup packed light brown sugar
1 large egg yolk
1 teaspoon vanilla extract
3 cups all-purpose flour
1/2 teaspoon kosher salt
1/2 teaspoon baking powder
1/2 cup jarred or canned dulce de leche
2 teaspoons flaked sea salt

1. Preheat the oven to 375°F with the oven racks in the top third and bottom third of the oven. Pulse the coconut in a food processor until finely chopped, about 10 times. Transfer to a shallow dish or bowl.
2. Beat the butter and both sugars with a mixer on medium speed until smooth, about 1 minute. Add the egg yolk and vanilla, and beat on low speed just until incorporated. Whisk together the flour, salt, and baking powder in a small bowl, and add to butter mixture, beating on low speed just until incorporated.
3. Drop the dough by tablespoonfuls into the chopped coconut, and roll lightly to coat. Place the cookies 1 inch apart on parchment paper-lined baking sheets. Press your thumb or the end of a wooden spoon into each ball, forming an indentation.
4. Bake at 375°F until the cookies are set and the coconut is browned, about 11 minutes, switching the pans top rack to bottom rack halfway through baking. Transfer the baking sheets to wire racks, and immediately reshape the indentations by pressing again with your thumb or spoon. Cool the cookies completely, about 30 minutes.
5. Fill each indentation with about 1/2 teaspoon of the dulce de leche. Sprinkle the cookies evenly with sea salt.

CHOCOLATE GANACHE THUMBPRINTS WITH CRUSHED PEPPERMINTS

This chocolate filling is impossibly rich and incredibly easy to make in the microwave. *(Pictured on page 133)*

MAKES 4 dozen cookies • **HANDS-ON** 40 minutes • **TOTAL** 1 hour, 47 minutes

1 cup unsalted butter, softened
3/4 cup powdered sugar
1/4 cup packed light brown sugar
1 large egg yolk
1 teaspoon vanilla extract
3 cups all-purpose flour
1/2 teaspoon kosher salt
1/2 teaspoon baking powder
1/2 cup semisweet chocolate chips
3 tablespoons heavy cream
1/4 cup crushed hard peppermint candies (about 12 candies)

1. Preheat the oven to 375°F with the oven racks in the top third and bottom third of the oven. Beat the butter and both sugars with a mixer on medium speed until smooth, about 1 minute. Add the egg yolk and vanilla, and beat on low speed just until incorporated. Whisk together the flour, salt, and baking powder in a small bowl, and gradually add to the butter mixture, beating on low speed just until incorporated after each addition.
2. Drop the dough by tablespoonfuls 1 inch apart onto the parchment paper-lined baking sheets. Press your thumb or the end of a wooden spoon into each ball, forming an indentation.
3. Bake at 375°F until the cookies are set and beginning to brown, about 12 minutes, switching the pans top rack to bottom rack halfway through baking. Cool on the pans on wire racks 5 minutes; remove the cookies to the wire racks, and cool completely, about 30 minutes.
4. Combine the chocolate chips and cream in a microwave-safe bowl, and microwave on MEDIUM (50% power) 1 to 1 1/2 minutes until melted and smooth, stirring at 30-second intervals. Cool 5 minutes. Fill each indentation with about 1/2 teaspoon of the ganache. Sprinkle the cookies evenly with the crushed peppermints, and let stand 15 minutes before serving.

TRIPLE MINT COOKIES

Mint lovers will fall head over heels for these rich, brownie-like cookies filled with chopped mint candies and topped with minty icing.

MAKES 30 cookies • **HANDS-ON** 30 minutes • **TOTAL** 2 hours, 15 minutes

- 1 cup 60% cacao bittersweet chocolate chips
- 1/2 cup unsalted butter
- 1 cup granulated sugar
- 2 large eggs
- 1 teaspoon vanilla extract
- 1/2 teaspoon mint extract
- 2 cups all-purpose flour
- 1/2 cup unsweetened cocoa
- 3/4 teaspoon baking powder
- 3/4 teaspoon kosher salt
- 1 cup chopped thin crème de menthe chocolate mints (such as Andes)
- 2 cups powdered sugar
- 3 to 4 tablespoons whole milk
- 5 to 6 drops of green liquid food coloring

1. Preheat the oven to 375°F with the oven racks in the top third and bottom third of the oven. Combine the chocolate chips and butter in a large microwave-safe bowl, and microwave at medium (50%) power 2 minutes or until melted and smooth, stirring at 30-second intervals. Whisk in the sugar, eggs, vanilla, and 1/4 teaspoon of the mint extract until smooth. Whisk together the flour, cocoa, baking powder, and salt in a medium bowl. Stir the flour mixture into the chocolate mixture; fold in the chopped mints. Drop the dough by tablespoonfuls 2 inches apart onto 2 parchment paper-lined baking sheets.

2. Bake at 375°F until the cookies are just set on top, about 10 minutes, switching the pans top rack to bottom rack halfway through baking. Remove the pans to wire racks, and immediately flatten the domed cookie tops with the bottom of a heatproof dry measuring cup. Cool the cookies on the pans 5 minutes; transfer the cookies to the wire racks, and cool completely, about 30 minutes.

3. Whisk together the powdered sugar, 3 tablespoons of the milk, and remaining 1/4 teaspoon mint extract in a small bowl. Stir in up to 1 more tablespoon of milk, 1 teaspoon at a time to the desired consistency. Transfer 2 tablespoons of the icing to a separate small bowl; stir in the desired amount of green food coloring.

4. Spoon the remaining white icing into a ziplock plastic freezer bag with 1 corner snipped or a piping bag. Pipe circles of the white icing over the cooled cookies. Add a little of the green icing onto the white icing circles, and swirl with a wooden pick to create freeform circles. Let stand at room temperature until set, about 1 hour.

Chocolate Ganache
Thumbprints with Crushed
Peppermints (page 131)
Triple Mint
Cookies
Raspberry Jam
Thumbprints
(page 130)
Coconut
Thumbprints with
Dulce De Leche
(center cookie,
page 131)

Spiced
Molasses Drops

SPICED MOLASSES DROPS

You've never had spice cookies like these. A secret ingredient—black pepper—adds just a hint of heat.

MAKES 4 dozen cookies • **HANDS-ON** 30 minutes • **TOTAL** 1 hour, 13 minutes

- 1/2 cup unsalted butter, softened
- 3/4 cup packed light brown sugar
- 1/4 cup light molasses
- 1 teaspoon vanilla extract
- 1 large egg
- 2 cups all-purpose flour
- 1 1/2 teaspoons baking powder
- 1/2 teaspoon baking soda
- 1/4 teaspoon kosher salt
- 1/4 teaspoon ground cinnamon
- 1/4 teaspoon ground ginger
- 1/4 teaspoon black pepper
- 1/2 cup sanding sugar or sparkling sugar

1. Preheat the oven to 375°F with oven racks in the top third and bottom third of the oven. Beat the butter and brown sugar with a mixer on medium speed until light and fluffy, about 2 minutes. Add the molasses and vanilla, and beat on low speed just until combined. Add the egg, and beat on medium speed until mixture thickens slightly, about 30 seconds. Whisk together the flour, baking powder, baking soda, salt, cinnamon, ginger, and pepper in a medium bowl. Gradually add to the butter mixture, and beat on low speed just until combined after each addition.

2. Place the sanding sugar in a shallow dish or bowl, and drop the dough by heaping tablespoonfuls into the sugar, rolling to coat. Place half of the coated dough balls about 2 inches apart on parchment paper-lined baking sheets.

3. Bake at 375°F until the cookies are just set, 8 to 9 minutes, switching the pans top rack to bottom rack halfway through baking. Cool on pans 5 minutes; remove the cookies to wire racks, and cool completely, about 30 minutes. Repeat with the remaining cookie dough.

PECAN TEA CAKES

We combined two classic Southern favorites—pecans and tea cakes—to make one irresistible cookie. If you're a fan of pecan Sandies, you'll love these. (Pictured on page 126)

MAKES 4 dozen cookies • **HANDS-ON** 1 hour • **TOTAL** 1 hour, 30 minutes

- 1 cup chopped toasted pecans, chopped
- 1/4 cup whole milk
- 1/2 cup unsalted butter, softened
- 3/4 cup granulated sugar, plus 1 tablespoon
- 1 large egg
- 1 teaspoon vanilla extract
- 2 cups self-rising flour
- 48 to 50 pecan halves (about 1 1/4 cups)
- 1 large egg white, lightly beaten

1. Place the chopped toasted pecans and milk in a small bowl, and let stand at room temperature until the milk is mostly absorbed, about 30 minutes.

2. Preheat the oven to 375°F with the oven racks in the top third and bottom third of the oven. Beat the butter and 3/4 cup of the sugar with a mixer on medium speed until light and fluffy, about 2 minutes. Add the egg and vanilla, and beat on low speed just until combined. Add the flour and chopped toasted pecans alternately to the butter mixture, beginning and ending with the flour. Beat on low speed just until incorporated after each addition. Drop by tablespoonfuls about 2 inches apart on parchment paper-lined baking sheets. Press 1 pecan half into the top of each cookie. Brush the pecans lightly with the egg white, and sprinkle evenly with the remaining 1 tablespoon sugar.

3. Bake at 375°F until the cookies are just set, about 10 minutes, switching the pans from top rack to bottom rack halfway through baking. Cool on the pans on wire rack 5 minutes; transfer the cookies to wire rack, and cool completely, about 30 minutes. Repeat with the remaining dough.

NUTTY CHOCOLATE THUMBPRINTS

No candy pieces here. These thumbprint cookies are topped with a delicious peanut butter-chocolate filling.

MAKES 30 cookies • **HANDS-ON** 40 minutes • **TOTAL** 1 hour, 30 minutes

COOKIES

1⅔ cups all-purpose flour
⅔ cup unsweetened cocoa
½ teaspoon baking powder
½ teaspoon table salt
½ cup butter, softened
1 cup packed light brown sugar
¾ cup powdered sugar
¾ cup creamy peanut butter
2 large eggs
1 teaspoon vanilla extract

FILLING

¼ cup creamy peanut butter
2 tablespoons butter, softened
½ (4-ounce) 60% cacao bittersweet chocolate baking bar, chopped
1½ cups powdered sugar
2 to 3 tablespoons milk, at room temperature

1. Make the Cookies: Preheat the oven to 350°F.
2. Whisk together the first 4 ingredients in a medium bowl. Beat the butter with a mixer on medium-high speed until fluffy. Add the brown sugar and ¾ cup of the powdered sugar; beat until well blended. Beat in the peanut butter, scraping down the sides as needed. Add the eggs, 1 at a time, beating until blended after each addition. Beat in the vanilla. Reduce the speed to medium-low, and gradually add the flour mixture, beating just until blended.
3. Shape the dough into 30 balls. Place 12 balls 2 inches apart on a parchment paper-lined baking sheet. Press your thumb or the end of a wooden spoon into each ball, forming an indentation. Bake at 350°F until set, 12 minutes; cool 5 minutes. Transfer the cookies to a wire rack, and cool 15 minutes. Repeat with the remaining dough.
4. Make the Filling: Beat the peanut butter and butter on medium speed until smooth. Microwave the chopped chocolate in a microwave-safe bowl at HIGH 1 to 2 minutes or until smooth, stirring at 30-second intervals. Add the melted chocolate to the peanut butter mixture, and beat at medium speed just until blended. Gradually add the powdered sugar to the peanut butter mixture alternately with 2 tablespoons of the milk, beginning with the sugar. Beat at low speed just until blended after each addition. Beat in up to 1 tablespoon milk, 1 teaspoon at a time to desired consistency. Spoon the filling into a ziplock plastic bag; snip 1 corner of the bag to make a small hole, and pipe the filling into the indentations in the cookies.

CREAM CHEESE-PEPPER JELLY THUMBPRINTS

This play on a traditional Southern appetizer has just enough of a savory element to be served before a meal. The pepper jelly can be replaced with a more kid-friendly option, such as strawberry jam, for a sweeter treat.

MAKES 3 1/2 dozen cookies • **HANDS-ON** 20 minutes • **TOTAL** 3 hours, 20 minutes, includes chilling

- 3/4 cup butter, softened
- 4 ounces cream cheese, softened
- 1/2 cup sugar
- 1 large egg
- 1 teaspoon vanilla extract
- 2 1/4 cups all-purpose flour
- 3/4 teaspoon baking powder
- 1/4 teaspoon table salt
- 1/2 cup red or green pepper jelly

1. Beat the first 3 ingredients on medium speed with a mixer 2 minutes or until light and fluffy. Beat in the egg and vanilla until blended. Combine the flour, baking powder, and salt; gradually add to butter mixture, beating at low speed until blended.
2. Shape the dough into a 1-inch-thick disk. Wrap tightly in plastic wrap, and chill 2 to 24 hours.
3. Preheat the oven to 350°F. Shape the chilled dough into 1-inch balls. Place 1 inch apart on parchment paper-lined baking sheets. Press your thumb or the end of a wooden spoon into each ball, forming an indentation.
4. Bake at 350°F for 10 minutes. Remove from the oven, and press indentations again, using the end of a wooden spoon. Bake 8 to 10 more minutes or until edges are golden brown. Cool on baking sheets 5 minutes; transfer to a wire rack, and cool completely, about 20 minutes.
5. Spoon 1/2 teaspoon pepper jelly into each indentation.

SANTA'S FAVORITE COOKIES

This is a "kitchen-sink" cookie of sorts. Swap out the mix-ins for your kids' favorites. The combination of cake flour and bread flour may seem odd, but it produces a cookie with the perfect tenderness and chew. This is the ideal make-ahead dough; it keeps very well in the refrigerator for up to two weeks. Have some on hand throughout the holiday season to bake fresh cookies at the spur of the moment for gifts, guests, or parties.

MAKES 4 dozen cookies • **HANDS-ON** 15 minutes • **TOTAL** 1 hour, 5 minutes

- 2 cups cake flour, plus 2 tablespoons
- 1 3/4 cups bread flour
- 1 1/2 teaspoons baking powder
- 1 1/4 teaspoons baking soda
- 1 teaspoon table salt
- 1 1/4 cups unsalted butter, softened
- 1 1/4 cups packed light brown sugar
- 1 cup granulated sugar
- 2 large eggs
- 2 teaspoons vanilla extract
- 1 1/4 cups chopped toasted pecans
- 1 cup red and green candy-coated milk chocolate pieces
- 3/4 cup sweetened flaked coconut
- 2 (4-ounce) bittersweet chocolate baking bars, chopped

1. Preheat the oven to 375°F. Whisk together the first 5 ingredients in a medium bowl. Beat together the butter and both sugars with a heavy-duty electric stand mixer on medium speed 3 to 5 minutes or until very light and fluffy. Beat in the eggs, 1 at a time, until blended. Beat in the vanilla. Gradually add the flour mixture, beating at low speed until blended. Stir in the pecans, milk chocolate pieces, coconut, and chopped chocolate baking bars.
2. Place heaping scoopfuls of the dough about 2 inches apart on large parchment paper-lined baking sheets, using a 1-ounce cookie scoop.
3. Bake at 375°F for 13 to 15 minutes or until golden brown but with centers still soft. Cool on baking sheet on a wire rack 5 minutes; transfer to the wire rack, and cool completely, about 20 minutes.

NOTE: If you don't have a cookie scoop, roll the dough into 1 1/2-inch balls.

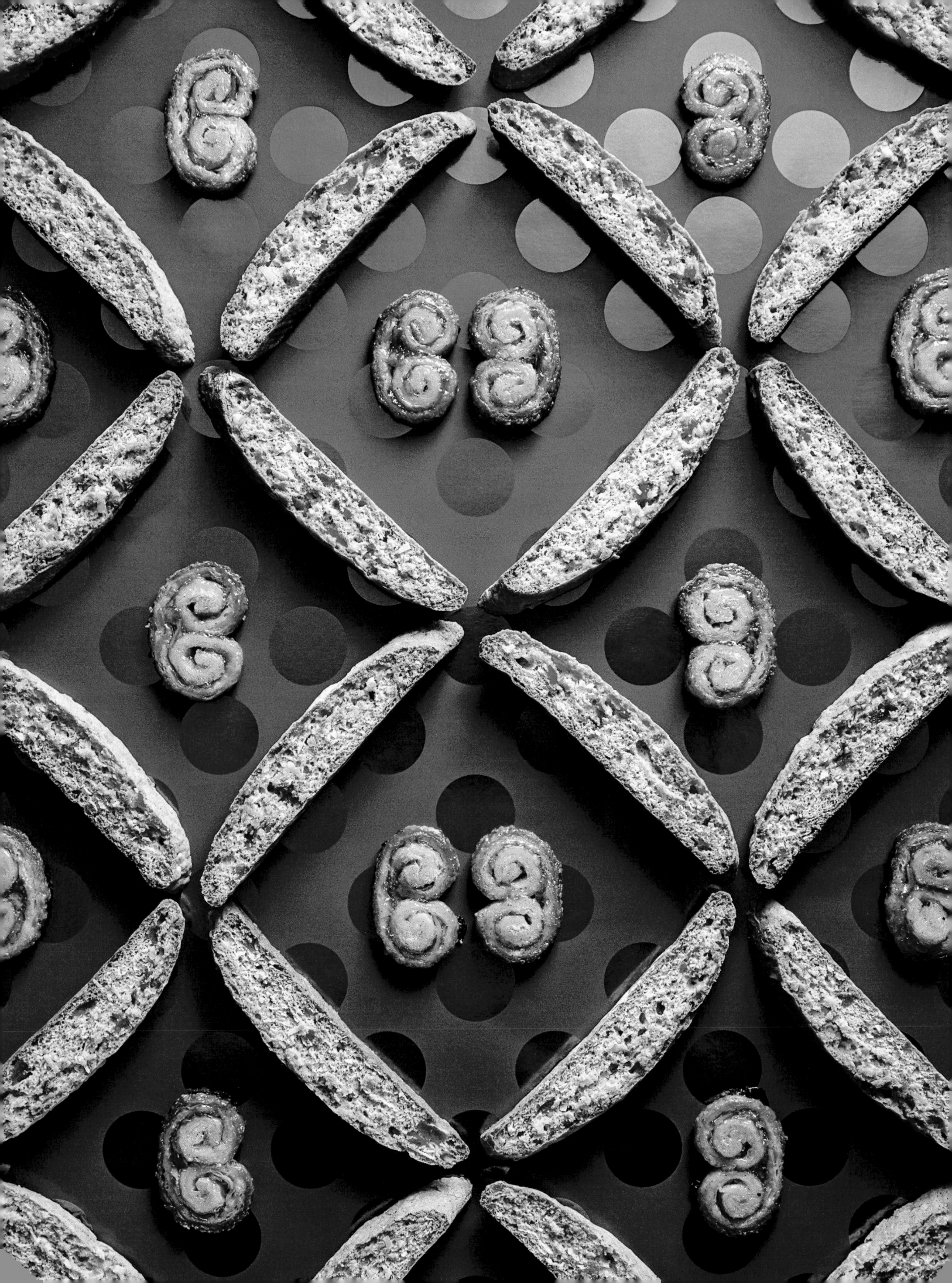

ORANGE PALMIERS

You'd never guess these impressive-looking cookies are made with just four ingredients. Demerara sugar is a coarse brown sugar; look for it in the baking aisle at the supermarket.

MAKES 40 cookies • **HANDS-ON** 20 minutes • **TOTAL** 2 hours, 4 minutes

- 3/4 cup Demerara sugar
- 1 teaspoon ground cinnamon
- 1 (17.3-ounce) package frozen puff pastry sheets, thawed
- 2/3 cup orange marmalade

1. Combine the sugar and cinnamon in a small bowl. Sprinkle 1/4 cup sugar mixture over a 12-inch square on a work surface. Unfold 1 pastry sheet on top of the sugar, and roll the sheet into a 12- x 9-inch rectangle. Spread 1/3 cup of the marmalade over the dough, leaving a 1/2-inch border around the edges. Starting with 1 long side, roll up the pastry, jelly-roll fashion, to the center of the pastry sheet. Roll the opposite side to the center. (The shape will resemble a scroll.) Wrap in plastic wrap, and freeze 20 minutes. Repeat the procedure with 1/4 cup of the sugar mixture and the remaining pastry sheet and 1/3 cup of the marmalade.
2. Preheat the oven to 375°F. Remove 1 pastry roll from the freezer, and cut into 1/2-inch-thick slices; place 2 inches apart on a parchment paper-lined baking sheet. Sprinkle each slice with a small amount of the remaining sugar mixture.
3. Bake at 375°F until light golden brown on the bottom, 14 to 16 minutes. Remove from the oven, and carefully turn each cookie over. Return to the oven, and bake until crisp and golden brown, 8 to 10 more minutes. Transfer the cookies to a wire rack, and cool completely, about 30 minutes. Repeat the procedure with the remaining pastry roll.

CHEWY AMBROSIA BISCOTTI

Make someone's Christmas extra merry by treating them to a batch of these biscotti with their favorite coffee or tea.

MAKES 22 biscotti • **HANDS-ON** 25 minutes • **TOTAL** 2 hours, 15 minutes

- 1 1/2 cups all-purpose flour
- 3/4 teaspoon baking powder
- 1/4 teaspoon table salt
- 1/4 teaspoon baking soda
- 3/4 cup granulated sugar
- 2 large eggs
- 1 teaspoon vanilla extract
- 1 cup sweetened shredded coconut
- 1/2 cup chopped maraschino cherries, drained and patted dry
- 1 tablespoon orange zest

1. Preheat the oven to 300°F. Stir together the flour, baking powder, salt, and baking soda in a small bowl. Beat the sugar, eggs, and vanilla in a large bowl with a mixer on medium speed until thick and pale, about 2 minutes. Stir in the flour mixture, coconut, cherries, and orange zest. (Dough will be very sticky.)
2. Turn the dough out onto a heavily floured surface; knead lightly 8 or 9 times. Shape the dough into a 15- x 3-inch loaf, using slightly dampened hands, and place on a parchment paper-lined baking sheet; pat to 3/4-inch thickness.
3. Bake at 300°F until the loaf is golden brown, about 40 minutes. Cool on the pan on a wire rack 5 minutes. Cut the loaf diagonally into 22 (1/2-inch-thick) slices with a serrated knife, using a gentle sawing motion. Place the slices in a single layer on the same parchment paper-lined baking sheet, and bake 20 minutes, turning the slices over halfway through baking. Remove from the baking sheet; cool the biscotti completely on a wire rack, about 20 minutes.

DARK CHOCOLATE SABLÉS

These French sugar cookies have a slightly crumbly texture ("sablé" means "sandy") and loads of chocolate flavor. The recipe makes a lot of cookies—ideal for a cookie exchange.

MAKES about 4½ dozen cookies • **HANDS-ON** 20 minutes • **TOTAL** 1 hour, 40 minutes

1 cup salted butter, softened
1 cup powdered sugar
1 teaspoon vanilla extract
2 cups all-purpose flour
⅓ cup unsweetened cocoa
½ teaspoon kosher salt
2½ (4-ounce) 60% cacao bittersweet chocolate baking bars
Sea salt or chopped toasted pecans (optional)

1. Beat the butter and sugar with a mixer on medium speed until creamy; add vanilla, and beat until combined. Stir together the flour, cocoa, and salt. Gradually add the flour mixture to butter mixture, beating at low speed until combined after each addition. Finely chop 1 of the bittersweet chocolate baking bars, and stir into cookie dough until well incorporated.
2. Divide the dough in half; shape each into an 8-inch-long log. Wrap each log tightly in plastic wrap, and freeze until firm, about 30 minutes. (Dough may be frozen up to 1 month.)
3. Preheat the oven to 350°F. Cut dough into ¼-inch-thick slices, and place 2 inches apart on parchment paper-lined baking sheets. (Keep the dough logs refrigerated while the cookies bake.)
4. Bake at 350°F until the bottoms are slightly firm, 11 to 13 minutes. Cool in the pans 5 minutes; remove the cookies to wire racks, and cool completely, about 20 minutes.
5. Chop the remaining 1½ bittersweet chocolate baking bars, and place in a small microwave-safe bowl. Microwave at HIGH 1 to 1½ minutes or until the chocolate is melted and smooth, stirring at 30-second intervals.
6. Dip half of the top side of each cookie in the melted chocolate. Sprinkle lightly with the sea salt or chopped toasted pecans, if desired. Place the cookies on a parchment paper-lined baking sheet, and chill just until the chocolate sets, about 15 minutes. Layer the cookies between wax paper, and store in an airtight container at room temperature up to 5 days.

PEPPERMINT CANDY CANE TWISTS

Using sugar cookie mix reduces the prep time on these cute cookies. Omit the peppermint extract if your kids prefer.

MAKES 1½ dozen cookies • **HANDS-ON** 20 minutes • **TOTAL** 1 hour

1 (16-ounce) package sugar cookie mix
½ cup softened butter
¼ cup all-purpose flour
1 teaspoon peppermint extract
1 large egg
Red food coloring paste

1. Preheat the oven to 375°F. Stir together the first 5 ingredients until a dough forms. Divide the dough in half; tint one half with the red food coloring paste. Roll level tablespoonfuls of both doughs into 6-inch ropes.
2. Twist 1 red rope with 1 white rope; pinch the ends to seal. Place on parchment paper-lined baking sheets, curving 1 end to form a candy cane.
3. Bake at 375°F for 9 to 11 minutes or until set. Cool completely on wire racks, about 20 minutes.

Dark Chocolate
Sablés

GINGERBREAD HOUSE CUTOUTS

Bake these cookies for kids to decorate. Tint the royal icing red and green, if desired. Keep the icing covered so it doesn't dry out.

MAKES 16 cookies • **HANDS-ON** 1 hour, 5 minutes • **TOTAL** 3 hours, 50 minutes, includes chilling

1 cup packed brown sugar
3/4 cup butter, softened
1/2 cup molasses
1 large egg
3 cups all-purpose flour
1 teaspoon baking soda
2 teaspoons ground ginger
2 teaspoons ground cinnamon
1/2 teaspoon table salt
1/2 teaspoon ground cloves
Garnishes: round gummy candies, assorted sprinkles, bite-size licorice pieces, striped candy sticks

EASY ROYAL ICING

1 (16-ounce) package powdered sugar
1/3 cup water
1/4 cup meringue powder

1. Beat the brown sugar and butter with a mixer on medium speed 3 minutes or until light and fluffy. Beat in the molasses and egg until well blended. Combine the flour and next 5 ingredients; gradually add to sugar mixture, beating at low speed until blended. Divide the dough in half, and shape into 2 flat disks; wrap in plastic wrap, and chill 2 hours or until firm.
2. Preheat the oven to 350°F. Roll the dough to 1/4-inch thickness on a lightly floured surface. Use a knife and a ruler to cut dough into gingerbread house shapes that are about 4- to 5-inches tall and 3- to 4-inches wide, rerolling the dough as needed. Place on parchment paper-lined baking sheets.
3. Bake at 350°F for 10 to 12 minutes or until set. Cool on the baking sheets 5 minutes; transfer to wire racks, and cool completely, about 20 minutes.
4. Meanwhile, make the Easy Royal Icing: Beat the powdered sugar, water, and meringue powder with a mixer on medium speed 2 minutes or until well blended and smooth. Once the cookies have cooled, decorate as desired using Easy Royal Icing and garnishes.

SPARKLING SNOWFLAKE SUGAR COOKIES

Adults will love these elegant cookies, made with a touch of brandy. And they're great for a Hanukkah party.

MAKES about 3½ dozen cookies • **HANDS-ON** 30 minutes • **TOTAL** 2 hours, 10 minutes, includes chilling

COOKIES

- 3 cups all-purpose flour
- 1 cup granulated sugar
- ½ teaspoon table salt
- 1 cup cold salted butter, cut into ½-inch pieces
- 2 large egg yolks
- 2 tablespoons brandy or whole milk

ICING

- 2 cups powdered sugar
- 4 teaspoons meringue powder
- 2 to 3 tablespoons water
- Blue liquid food coloring
- Blue sparkling sugar
- White sparkling sugar

1. Make the Cookies: Pulse the flour, granulated sugar, and salt in a food processor until combined, 3 or 4 times. Add the butter, and pulse until the mixture resembles coarse sand, 5 or 6 times. Add the egg yolks and brandy; process until clumps begin to form, 30 seconds to 1 minute. Turn the mixture out onto a lightly floured work surface; knead until the dough comes together, 3 to 4 times. Divide the dough in half; shape each half into a 6-inch disk. Wrap each disk with plastic wrap, and chill 1 hour.

2. Preheat the oven to 350°F. Let 1 dough disk stand at room temperature 10 minutes. Unwrap the dough disk, and roll to ¼-inch thickness on a lightly floured surface. Cut with a 3½-inch snowflake-shaped cutter, rerolling the scraps once. Place the cookies 2 inches apart on parchment paper-lined baking sheets.

3. Bake at 350°F until set and beginning to brown on the edges, 9 to 10 minutes, switching the pans top rack to bottom rack halfway through baking. Cool on the pans 2 minutes; remove the cookies to wire racks, and cool completely, about 20 minutes. Repeat the process with the remaining dough disk.

4. Make the Icing: Beat the powdered sugar, meringue powder, and 2 tablespoons of the water on medium speed in a bowl until well combined, 3 to 4 minutes. Add up to 1 tablespoon of the water, ¼ teaspoon at a time, to the desired consistency. Add the food coloring, 1 drop at a time, and beat until the frosting is the desired color. Spread the icing on the cookies, and sprinkle with the sparkling sugars.

CHAI-SPICED SPRITZ COOKIES

Be sure to use ungreased baking sheets (not lined with parchment paper). Otherwise, the dough won't release from the cookie press and adhere to the baking sheet.

MAKES 7 dozen cookies • **HANDS-ON** 20 minutes • **TOTAL** 1 hour, 20 minutes

- 1 cup butter, softened
- 1 cup powdered sugar
- 1 large egg
- 1 teaspoon vanilla extract
- 2 cups all-purpose flour
- ¾ teaspoon ground cinnamon
- ½ teaspoon table salt
- ½ teaspoon ground cardamom
- ½ teaspoon ground ginger
- ¼ teaspoon ground cloves
- ¼ teaspoon freshly ground black pepper
- Sanding sugar

1. Preheat the oven to 375°F. Beat the butter and powdered sugar with a mixer on medium speed until light and fluffy. Beat in the egg and vanilla. Combine the flour, cinnamon, salt, cardamom, ginger, cloves, and black pepper; gradually add to the butter mixture, beating at low speed until blended.

2. Use a cookie press to shape the dough into the desired shapes, following manufacturer's instructions. Place on ungreased baking sheets. Sprinkle with the sanding sugar.

3. Bake at 375°F for 10 to 12 minutes or until the edges are lightly browned. Cool on the baking sheets 5 minutes; transfer to wire racks. Cool completely, about 15 minutes.

Sparkling Snowflake Sugar Cookies

Chocolate Cutout Cookies (page 147), Almond Stars (page 148)

CHOCOLATE CUTOUT COOKIES

Cutout cookies don't have to be vanilla. This year, try a deep, dark chocolate version.

MAKES 40 cookies • **HANDS-ON** 30 minutes • **TOTAL** 3 hours, 13 minutes, includes chilling

COOKIES

3/4 cup salted butter
1/2 (4-ounce) 60% cacao bittersweet chocolate baking bar, finely chopped
2 (1-ounce) unsweetened chocolate baking squares, finely chopped
1 cup granulated sugar
1 cup packed light brown sugar
2 large eggs
1 teaspoon vanilla extract
1 1/2 cups all-purpose flour
1 teaspoon baking soda
1/2 teaspoon table salt
1 cup unsweetened cocoa

ICING

1 1/2 cups powdered sugar
1 tablespoon meringue powder
4 to 5 teaspoons water
Red liquid food coloring
Green liquid food coloring

Red and green sparkling sugar

1. Make the Cookies: Combine the butter, bittersweet chocolate, and unsweetened chocolate in a microwave-safe bowl, and microwave at HIGH 1 minute or until the chocolate melts and the mixture is smooth, stirring at 15-second intervals.

2. Beat the chocolate mixture, granulated sugar, and brown sugar with a mixer on medium speed until well combined, about 3 minutes. Add eggs, 1 at a time, beating well after each addition. Add the vanilla; beat until combined.

3. Whisk together the flour, baking soda, salt, and 3/4 cup of the cocoa in a bowl. Add the flour mixture to the chocolate mixture; beat on low speed until well combined, about 2 minutes. (Dough will be very soft.) Divide the dough in half; shape each half into a disk. Wrap with plastic wrap. Chill the dough 2 hours.

4. Preheat the oven to 325°F. Let 1 dough disk stand at room temperature 10 minutes. Sprinkle a work surface with 2 tablespoons of the cocoa. Unwrap the dough disk, and roll to 1/4-inch thickness on the cocoa. Cut with a 2 1/2-inch round cutter, rerolling the scraps once. Place the cookies 2 inches apart on parchment paper-lined baking sheets.

5. Bake at 325°F until just set, about 8 minutes, switching the pans top rack to bottom rack halfway through baking. Cool on the pans 5 minutes; remove the cookies to wire racks, and cool completely, about 30 minutes. Repeat the process with the remaining dough disk and 2 tablespoons cocoa.

6. Make the Icing: Beat the powdered sugar, meringue powder, and 4 teaspoons of the water on medium speed until well combined, 3 to 4 minutes. Add up to 1 teaspoon more water, 1/4 teaspoon at a time, and beat to desired consistency. Divide the icing between 2 bowls. Stir in the food coloring, 1 drop at a time, until the icing reaches the desired shades of red and green. Place the icing into piping bags, and pipe trees onto the tops of the cookies. Sprinkle with sparkling sugar.

ALMOND STARS

These aromatic cookies are made with almond flour (found in the gluten-free section of the supermarket) and almond paste. *(Pictured on page 146)*

MAKES about 2 dozen cookies • **HANDS-ON** 30 minutes • **TOTAL** 2 hours, 10 minutes, includes chilling

COOKIES
1 cup almond flour
1½ cups salted butter, softened
½ cup almond paste, crumbled
2 teaspoons vanilla extract
2 cups powdered sugar
2¼ cups all-purpose flour
½ teaspoon table salt

ICING
2 cups powdered sugar
4 teaspoons meringue powder
6 to 7 teaspoons water

1 cup sliced almonds, toasted

1. Make the Cookies: Preheat the oven to 350°F. Spread the almond flour in an even layer on a parchment paper-lined baking sheet. Bake at 350°F until lightly toasted, about 10 minutes.
2. Beat the butter, almond paste, and vanilla with a mixer on medium-low speed until well combined, about 4 minutes. Add the powdered sugar; beat on low speed until well combined, about 2 minutes.
3. Whisk together the all-purpose flour, toasted almond flour, and salt in a bowl. Add the flour mixture to butter mixture; beat on low speed until just combined. Turn the dough out onto a work surface; knead until the dough comes together, 4 or 5 times. Divide the dough in half. Shape each half into a 6-inch disk, and wrap each disk in plastic wrap. Chill 1 hour.
4. Preheat the oven to 350°F. Let 1 dough disk stand at room temperature 10 minutes. Unwrap the dough disk, and roll to ¼-inch thickness on a lightly floured surface. Cut with a 3½-inch star-shaped cookie cutter, rerolling the scraps once. Place the cookies 2 inches apart on parchment paper-lined baking sheets.
5. Bake at 350°F until the edges are golden brown, 9 to 10 minutes, switching the pans top rack to bottom rack halfway through baking. Cool on pans 2 minutes. Remove the cookies to wire racks, and cool completely, about 20 minutes. Repeat the process with the remaining dough disk.
6. Make the Icing: Beat the powdered sugar, meringue powder, and 6 teaspoons water on medium speed until well combined, 3 to 4 minutes. Add up to 1 teaspoon of the water, ¼ teaspoon at a time, and beat to the desired consistency. Spread the icing over the cookies, and top with the toasted almonds.

PECAN LINZER COOKIES

Use any flavor jam or jelly you prefer on this traditional cookie with a Southern twist.

MAKES 2 dozen cookies • **HANDS-ON** 25 minutes • **TOTAL** 3 hours, includes chilling

2½ cups all-purpose flour
¾ cup pecan halves
½ teaspoon baking powder
½ teaspoon table salt
¼ teaspoon ground cinnamon
1 cup butter, softened
½ cup granulated sugar
1 large egg
1 teaspoon vanilla extract
1 tablespoon powdered sugar
½ cup cherry jam

1. Pulse the flour, pecan halves, baking powder, salt, and cinnamon in a food processor until the pecans are finely ground.
2. Beat the butter and granulated sugar at medium speed with an electric mixer 3 minutes or until light and fluffy. Beat in the egg and vanilla. Gradually add the flour mixture, beating on low speed just until combined.
3. Divide the dough in half; shape into 2 (¾-inch-thick) disks. Wrap each disk in plastic wrap, and chill 2 hours.
4. Preheat the oven to 350°F. Roll each disk to ⅛-inch thickness on a floured surface. Cut each disk into 24 (2½-inch) fluted rounds, rerolling the scraps as needed. Place the dough rounds 1 inch apart on parchment paper-lined baking sheets. Cut the centers out of half of the cookies using 1½-inch shaped cutters.
5. Bake at 350°F for 12 to 14 minutes or until the edges are golden. (If desired, place the cut centers of the dough on a separate parchment paper-lined baking sheet, and bake 9 to 11 minutes.) Cool on the baking sheet on a wire rack 5 minutes; transfer to the rack, and cool completely, about 20 minutes.
6. Sprinkle the powdered sugar over the hollow cookies. Puree the jam in a food processor. Spread 1 teaspoon jam onto each solid cookie; top with a cutout cookie.

Pecan Linzer Cookies

PEANUT BUTTER-AND-JELLY LINZER COOKIES

We gave the classic linzer cookie a makeover with the flavors of a childhood favorite: PB&J. Use a low-sugar strawberry jam for the brightest red color.

MAKES 18 cookies • **HANDS-ON** 40 minutes • **TOTAL** 1 hour, 30 minutes

1 cup unsalted butter, softened
1/2 cup granulated sugar
1/2 cup packed light brown sugar
1/2 cup creamy peanut butter
1 large egg yolk
1 teaspoon vanilla extract
3 cups all-purpose flour
1/2 teaspoon kosher salt
1/2 teaspoon baking powder
1/2 cup powdered sugar
1/2 cup strawberry jam

1. Preheat the oven to 375°F with the oven racks in the top third and bottom third of the oven. Beat the butter, granulated sugar, brown sugar, and peanut butter with a mixer on medium speed until smooth, about 1 minute. Add the egg yolk and vanilla, and beat on low speed just until incorporated. Whisk together the flour, salt, and baking powder, and gradually add to butter mixture, beating on low speed just until incorporated.
2. Place the dough on a well-floured surface, and roll to 1/4-inch thickness. Cut the dough with a 2 1/2-inch round cutter. Gently reroll the scraps once, and repeat the process with the round cutter. Place half of the dough rounds on parchment paper-lined baking sheets. Using a 1-inch star-shaped cutter, cut out and remove the dough star shapes from the center of the remaining half of the dough rounds. (Reserve and bake the dough star cutouts for later, if desired.) Transfer the dough rounds with the star cutouts removed to the lined baking sheets.
3. Bake the cookies at 375°F until the cookies are set and beginning to brown, 12 to 13 minutes, switching the pans top rack to bottom rack halfway through baking. Transfer the pans to the wire racks; cool the cookies completely, about 30 minutes.
4. Sift the powdered sugar over the cookies with the star cutouts. Spread 1 1/2 teaspoons of the jam on 1 side of the remaining cookies. Place a star cutout cookie, powdered sugar side up, over each jam covered cookie, and gently press.

LEMONY SANDWICH COOKIES

These soft cookies have a creamy lemon filling made with fresh zest and juice. We also admire their beautifully crackled and crunchy tops.

MAKES about 20 sandwich cookies • **HANDS-ON** 40 minutes • **TOTAL** 1 hour, 30 minutes

- 1 cup granulated sugar
- 3/4 cup unsalted butter, at room temperature
- 1 large egg
- 1 large egg yolk
- 1 teaspoon vanilla extract
- 1/8 teaspoon yellow food coloring gel
- 2 tablespoons lemon zest, plus 1 teaspoon fresh juice (from 1 lemon)
- 2 cups self-rising flour
- 1/2 cup sanding or sparkling sugar
- 1 cup powdered sugar
- 4 teaspoons whole milk

1. Preheat the oven to 375°F with the oven racks in the top third and bottom third of the oven. Beat the granulated sugar and 1/2 cup of the butter with a mixer on medium speed until light and fluffy. Add the egg, egg yolk, vanilla, food coloring gel, and 1 tablespoon of the lemon zest, and beat on low speed until just combined. Add the flour to the butter mixture, beating on low speed just until the flour is incorporated. Place the sanding sugar in a shallow dish. Drop the dough by tablespoonfuls into the sugar, rolling to coat, and place 2 inches apart on parchment paper-lined baking sheets.
2. Bake at 375°F until the cookies are just set, about 8 minutes, switching the pans top rack to bottom rack halfway through baking. Transfer to wire racks, and cool the cookies on the pans 5 minutes. Remove the cookies from the pans to the wire racks, and cool completely.
3. Beat the powdered sugar, milk, lemon juice, and remaining 1/4 cup butter and 1 tablespoon lemon zest on medium speed until light and fluffy. Pipe 2 teaspoons lemon filling onto the flat side of half of the cookies. Cover with the remaining half of cookies, flat side down, and gently press.

EGGNOG WHOOPIE PIES

The rich, creamy filling can be made up to three days ahead and then piped onto fresh, cooled cookies. Bourbon makes the filling lick-the-bowl good, but you can omit the booze for a kid-friendly treat.

MAKES about 22 cookie pies • **HANDS-ON** 45 minutes • **TOTAL** 1 hour, 15 minutes

- 1/2 cup unsalted butter, softened
- 1 cup granulated sugar
- 1/2 cup packed light brown sugar
- 2 large eggs
- 2 teaspoons vanilla extract
- 2 1/2 cups all-purpose flour
- 1 teaspoon baking powder
- 1/4 teaspoon baking soda
- 1/4 teaspoon ground cinnamon
- 1 teaspoon kosher salt
- 1/3 cup whole milk
- 4 ounces cream cheese, softened
- 2 tablespoons bourbon
- 1/4 teaspoon ground nutmeg
- 1 1/3 cups powdered sugar
- 1/2 cup heavy cream

1. Preheat the oven to 375°F with the oven racks in the top third and bottom third of the oven. Beat the butter, granulated sugar, and brown sugar with a mixer on medium speed until smooth, about 1 minute. Add the eggs, 1 at a time, beating on low speed just until incorporated. Add 1 teaspoon of the vanilla, and beat just until combined. Whisk together the flour, baking powder, baking soda, cinnamon, and 3/4 teaspoon of the salt, and add to the butter mixture alternately with the milk, beginning and ending with the flour mixture and beating on low speed just until each is incorporated.
2. Using a 1-inch cookie scoop, drop the dough about 3 inches apart onto parchment paper-lined baking sheets. Bake at 375°F until the cookies are just set and beginning to brown, 9 to 11 minutes, switching the pans top rack to bottom rack halfway through baking. Transfer to wire racks, and cool the cookies on the pans 5 minutes. Remove the cookies from the pans to the wire racks, and cool completely, about 30 minutes.
3. Beat the cream cheese on medium speed until fluffy, about 2 minutes, scraping down the sides of the bowl as needed. Add the bourbon, nutmeg, 1 cup of the powdered sugar, and remaining 1 teaspoon vanilla and 1/4 teaspoon salt; beat until smooth. Beat the heavy cream in a small bowl until stiff peaks form; fold into the cream cheese mixture. Pipe 1 tablespoon of the cream cheese filling onto the flat side of half of the cookies. Cover with the remaining half of cookies, flat side down, and gently press. Sift the remaining 1/3 cup powdered sugar evenly onto the "pies."

RED VELVET CRACKLE SANDWICH COOKIES

These treats have all the flavors of red velvet cake in a bite-size package. Use a small trigger-handled ice cream scoop for uniform cookies.

MAKES 21 sandwich cookies • **HANDS-ON** 30 minutes • **TOTAL** 1 hour, 10 minutes

3 ounces semisweet baking chocolate, chopped
1/4 cup unsalted butter
1 cup granulated sugar
2 large eggs
1 tablespoon red liquid food coloring
2 cups all-purpose flour
2 tablespoons unsweetened cocoa
1 teaspoon baking powder
1/2 teaspoon baking soda
1/2 teaspoon kosher salt
2 cups powdered sugar
4 ounces cream cheese, softened

1. Preheat the oven to 375°F with the oven racks in the top third and bottom third of the oven. Melt the chocolate and butter in a large microwave-safe glass bowl on MEDIUM (50% power) 1 1/2 minutes or until melted and smooth, stirring at 30-second intervals. Whisk in the granulated sugar, eggs, and food coloring until smooth.
2. Whisk together the flour, cocoa, baking powder, baking soda, and salt, and add to the butter mixture, stirring gently just to combine.
3. Place 1 cup of the powdered sugar in a small bowl. Drop the dough by tablespoonfuls into the powdered sugar, rolling to coat, and place 1 inch apart on parchment paper-lined baking sheets. Using the heel of your hand, gently flatten the domed tops of the dough. Bake at 375°F until the cookies are almost set and the outsides are crackled, 10 to 11 minutes. Transfer the pans to wire racks, and cool the cookies completely, about 30 minutes.
4. Beat the cream cheese and remaining 1 cup powdered sugar with a mixer on medium speed until smooth. Spread 1 1/2 teaspoons of the cream cheese filling onto the flat side of half of the cookies. Cover with the remaining half of cookies, flat side down, and gently press.

CHOCOLATE CRÈME-FILLED SANDWICH COOKIES

The classic combination of chocolate and crème will be a surefire crowd-pleaser at all your holiday parties.

MAKES 48 sandwich cookies • **HANDS-ON** 25 minutes • **TOTAL** 3 hours, 11 minutes, includes chilling

COOKIES

- 1¾ cups all-purpose flour
- ¾ cup sugar
- ⅔ cup unsweetened dark cocoa powder
- ½ teaspoon baking soda
- ¼ teaspoon table salt
- 12 tablespoons unsalted butter, cut into small pieces
- 1 large egg white
- 1 tablespoon water

FILLING

- ⅓ cup vegetable shortening, at room temperature
- 5½ tablespoons unsalted butter, at room temperature
- 1⅔ cups confectioners' sugar
- 1 teaspoon vanilla extract

1. Make the Cookies: Beat together the flour, sugar, cocoa powder, baking soda, salt, and butter with a mixer at low speed until crumbly. Add the egg white and water; beat until blended.
2. Divide the dough in half. Roll each piece into an 8½-by-1½-inch log. Wrap in plastic wrap; chill for 2 hours.
3. Line 2 baking sheets with parchment paper. Place racks in the upper and lower thirds of the oven and preheat to 350°F. Cut each log into 48 slices (about ⅛ inch thick). Place on the prepared sheets, about 2 inches apart.
4. Bake at 350°F until the cookies are set, 10 to 12 minutes, rotating the sheets once. Let the cookies cool on the sheets on wire racks for 2 minutes, then transfer to the wire racks to cool completely.
5. Make the Filling: Beat together the shortening and butter with a mixer on medium speed until smooth. Gradually add the sugar, beating on low speed until blended. Beat in the vanilla.
6. Spread 1½ teaspoons of the filling onto the flat side of 48 cookies; top with the remaining 48 cookies, flat side down, and gently press.

SPARKLING ORNAMENT COOKIES

These richly colored vanilla and almond-flavored cookies are perfect for little hands—the more sprinkles, the better!

MAKES about 4 dozen cookies • **HANDS-ON** 30 minutes • **TOTAL** 2 hours, 35 minutes, includes chilling

- 1½ cups salted butter, softened
- ¾ cup granulated sugar
- ½ teaspoon vanilla extract
- ⅛ teaspoon almond extract
- 3¾ cups all-purpose flour
- Food coloring gel in blue, red, green, and yellow
- White sparkling sugar or sanding sugar
- Assorted sprinkles, sugar pearls, silver dragées

1. Beat the butter and sugar with a heavy-duty stand mixer on medium speed until creamy; add the vanilla and almond extracts, and beat until incorporated. Gradually add the flour; beat on low speed until incorporated after each addition.
2. Divide the dough into 4 equal portions, and place each portion in a small bowl. Add the desired amount of the food coloring gel to each bowl, and stir with a fork until the food coloring is incorporated. Cover the bowls, and chill 1 hour.
3. Preheat the oven to 250°F. Shape 1 dough portion into about 12 (1½-inch) balls, and roll in the sparkling sugar or sanding sugar. Press the sprinkles, sugar pearls, or silver dragées into the dough balls. Place the decorated balls about 2 inches apart on parchment paper-lined baking sheets. Repeat with the remaining dough portions.
4. Bake at 250°F until lightly browned on the bottom, 25 to 30 minutes, switching the pans top rack to bottom rack halfway through baking. Cool on the pans 5 minutes. Remove the cookies to wire racks; cool completely, about 30 minutes.

CHOCOLATE-BOURBON-FUDGE BALLS

These delightfully tipsy, no-bake treats will be a hit at holiday parties. Make the mixture up to two days in advance. Store the fudge balls in the refrigerator for up to five days in an airtight container.

MAKES about 40 cookies • **HANDS-ON** 25 minutes • **TOTAL** 4 hours, 25 minutes, includes chilling

- 2 (4-ounce) bittersweet chocolate baking bars, chopped
- 1 (4-ounce) semisweet chocolate baking bar, chopped
- 1½ tablespoons salted butter, cubed
- 9 tablespoons heavy cream
- ¼ cup bourbon
- 2 teaspoons vanilla extract
- 1 (5.3-ounce) package pure butter shortbread cookies (such as Walkers), finely crushed
- ½ teaspoon fine sea salt
- 2 cups finely chopped toasted pecans

1. Combine the chopped bittersweet chocolate, semisweet chocolate, and butter in a large glass bowl. Cook the cream and bourbon in a small saucepan over medium until the mixture is hot but not boiling, 3 to 4 minutes. (Bubbles will form around the edge.) Pour the mixture over the chocolate. Let stand 1 minute.
2. Stir the chocolate mixture until melted and smooth. (If the mixture doesn't melt completely, microwave at HIGH 30 seconds to 1 minute, stirring at 30-second intervals.) Stir in the vanilla. Stir in the crushed cookies. Cover and chill 3 hours or until firm. (Mixture can be prepared and chilled up to 2 days ahead.)
3. Shape the mixture into about 40 (1-inch) balls. Sprinkle each ball with a very small amount of sea salt, and coat the balls in the chopped pecans. Place on wax paper-lined baking sheets, and chill 1 hour. Refrigerate in an airtight container up to 5 days.

KEY LIME TASSIES

If you love Key lime pie, then you must make these. The best part is they're truly make-ahead: The tart shells can be made and frozen up to a month in advance, and the Key lime curd can be made up to two weeks ahead and stored in the refrigerator.

MAKES 5 dozen cookies • **HANDS-ON** 45 minutes • **TOTAL** 6 hours, 45 minutes, includes chilling

CURD

- 2 cups granulated sugar
- 1/2 cup salted butter, softened
- 4 large eggs, at room temperature
- 1 cup bottled Key lime juice (such as Nellie & Joe's Famous Key West Lime Juice), at room temperature

CREAM CHEESE PASTRY

- 1 (8-ounce) package cream cheese, softened
- 1 cup salted butter, softened
- 1/4 cup granulated sugar
- 3 1/2 cups all-purpose flour

Garnishes: powdered sugar, lime zest

1. Make the Curd: Beat 2 cups granulated sugar and 1/2 cup butter with a mixer on medium speed until blended. Add the eggs, 1 at a time, beating just until blended after each addition. Gradually add the Key lime juice to the butter mixture, beating at low speed just until blended after each addition. (Mixture may separate at this stage, but will emulsify as it is heated and whisked.)

2. Transfer the mixture to a heavy 4-quart saucepan. Cook over medium-low, whisking constantly, until the mixture thickens and just begins to bubble, 14 to 16 minutes. Remove the saucepan from the heat, and cool the curd 30 minutes. Place plastic wrap directly on the surface of the warm curd (to prevent a film from forming), and chill until firm, about 4 hours. Refrigerate in an airtight container up to 2 weeks.

3. Make the Cream Cheese Pastry: Beat the cream cheese, 1 cup butter, and 1/4 cup granulated sugar with a heavy-duty stand mixer on medium speed until creamy. Gradually add the flour to the butter mixture, beating at low speed just until blended after each addition. Shape the dough into 60 (1-inch) balls, and place on a baking sheet; cover and chill 1 hour.

4. Preheat the oven to 400°F. Place 1 chilled dough ball into each cup of lightly greased miniature muffin pans; press the dough into the bottoms and up the sides of the cups, forming the shells.

5. Bake at 400°F until lightly browned, 10 to 12 minutes. Remove the shells from the pans to wire racks, and cool completely, about 20 minutes.

6. Spoon about 1 1/2 teaspoons of the curd into each pastry shell. Cover the filled shells, and chill until ready to serve. Just before serving, sprinkle the filled shells evenly with the powdered sugar. Garnish, if desired.

NOTE: You will have leftover curd. It is great as a spread on warm biscuits or scones, as a topping for pound cake, or as a dip for fresh fruit.

GIFTS FROM THE KITCHEN

Looking for a thoughtful gift for that special friend, a neighbor, or your child's teacher? These recipes for crackers, infused oil, candies, and more are sure to please everyone on your list.

MUSTARD-DILL SAUCE

Use this sauce as a base or starter for vinaigrettes, sauces, or marinades, or use it on its own with gravlax and toasted rye bread as a quick appetizer.

MAKES 6 cups • **HANDS-ON** 10 minutes • **TOTAL** 10 minutes

3 cups Dijon mustard
1½ cups chopped fresh dill (about 2 [1-ounce] packages)
1 cup honey
½ cup extra-virgin olive oil
½ cup white wine vinegar
2 tablespoons dry white wine

Stir together all the ingredients in a large bowl. Divide the sauce among small jars, label, and store in a cool, dry place until ready to use.

GARLIC-AND-HERB-INFUSED OIL

Be sure to thoroughly wash and dry the herbs before adding to the oil to prevent bacterial growth.

MAKES about 3 cups • **HANDS-ON** 10 minutes • **TOTAL** 4 hours, 10 minutes, includes cooling

3 cups extra-virgin olive oil
5 garlic cloves, smashed
3 fresh thyme sprigs
3 fresh rosemary sprigs
3 fresh sage sprigs
2 bay leaves
1 teaspoon fennel seeds
1 teaspoon coriander seeds
1 teaspoon crushed red pepper
Cheesecloth

1. Heat the first 9 ingredients in a large, deep skillet over medium 5 minutes or until the oil warms and the garlic and herbs begin to sizzle.
2. Remove from the heat, and cool completely, about 4 hours.
3. Pour the oil through a cheesecloth-lined strainer into a bowl; discard the solids. Transfer the infused oil into small bottles, and label. Store in the refrigerator up to 1 month.

SMOKY PORCINI SALT

This salt will add a slight smoky umami flavor to foods. It's perfect on steak, chicken, and buttered bread.

MAKES 1¾ cups • **HANDS-ON** 15 minutes • **TOTAL** 15 minutes

½ cup hickory wood chips
1 (8.5-ounce) box flaky sea salt
1 (1-ounce) package dried porcini mushrooms

1. Pierce 10 holes in bottom of a 13- x 9-inch disposable aluminum pan. Arrange the wood chips over the holes. Place the salt on the opposite side of the pan.
2. Place the pan on stove-top burner with the holes over the burner; heat the burner to medium until the wood chips begin to smoke. Reduce the heat to medium-low; cover the pan with aluminum foil, and seal tightly. Cook 4 minutes or until the salt is a light tan color and tastes smoky. Remove from the heat, and transfer the salt to a bowl.
3. Grind the mushrooms into a fine powder in a spice grinder (about ⅓ cup). Combine the porcini powder and smoked salt, and transfer to small jars.

Garlic-and-Herb-Infused Oil
Homemade Bourbon "Irish" Crème (page 165)
NAUGHTY AND NICE
Mustard-Dill Sauce
DASH
Smoky Porcini Salt

Herb-Dusted Potato Chips

HOMEMADE BOURBON "IRISH" CRÈME

You'll wow your friends with this fun party gift. Use as you would Baileys Irish Cream. (Pictured on page 163)

MAKES 4 cups • **HANDS-ON** 5 minutes • **TOTAL** 5 minutes

- $1\frac{2}{3}$ cups bourbon
- 1 (14-ounce) can sweetened condensed milk
- 1 cup heavy cream
- 2 tablespoons chocolate syrup
- 1 teaspoon instant coffee
- 2 teaspoons vanilla extract

Process all the ingredients in a blender until smooth. Pour into individual bottles. Store in the refrigerator up to 2 weeks.

HERB-DUSTED POTATO CHIPS

The herb dust makes these chips unique and so flavorful. For giving, double or triple the recipe. Let the chips cool before packaging to send home with your guests.

SERVES 10 • **HANDS-ON** 30 minutes • **TOTAL** 30 minutes

- 1 teaspoon fine sea salt
- 1 teaspoon dried parsley
- 1 teaspoon dried dill
- $\frac{1}{2}$ teaspoon garlic salt
- $\frac{1}{2}$ teaspoon dried Italian seasoning
- $\frac{1}{2}$ teaspoon dried oregano
- $\frac{1}{4}$ teaspoon freshly ground black pepper
- 2 medium-size Yukon gold potatoes (about $1\frac{1}{4}$ pounds)
- Vegetable oil

1. Combine the first 7 ingredients in a small bowl.
2. Cut the potatoes into $\frac{1}{16}$-inch-thick slices, using a mandoline.
3. Pour the oil to a depth of 4 inches into a Dutch oven; heat to 360°F. Fry the potatoes in the hot oil, in batches, 1 to 2 minutes or until golden brown, turning occasionally with a slotted spoon. Remove with the slotted spoon; drain on paper towels. Immediately sprinkle with the herb mixture. Serve warm or at room temperature.

ROSEMARY-BLUE CHEESE CRACKERS

Give these crackers in glassine bags tied with string for a festive party gift.

MAKES 8 dozen crackers • **HANDS-ON** 15 minutes • **TOTAL** 2 hours, 45 minutes, includes chilling

16 ounces blue cheese, softened and crumbled
1 cup unsalted butter, softened
2 tablespoons finely chopped fresh rosemary
2 teaspoons kosher salt
1½ teaspoons freshly ground black pepper
3 cups all-purpose flour

1. Beat the first 5 ingredients with a heavy-duty stand mixer at medium speed, using the paddle attachment, 2 to 3 minutes or until creamy and well blended. Gradually add the flour, beating at low speed just until blended and the dough comes together. Divide the dough in half; roll each half into a 12-inch-long, 1½-inch-thick log. Wrap in plastic wrap, and chill until firm (at least 2 hours).
2. Preheat the oven to 350°F. Cut logs into ¼-inch-thick slices using a sharp knife; place on parchment paper-lined baking sheets. (Work with 1 log at a time to ensure that the slices remain chilled before baking.)
3. Bake at 350°F for 18 to 20 minutes or until the edges are deep golden brown. Cool on the baking sheets 5 minutes; transfer to wire racks, and cool completely, about 15 minutes. (The crackers will crisp as they cool.)

NOTE: You can keep these logs on hand in your freezer for last-minute gifts and appetizer options. Let them stand at room temperature 15 minutes or until sliceable. For a decorative touch, press a couple of fresh rosemary leaves onto each cracker before baking.

PARMESAN AND CARAMELIZED SHALLOT PALMIERS

Double this recipe to use the entire box of puff pastry. These also make an excellent holiday appetizer.

MAKES 2 dozen palmiers • **HANDS-ON** 30 minutes • **TOTAL** 2 hours, 5 minutes

2 tablespoons butter
1½ cups finely chopped shallots (about 7 medium shallots)
2 teaspoons chopped fresh thyme
½ teaspoon table salt
¼ teaspoon freshly ground black pepper
½ (17.3-ounce) package puff pastry sheets, thawed (1 sheet)
1 large egg, lightly beaten
1 cup grated Parmigiano-Reggiano cheese (about 4 ounces)

1. Melt the butter in a medium skillet over medium. Add the shallots; cook, stirring often, 15 minutes or until caramelized. Remove from the heat, and stir in the thyme, salt, and pepper. Cool 10 minutes.
2. Unroll the pastry on a lightly floured surface; brush lightly with the egg. Spread the shallot mixture over the pastry, leaving a ½-inch border around the edges; sprinkle with the cheese. Starting with 1 long side, roll up the pastry, jelly-roll fashion, to the center of the pastry sheet. Roll the opposite side to the center. (The shape will resemble a scroll.) Roll in two opposite sides, jelly-roll fashion, to meet in the center. Brush the beaten egg between the rolled sides; press lightly to seal. Wrap in plastic wrap, and freeze for 45 minutes or until well chilled and almost firm.
3. Preheat the oven to 400°F. Cut the pastry into 24 slices (about ⅜ inch thick) using a sharp knife; place on a parchment paper-lined baking sheet. Brush lightly with the egg.
4. Bake at 400°F for 18 to 20 minutes or until golden brown. Cool on the baking sheet 5 minutes; transfer to a wire rack, and cool completely, 15 minutes.

SAVORY HERBED BISCOTTI

This delightful take on a simple crostini will complement your aperitifs during the cocktail hour. As these are not meant to be dipped in a liquid, they are more tender than you might expect from biscotti. Serve with your favorite Camembert or other soft-ripened cheese. Be sure to use whole dates, not prechopped, for the best results.

MAKES about 3 dozen biscotti • **HANDS-ON** 30 minutes • **TOTAL** 2 hours, 30 minutes

4 cups all-purpose flour
2 tablespoons finely chopped fresh flat-leaf parsley
1 tablespoon baking powder
2 teaspoons finely chopped fresh rosemary
1½ teaspoons kosher salt
½ cup chopped pitted dates (about 6 Medjool dates)
1 cup unsalted butter, softened
4 ounces goat cheese, softened
3 tablespoons sugar
3 tablespoons honey
4 large eggs, at room temperature

1. Preheat the oven to 350°F. Whisk together the first 5 ingredients in a medium bowl. Stir in the dates.
2. Beat the butter and goat cheese with a heavy-duty stand mixer on medium speed until smooth, using the paddle attachment. Add the sugar and honey; beat at medium speed until well blended. Add the eggs, 1 at a time, beating well after each addition. Gradually add the flour mixture, beating at medium-low speed until just blended.
3. Divide the dough in half. Shape each portion into 2 (14- x 2-inch) slightly flattened logs on a parchment paper-lined baking sheet, using your slightly dampened hands.
4. Bake at 350°F for 30 minutes or until light golden brown and the logs resist slightly when touched. Cool on the baking sheets on a wire rack 30 minutes.
5. Reduce the oven temperature to 300°F. Cut each log diagonally into ½-inch-thick slices with a serrated knife, using a gentle sawing motion. Place the slices on ungreased baking sheets.
6. Bake at 300°F for 15 minutes; turn over, and bake 15 more minutes or until golden brown. Transfer to wire racks, and cool completely, about 30 minutes.

GINGER-MOLASSES BISCOTTI

Turbinado sugar, found in supermarkets, is a raw sugar product with coarse, light brown crystals. We love it for its subtle molasses flavor. Store crunchy biscotti in an airtight container for up to one week.

MAKES 14 biscotti • **HANDS-ON** 15 minutes • **TOTAL** 2 hours, 16 minutes

1 (16.5-ounce) package refrigerated chocolate chip cookie dough
1/3 cup chopped crystallized ginger
2 tablespoons molasses
1 1/2 teaspoons bourbon
1/2 teaspoon ground cinnamon
1/4 teaspoon ground nutmeg
2 teaspoons turbinado sugar

1. Tear the cookie dough into pieces in a large bowl. Stir in the ginger, molasses, bourbon, cinnamon, and nutmeg until well combined.
2. Press onto the bottom of a lightly greased 1-quart baking dish. Sprinkle evenly with the turbinado sugar.
3. Bake at 350°F for 40 minutes or until a wooden pick inserted in the center comes out clean. Cool in the baking dish on a wire rack 20 minutes. Remove from the baking dish to the wire rack, and cool 10 more minutes. Reduce the oven temperature to 300°F.
4. Cut the cookie into 14 (1/4-inch-wide) slices with a serrated knife using a gentle sawing motion. Place the slices on a baking sheet.
5. Bake at 300°F for 18 minutes on each side. Remove to wire racks, and let cool 15 minutes or until completely cool.

NOTE: 2 teaspoons granulated sugar may be substituted.

SPICED HOLIDAY NUTS

This nut mix is incredibly addictive—you may want to make a quadruple batch. We tested with one cup each cashews, pecans, and walnuts.

MAKES 5½ cups • **HANDS-ON** 15 minutes • **TOTAL** 2 hours, includes cooling

- ½ cup packed dark brown sugar
- 1½ teaspoons kosher salt
- 1 teaspoon ancho chili powder
- ½ teaspoon ground cinnamon
- ½ teaspoon freshly ground black pepper
- ¼ teaspoon cayenne pepper
- 1 large egg white, at room temperature
- 1 tablespoon water
- 1 pound raw mixed nuts (such as cashews, pecans, and walnuts)

1. Preheat the oven to 300°F. Stir together the first 6 ingredients.
2. Whisk together the egg white and water in a large bowl until frothy but not stiff, about 1 minute. Add the nuts, and stir to coat. Add the sugar mixture, and toss until evenly coated.
3. Lightly grease a parchment paper-lined baking sheet, and spread the nuts in a single layer on parchment paper.
4. Bake at 300°F for 45 minutes, stirring every 8 minutes. Remove from the oven, and cool completely, about 1 hour, breaking up any nuts that clump together.

HERBED PECORINO GRISSINI

These long, thin Italian-style breadsticks make a lovely gift when wrapped in parchment paper and tied with ribbon.

MAKES 36 pieces • **HANDS-ON** 25 minutes • **TOTAL** 2 hours, 15 minutes

- 2⅔ cups bread flour
- ⅓ cup finely grated Pecorino Romano cheese
- 3 teaspoons active dry yeast
- 1½ teaspoons minced fresh rosemary
- 1½ teaspoons minced fresh sage
- 1 teaspoon table salt
- ½ teaspoon garlic powder
- ½ teaspoon freshly ground black pepper
- 1 cup warm milk (105° to 110°F)
- 3 tablespoons olive oil

1. Combine the first 8 ingredients in bowl of a heavy-duty stand mixer. Beat at low speed 1 minute until blended, using the dough hook attachment. Add the milk and oil; beat 1 to 2 minutes or until the dough comes together. Increase the speed to medium-low, and beat 3 to 5 minutes or until the dough is smooth.
2. Place the dough in a lightly greased large bowl, turning to grease the top. Cover the bowl with plastic wrap, and let rise in a warm place (80° to 85°F), free from drafts, 45 minutes to 1 hour or until doubled in bulk.
3. Preheat the oven to 400°F. Turn the dough out onto a lightly floured surface, and knead lightly 1 minute. Roll the dough into a 15- x 12-inch rectangle, about ¼ inch thick. Cut the dough into 36 strips (just under ½-inch wide), using a sharp knife or pizza cutter. Roll the strips back and forth on the surface until slightly rounded. Place 1 inch apart on parchment paper-lined baking sheets. Cover loosely with plastic wrap; let rise 15 to 20 minutes.
4. Bake at 400°F for 18 to 23 minutes or until golden brown and crisp, turning halfway through. Cool on the baking sheets 2 minutes; transfer to wire racks, and cool completely, about 20 minutes.

Cranberry Shortbread Bars

CRANBERRY SHORTBREAD BARS

Freeze the shortbread dough, and then grate it in a food processor to get the most tender crust.

MAKES 24 bars • **HANDS-ON** 20 minutes • **TOTAL** 2 hours, 5 minutes, includes chilling

- 1½ cups fresh or frozen cranberries, thawed
- ¼ cup water
- 1 cup granulated sugar
- ¾ cup salted butter, softened, plus more for greasing pan
- ¼ teaspoon table salt
- 2 large egg yolks
- 1 teaspoon vanilla extract
- 1¾ cups all-purpose flour

1. Bring the cranberries, water, and ¼ cup of the sugar to a boil in a small saucepan over medium-high. Cook, stirring and smashing the berries occasionally, until the mixture thickens, 10 to 12 minutes. Remove from the heat, and cool completely.
2. Beat the butter, salt, and the remaining ¾ cup sugar in a large bowl with a mixer on medium speed until light and fluffy, 3 to 5 minutes. Add the egg yolks and vanilla; beat on low speed until combined. Add the flour to the butter mixture; beat on low speed until combined.
3. Turn the dough out onto a lightly floured surface; knead until the dough comes together, 3 or 4 times. Shape into a 14-inch-long log. Cover with plastic wrap, and freeze at least 1 hour or overnight.
4. Preheat the oven to 350°F. Line a 9-inch square baking pan with parchment paper, allowing the paper to extend over the sides of the pan. Grease the paper.
5. Remove the plastic wrap from the dough log; cut in half crosswise, and cut each piece in half lengthwise. Feed the dough log quarters through the chute of a food processor fitted with a shredding blade. Press half of the grated dough into the bottom of the prepared pan. Spread the cranberry mixture over the dough, leaving a ½-inch border. Top with the remaining half of the grated dough, pressing to seal the edges.
6. Bake in the preheated oven until firm and golden brown, 33 to 35 minutes. Cool in the pan. Lift the cranberry shortbread from the pan using the parchment as handles; cut into rectangles; then cut into triangles.

WHITE CHOCOLATE-PEPPERMINT BLONDIES

We gave the classic blondie a Christmas makeover. *(Pictured on page 160)*

MAKES about 4½ dozen blondies • **HANDS-ON** 20 minutes • **TOTAL** 1 hour, 40 minutes

BLONDIES

- 1 cup salted butter, softened, plus more for greasing pan
- 1 cup granulated sugar
- 2 large eggs
- 2 teaspoons vanilla extract
- ½ teaspoon table salt
- 2¼ cups all-purpose flour
- ½ cup white chocolate chips
- 1 cup coarsely crushed peppermint candies (about 40 candies)

ICING

- 2 cups powdered sugar
- ¼ cup salted butter, softened
- 1 teaspoon vanilla extract
- ¼ teaspoon peppermint extract
- 2 to 3 tablespoons heavy cream

1. Preheat the oven to 350°F. Grease a 13- x 9-inch baking pan with butter. Line the pan with parchment paper, allowing the paper to extend over the sides of the pan. Grease the paper.
2. Make the Blondies: Combine the butter and granulated sugar in a large bowl. Beat with a mixer on medium speed until well combined, about 3 minutes. Add the eggs, 1 at a time, beating until combined after each addition. Beat in the vanilla and salt. Add the flour; beat on low speed just until combined, 1 to 2 minutes. Stir in the white chocolate chips and ½ cup of the crushed candies.
3. Spread the batter in the prepared pan; smooth the top with a spatula. Bake at 350°F until a wooden pick inserted in the center comes out clean, 20 to 22 minutes. Cool completely in the pan. Lift the blondies from the pan using the parchment paper as handles. Discard the paper; trim the browned edges.
4. Make the Icing: Combine the powdered sugar, butter, vanilla, and peppermint extract in a medium bowl; beat on medium speed until smooth. Beat in 2 tablespoons of the cream. Add up to 1 additional tablespoon of the cream, if necessary, until the icing reaches a spreadable consistency. Spread Icing over the top of the blondies. Sprinkle with the remaining crushed candies. Cut into 3-inch squares; cut the squares into triangles.

NO-BAKE FUDGY TOFFEE BARS

These gooey bars will be your new favorite no-bake cookie. Serve chilled for less mess.

SERVES 16 bars • **HANDS-ON** 30 minutes • **TOTAL** 4 hours, 30 minutes, includes chilling

Salted butter for greasing pan
1½ cups heavy cream
3 tablespoons powdered sugar
3 (4-ounce) semisweet chocolate baking bars, finely chopped
1 teaspoon vanilla extract
2 (11-ounce) packages caramels
⅓ cup evaporated milk
17 graham cracker sheets
2 (1.4-ounce) chocolate-covered toffee candy bars (such as Heath), coarsely chopped

1. Line a 9-inch square baking pan with parchment paper, allowing the parchment to extend over the sides of the pan. Grease the paper with butter.
2. Combine the heavy cream and powdered sugar in a small saucepan. Bring to a simmer over medium-low, stirring occasionally. (Do not bring to a boil.) Place the chopped chocolate in a medium bowl. Pour the cream mixture over the chocolate; let stand 1 minute. Gently stir the mixture until the chocolate melts and the mixture is smooth. Stir in the vanilla.
3. Combine the caramels and evaporated milk in a saucepan over medium-low. Cook, stirring often, until the caramels melt and the mixture is smooth, 9 to 10 minutes. Remove from the heat; let stand 10 minutes.
4. Place 1 layer of the graham cracker sheets in the bottom of the prepared pan, breaking the crackers to fit as needed. Pour one-third of the caramel mixture over the crackers. Using an offset spatula, smooth the caramel to the edges of the pan. Pour one-third of the chocolate mixture over the caramel; smooth the chocolate to the edges of the pan. Repeat the layers 2 times with the remaining graham cracker sheets, caramel mixture, and chocolate mixture, ending with the chocolate. Sprinkle the chopped toffee candy bars over the top. Chill, uncovered, 4 hours or overnight.
5. Lift the toffee bar mixture from the pan using the parchment as handles. Trim the edges if necessary. Cut into 16 bars. Serve chilled.

WHITE CHOCOLATE SALTIES

Be sure to buy the salted variety of pretzels to get that crave-worthy salty-sweet combo.

MAKES 1½ pounds • **HANDS-ON** 15 minutes • **TOTAL** 35 minutes

1 pound vanilla candy coating, chopped
3 cups thin pretzel sticks
6 ounces cocktail peanuts

Microwave the candy coating in a microwave-safe bowl at MEDIUM 3 minutes, stirring every 30 seconds or until melted. Stir in the pretzels and peanuts. Drop by tablespoonfuls onto parchment paper-lined baking sheets. Chill 20 minutes or until firm.

No-Bake Fudgy
Toffee Bars

LEMON CRUMBLE BARS

Lemon bars are always a crowd-pleaser, and they'll be even more popular topped with a sweet oat crumble.

MAKES 16 bars • **HANDS-ON** 25 minutes • **TOTAL** 1 hour, 25 minutes

COOKIE BASE

- 1¼ cups all-purpose flour
- ½ cup powdered sugar
- ¼ teaspoon table salt
- 10 tablespoons cold salted butter, cut into ½-inch pieces, plus more for greasing pan

FILLING

- 1 cup granulated sugar
- ⅔ cup fresh lemon juice (from about 4 lemons)
- ¼ cup cornstarch
- ¼ teaspoon table salt
- 2 large eggs
- 2 large egg yolks
- 1 tablespoons salted butter

TOPPING

- ½ cup all-purpose flour
- 3 tablespoons powdered sugar
- 2 teaspoons lemon zest
- ⅛ teaspoon table salt
- ⅜ cup salted butter
- ½ cup uncooked regular oats

1. Make the Cookie Base: Preheat oven to 350°F. Grease an 8-inch square baking pan with butter. Line the pan with parchment paper, allowing the paper to extend over the sides of the pan. Grease the parchment. Pulse the flour, powdered sugar, and salt in a food processor until combined, about 3 times. Add the butter; pulse until the mixture resembles coarse sand, 6 or 7 times. Press the flour mixture into the prepared pan. Bake in the preheated oven 15 minutes.
2. Make the Filling: Combine the granulated sugar, lemon juice, cornstarch, and salt in a medium saucepan; bring to simmer over medium-high. (Do not bring to a boil.) Lightly beat the eggs and yolks in a medium bowl. Add ½ cup of the hot sugar mixture to the eggs, whisking constantly. Gradually add the egg mixture to the remaining sugar mixture in the saucepan, whisking constantly. Cook, whisking constantly, until thick and bubbly, about 2 minutes. Remove from the heat. Stir in the butter until melted and combined. Spread the hot filling evenly over the prepared cookie base.
3. Make the Topping: Pulse the flour, powdered sugar, lemon zest, and salt in a food processor until combined, 5 or 6 times. Add the butter; pulse until the mixture forms pea-size pieces, 4 or 5 times. Add the oats; pulse until combined, 2 or 3 times. Using your hands, press the mixture together into small clumps. Sprinkle the clumps evenly over the filling, pressing lightly to adhere. Bake at 350°F until the top is lightly browned, 35 to 40 minutes.
4. Cool completely in the pan. Lift the Lemon Crumble Bars from the pan using the parchment as handles. Trim the edges, if necessary, and cut into 16 bars.

DIVINE DIVINITY

These little goodies had their heyday back in the seventies, but they've not since lost an ounce of their appeal.

MAKES 3 dozen candies • **HANDS-ON** 20 minutes • **TOTAL** 20 minutes

- 2½ cups sugar
- ½ cup light corn syrup
- ½ cup water
- 2 large egg whites
- 2 teaspoons vanilla extract
- 1 cup chopped toasted pecans

1. Combine the sugar, corn syrup, and water in a 2-quart saucepan. Bring to a boil over medium-high; reduce the heat to medium, and cook 3 minutes or until a candy thermometer registers 234°F (thread stage).
2. Meanwhile, place the egg whites in the bowl of a heavy-duty stand mixer. Beat on medium-high speed until soft peaks form. Slowly pour half of the hot sugar mixture into the egg whites in a thin stream, beating at medium-high speed. Reduce the mixer speed to low.
3. Return the sugar mixture to medium heat; cook 3 minutes or until a candy thermometer registers 265°F (hard ball stage). Increase the mixer speed to medium-high; slowly pour the remaining sugar mixture into the egg whites in a thin stream. Beat 7 minutes or until mixture just begins to hold its shape (do not overbeat; mixture will become more firm as it cools). Beat in the vanilla.
4. Fold in the pecans. Quickly drop by tablespoonfuls onto parchment paper-lined baking sheets. Let cool completely.

MEXICAN PECAN CANDY

Pecans give these soft, dense pralines a nice crunch.

MAKES 2 dozen pieces • **HANDS-ON** 21 minutes • **TOTAL** 1 hour, 21 minutes, includes cooling

- 2 cups sugar
- 1 cup milk
- 2 tablespoons butter
- 2 tablespoons light corn syrup
- 1/2 teaspoon table salt
- 1/4 teaspoon baking soda
- 1 cup chopped pecans
- 1 teaspoon vanilla extract

1. Line the bottom and sides of an 8-inch square pan with parchment paper, allowing 2 to 3 inches to extend over the sides.
2. Combine the sugar and the next 5 ingredients in a large saucepan; bring to a boil over medium-high heat. Stir in the pecans; cook 8 minutes, stirring constantly, or until a candy thermometer registers 234°F (soft ball stage). Remove from the heat; stir in the vanilla. Beat 3 to 4 minutes with a wooden spoon or until creamy and beginning to thicken. Pour into the pan, spreading evenly. Cool completely, about 1 hour. Lift out of the pan using the parchment as handles; cut into small rectangles.

TURTLE CANDIES

Make these cute, turtle-shaped delights with house guests for a fun activity.

MAKES 16 candies • **HANDS-ON** 20 minutes • **TOTAL** 1 hour, 10 minutes, includes chilling

- 1 (12-ounce) package semisweet chocolate morsels
- 1 1/4 cups pecan halves, toasted
- 28 caramels, unwrapped
- 2 tablespoons whipping cream

1. Microwave the chocolate chips in a microwave-safe bowl at HIGH 1 to 1 1/2 minutes or until melted and smooth, stirring in 30-second intervals. Cool 10 minutes, stirring occasionally, until slightly thickened.
2. Drop the chocolate by tablespoonfuls onto a parchment paper-lined baking sheet, shaping into 16 (1 1/2-inch) circles. Reserve the remaining chocolate. Arrange 4 pecans over each circle; chill 15 minutes or until firm.
3. Microwave the caramels and whipping cream in a medium-size microwave-safe bowl at HIGH 2 minutes or until the caramels melt, stirring after 1 minute. Let stand 5 minutes or until slightly thickened. Spoon the caramel mixture evenly over the pecans.
4. Microwave the remaining chocolate at HIGH 1 minute until melted and smooth, stirring after 30 seconds; quickly spread the chocolate over the caramel mixture. Chill 30 minutes or until firm.

ROCKY ROAD PEANUT BUTTER CANDY CUPS

Fans of the classic chocolate-peanut butter combo will love these.

MAKES 3 dozen candies • **HANDS-ON** 15 minutes • **TOTAL** 1 hour, 15 minutes, includes chilling

- 1 (11-ounce) package peanut butter and milk chocolate chips
- 2 tablespoons creamy peanut butter
- 1 cup crisp rice cereal
- 1 cup miniature marshmallows
- 3/4 cup chopped unsalted roasted peanuts

Microwave the peanut butter and chocolate chips in a large glass bowl at HIGH 1 to 1 1/2 minutes or until melted, stirring every 30 seconds. Stir in the peanut butter until well blended. Stir in the rice cereal, marshmallows, and chopped peanuts. Spoon the mixture evenly into miniature paper candy cups. Chill 1 hour or until firm.

DARK CHOCOLATE TRUFFLES WITH FLEUR DE SEL

It's important to keep the saucepan of melted chocolate at 115°F for coating the truffles. As your guide, use a candy or digital thermometer, easily found at your local kitchen supply store.

MAKES about 2 dozen candies • **HANDS-ON** 30 minutes • **TOTAL** 3 hours, 30 minutes, includes chilling

- 8 ounces bittersweet chocolate, chopped
- 1/4 cup sugar
- 1 tablespoon water
- 2/3 cup heavy whipping cream
- 1/4 teaspoon fleur de sel or coarse sea salt
- 1/2 cup Dutch-process cocoa, sifted
- 12 ounces bittersweet chocolate, broken
- Fleur de sel or coarse sea salt

1. Microwave the 8 ounces chocolate in a glass bowl at HIGH 1 minute or until melted and smooth, stirring at 30-second intervals.

2. Combine the sugar and water in a small heavy saucepan; cook over medium until the sugar dissolves, stirring gently. Continue to simmer, without stirring, about 7 minutes or until the syrup is golden, brushing down the sides of the pan with a pastry brush dipped in water; remove the pan from the heat. Carefully add the cream (the mixture will bubble). Return the pan to low, and simmer, stirring until smooth. Stir in the 1/4 teaspoon fleur de sel. Remove from the heat. Add the cream mixture to the melted chocolate; stir until smooth, and let cool. Cover and chill 3 hours or until firm.

3. Place the cocoa in a bowl. Shape the chocolate mixture into 1-inch balls (we used a 1-inch icecream scoop); roll in the cocoa. Place the truffle balls on a baking sheet; chill until firm.

4. Place the 12 ounces chocolate in the top of a double boiler over simmering water until a thermometer inserted into the chocolate registers 115°F. Remove the top insert; working quickly, dip the truffles in the melted chocolate, coating completely. Lift out the truffles with a small fork, letting the excess chocolate drip off. Tilt the double boiler insert, if needed, to make dipping and coating easier. Return the top insert to the heat every few minutes to keep the chocolate at 115°F. Transfer the truffles to the parchment paper. Sprinkle the truffles lightly with additional fleur de sel. Let stand until the chocolate coating is set.

SPICED PRALINE DELIGHTS

These are best enjoyed as an after dinner-treat along with a cup of coffee.

MAKES 2 1/2 dozen candies • **HANDS-ON** 18 minutes • **TOTAL** 38 minutes

- 1 cup evaporated milk
- 1 (16-ounce) package light brown sugar
- 1/4 cup butter
- 12 large marshmallows
- 1 teaspoon ground cinnamon
- 1/4 teaspoon ground nutmeg
- 2 cups coarsely chopped toasted pecans

1. Combine the milk and sugar in a 4-quart saucepan; bring to a boil over medium-high heat, stirring constantly. Reduce the heat to medium and cook 7 minutes, stirring constantly, or until a candy thermometer registers 234°F (soft ball stage).

2. Remove from the heat; stir in the butter, marshmallows, cinnamon, and nutmeg until melted. Stir in the pecans. Beat with a wooden spoon 3 to 5 minutes or until the mixture is creamy and begins to thicken. Quickly drop the mixture by rounded tablespoonfuls onto parchment paper-lined baking sheets; cool completely, about 20 minutes.

Dark Chocolate Truffles
with Fleur de Sel

BOURBON BALLS

Put a few of these rich balls into cellophane bags and tie them with red and green ribbon. Place the bags in a large bowl by the front door for guests to grab as they leave.

MAKES 5 dozen • **HANDS-ON** 25 minutes • **TOTAL** 25 minutes

60 vanilla wafers, finely crushed (2 cups)
2 cups chopped toasted walnuts
2 cups powdered sugar
1/4 cup unsweetened cocoa
6 tablespoons bourbon
3 tablespoons light corn syrup
Powdered sugar

Combine the vanilla wafers, walnuts, sugar, and cocoa in a large bowl; mix well. Combine the bourbon and corn syrup; add to the crumb mixture, stirring until well blended. Shape into 1-inch balls; roll in the powdered sugar. Store in an airtight container.

CITRUS BONBONS

The bright flavors of lemon and orange are a perfect compliment to the sugary sweetness of these candies.

MAKES 4 dozen • **HANDS-ON** 20 minutes • **TOTAL** 1 hour, 20 minutes, includes standing

1 (11-ounce) box vanilla wafers, finely crushed (3 cups)
1 cup powdered sugar
1 cup finely chopped toasted pecans
1/4 cup fresh lemon juice
1/4 cup fresh orange juice
1 tablespoon orange zest
1/2 cup granulated sugar

Combine the vanilla wafers, powdered sugar, pecans, lemon juice, orange juice, and orange zest in a large bowl; mix well. Shape into 1-inch balls; roll in the granulated sugar. Place on parchment paper-lined baking sheets, and let stand 1 hour. Store in an airtight container.

COLA CANDY

Pair a few of these candies, wrapped in red and white tissue paper and tied with a green ribbon, with a miniature glass bottle of classic cola for a cute and creative gift.

MAKES 2 dozen • **HANDS-ON** 15 minutes • **TOTAL** 50 minutes

1 (11-ounce) box vanilla wafers, finely crushed (3 cups)
2 cups powdered sugar
1 cup chopped toasted pecans
1/2 cup cola soft drink
2 tablespoons butter, melted

COLA FROSTING
3/4 cup powdered sugar
1/4 cup butter, softened
2 to 3 tablespoons cola soft drink
1/4 teaspoon vanilla extract

1. Prepare the Cola Frosting: Beat the powdered sugar and butter at medium speed with an electric mixer until smooth. Beat in 2 tablespoons of the cola and vanilla until blended, adding an additional 1 tablespoon of the cola if needed to reach the desired consistency.
2. Stir together the vanilla wafers, powdered sugar, pecans, cola soft drink, and melted butter; shape the mixture into 1-inch balls. Cover and chill at least 30 minutes. Dip the balls in the Cola Frosting, and chill until ready to serve.

YULE STREET TRUFFLES

Burning a Yule log during the Christmas season is a tradition that stretches back to the days of the Vikings. In those times, Northern Europeans would cut down trees and burn them in celebration of the Winter Solstice.

MAKES 3 dozen • **HANDS-ON** 15 minutes • **TOTAL** 45 minutes, includes chilling

- 1 cup semisweet chocolate morsels
- 2 tablespoons butter
- 1 tablespoon brandy
- 1⅓ cups almonds, toasted and chopped
- ¼ cup powdered sugar
- ½ cup flaked coconut
- ½ cup whole pitted dates, chopped
- ¼ cup chopped red candied cherries

Microwave the chocolate morsels and butter in a microwave-safe bowl at HIGH 1 to 1½ minutes, stirring every 30 seconds, until melted. Stir in the brandy. Stir in ⅓ cup of the almonds and remaining ingredients. Shape the mixture into ¾-inch balls, and roll in the remaining almonds. Chill 30 minutes or until firm. Store in an airtight container in the refrigerator.

CHOCOLATE-ESPRESSO POUND CAKE TRUFFLES

Rolling each truffle in the Dutch process cocoa twice helps to get a good coating.

MAKES about 3 dozen • **HANDS-ON** 35 minutes • **TOTAL** 2 hours, 50 minutes, includes cooling

MILLION DOLLAR POUND CAKE

- 1 cup butter, softened
- 1½ cups sugar
- 3 large eggs
- 2 cups all-purpose soft-wheat flour
- ½ cup milk
- ½ teaspoon almond extract
- ½ teaspoon vanilla extract

VANILLA BUTTERCREAM FROSTING

- 1 cup butter, softened
- ¼ teaspoon table salt
- 1 (32-ounce) package powdered sugar
- 6 to 7 tablespoons milk
- 1 tablespoon vanilla extract

TRUFFLES

- 1 (4-ounce) semisweet chocolate baking bar
- 3 tablespoons heavy cream
- 1 single-serve packet from a 0.93-ounce package of ready-brew Colombian medium-roast instant coffee (such as Starbucks Via)
- Dutch process cocoa

1. Prepare the Million Dollar Pound Cake: Preheat the oven to 300°F. Beat the butter at medium speed with a heavy-duty electric stand mixer until creamy. Gradually add the sugar, beating 3 to 5 minutes or until light and fluffy. Add the eggs, 1 at a time, beating just until the yellow disappears.

2. Add the flour to the butter mixture alternately with the milk, beginning and ending with the flour. Beat at low speed just until blended after each addition. Stir in the extracts. Pour the batter into a lightly greased and floured 9-inch round cake pan.

3. Bake at 300°F for 50 to 60 minutes or until a wooden pick inserted in the center comes out clean. Cool in the pan on a wire rack 10 minutes. Remove from the pan to the wire rack, and cool completely (about 1 hour).

4. Meanwhile, prepare the Vanilla Buttercream Frosting: Beat the butter and salt at medium speed with an electric mixer 1 to 2 minutes or until creamy; gradually add the powdered sugar alternately with 6 tablespoons of the milk, beating at low speed until blended and smooth after each addition. Stir in the vanilla. If desired, beat in the remaining 1 tablespoon milk, 1 teaspoon at a time, until the frosting reaches the desired consistency.

5. Prepare the Truffles: Crumble half of the Million Dollar Pound Cake into a large bowl. Microwave the baking bar and heavy cream in a medium-size microwave-safe bowl at HIGH 1 to 1½ minutes or until melted and smooth, stirring at 30-second intervals.

6. Stir in the instant coffee. Stir ⅓ cup of the Vanilla Buttercream Frosting and the chocolate mixture into the crumbled cake until the mixture holds its shape. Shape into 1-inch balls. Roll each truffle in the cocoa 2 times.

NOTE: We tested with White Lily all-purpose wheat flour.

Buckeye Balls

BUCKEYE BALLS

Make these balls ahead of time, and whip them out for a last minute dessert or a treat for an unexpected visitor.

MAKES 7 dozen candies • **HANDS-ON** 45 minutes • **TOTAL** 1 hour, 15 minutes, includes chilling

- 1 (16-ounce) jar creamy peanut butter
- 1 cup butter, softened
- 6½ cups powdered sugar
- 1 (12-ounce) package semisweet chocolate chips
- 2 tablespoons shortening

1. Beat the peanut butter and butter at medium speed with an electric mixer until blended. Gradually add the powdered sugar, beating until blended. Shape into 1-inch balls; place on parchment paper-lined baking sheets. Chill 20 minutes or until firm.

2. Microwave the chocolate and shortening in a medium-size microwave-safe bowl at HIGH 1 to 1½ minutes or until melted and smooth, stirring at 30-second intervals. Remove several balls from refrigerator at a time; dip each ball in the chocolate mixture until partially coated, and place on parchment paper-lined baking sheets. Let stand 10 minutes or until set. Store in an airtight container.

KENTUCKY COLONELS

Named for the origin of their bourbon flavor, these boozy sweets are also a fantastic party starter.

MAKES 6 dozen candies • **HANDS-ON** 30 minutes • **TOTAL** 1 hour, 30 minutes, includes chilling

- ½ cup butter, softened
- 6 tablespoons bourbon
- 3 tablespoons sweetened condensed milk
- 7½ cups powdered sugar
- ½ cup finely chopped toasted pecans
- 2 (12-ounce) packages semisweet chocolate morsels
- ¼ cup shortening
- Toasted pecan halves

1. Beat the butter, bourbon, and condensed milk with a heavy-duty stand mixer fitted with a paddle attachment until blended (the mixture may not be smooth). Gradually add the powdered sugar, beating on low speed until blended and smooth. Beat in the chopped pecans. Shape the mixture into 1-inch balls; place on parchment paper-lined baking sheets. Chill 30 minutes or until firm.

2. Microwave the chocolate chips and shortening in a medium-size microwave-safe bowl at HIGH 1½ to 2 minutes or until melted and smooth, stirring at 30-second intervals. Remove several balls from the refrigerator at a time. Using a wooden pick, dip each ball into the chocolate mixture, shaking off the excess. Place on the parchment paper-lined baking sheets. Remove the wooden pick, and gently press a pecan half on each. Chill 30 minutes or until firm. Store in an airtight container in a cool place or in refrigerator.

NOTE: You will need 6 dozen pecan halves for this recipe.

BACON-PEANUT TRUFFLES

Chocolate, peanut butter, bacon—need we say more?

MAKES 2 dozen candies • **HANDS-ON** 30 minutes • **TOTAL** 4 hours, includes chilling

- 3/4 cup honey-roasted peanuts
- 2 tablespoons dark brown sugar
- 1/4 teaspoon table salt
- 8 thick bacon slices, cooked
- 1/3 cup creamy peanut butter
- 6 ounces bittersweet chocolate, chopped

1. Process the first 3 ingredients and 6 of the bacon slices in a food processor 20 to 30 seconds or until finely ground. Stir together the bacon mixture and peanut butter in a small bowl until smooth. Cover and chill 2 hours.

2. Shape rounded teaspoonfuls of the bacon mixture into 3/4-inch balls. Place on a parchment paper-lined baking sheet; chill 1 hour.

3. Chop the remaining 2 bacon slices. Microwave the chocolate in a microwave-safe bowl at HIGH 1 to 1½ minutes or until melted and smooth, stirring at 30-second intervals. Dip the chilled bacon balls into the chocolate. Place on a parchment paper-lined baking sheet. Immediately sprinkle the tops with the bacon. Chill 30 minutes before serving. Store in an airtight container in refrigerator up to 2 weeks.

CHOCOLATE TRUFFLES

These classic treats are deserving of standby status for any party.

MAKES 2 dozen candies • **HANDS-ON** 15 minutes • **TOTAL** 3 hours, 15 minutes, includes chilling

3 ounces unsweetened chocolate baking bar, chopped
1¼ cups powdered sugar
⅓ cup butter, softened
2 tablespoons light corn syrup
½ teaspoon vanilla extract
¾ cup chopped toasted hazelnuts

1. Microwave the chocolate in a microwave-safe bowl at HIGH 1 minute or until melted and smooth, stirring after at 30-second intervals.
2. Beat the powdered sugar and butter at medium speed with an electric mixer until smooth. Beat in the corn syrup and vanilla. Stir in the chocolate. Place plastic wrap on the surface of the mixture; chill 3 hours or until firm.
3. Shape the mixture into 1-inch balls with a small cookie scoop; roll in the hazelnuts. Store in an airtight container in a cool place.

COFFEE BUTTONS

Fill an empty vintage coffee tin with these treats surrounded in crinkle cut paper. Attach a gift card with twine wrapped around the canister, and gift to your coffee-loving friends.

MAKES 2½ dozen candies • **HANDS-ON** 30 minutes • **TOTAL** 1 hour, 30 minutes

2 tablespoons instant coffee granules
½ cup butter, softened
3 cups powdered sugar
2 tablespoons coffee liqueur
Powdered sugar
16 ounces vanilla candy coating, chopped
4 ounces chocolate candy coating, chopped

1. Crush the instant coffee granules with the back of a spoon or with a mortar and pestle to make coffee powder.
2. Beat the butter at medium speed with a mixer until creamy; gradually add 1½ cups of the powdered sugar, beating until smooth. Add the liqueur and coffee powder; beat until blended. Add the remaining 1½ cups powdered sugar, beating at low speed until blended. Shape the mixture into 1-inch balls; roll in the powdered sugar. Place on a parchment paper-lined baking sheet. Flatten to ¼-inch thickness; freeze 30 minutes or until firm.
3. Microwave the vanilla candy coating in a medium-size microwave-safe bowl according to the package directions. Place the coffee rounds on the tines of a fork; dip the rounds in the coating, letting the excess drip off. Return to the baking sheet, and let stand 20 minutes or until set.
4. Place the chocolate coating in a ziplock plastic freezer bag; seal the bag. Submerge in hot water until the chocolate melts. Snip a tiny hole in 1 corner of the bag; drizzle the chocolate over the rounds. Let stand 10 minutes or until set. Store in an airtight container.

CHAI TEA TRUFFLES

This is a must-try for chai lovers.

MAKES 4 dozen candies • **HANDS-ON** 15 minutes • **TOTAL** 2 hours, 35 minutes, includes chilling

- 3/4 cup whipping cream
- 1 1/2 teaspoons ground cardamom
- 1 teaspoon ground ginger
- 2 teaspoons ground cinnamon
- 2 1/4 teaspoons black pepper
- 2 (12-ounce) packages semisweet chocolate chips
- 2/3 cup Dutch-process cocoa
- 1/2 cup powdered sugar
- 1/4 teaspoon kosher salt

1. Bring the cream, 1 teaspoon of the cardamom, ginger, 1/2 teaspoon of the cinnamon, and 1/4 teaspoon of the pepper to a boil; remove from the heat. Add the semisweet chocolate morsels, and stir until melted. Pour into a lightly greased 11- x 7-inch baking dish. Chill 2 hours.
2. Remove from the refrigerator, and let stand at room temperature for 20 minutes. Shape into 1-inch balls (about 2 teaspoons per ball).
3. Whisk together the cocoa, powdered sugar, remaining 2 teaspoons pepper, remaining 1 1/2 teaspoons cinnamon, remaining 1/2 teaspoon cardamom, and salt in a shallow dish, stirring with a whisk. Roll the balls in the cocoa mixture.

ORANGE-PECAN TRUFFLES

A small bag of these truffles makes a perfect stocking stuffer.

MAKES 3 dozen candies • **HANDS-ON** 20 minutes • **TOTAL** 2 hours, 20 minutes, includes chilling

- 8 ounces semisweet chocolate baking bar, chopped
- 1/3 cup butter
- 1 1/4 cups finely chopped toasted pecans
- 1/4 cup orange marmalade
- 2 tablespoons orange liqueur
- 1/2 teaspoon orange zest

1. Microwave the chocolate and butter in a medium-size microwave-safe bowl at HIGH 1 minute or until melted and smooth, stirring at 30-second intervals. Stir in 1/2 cup of the pecans, marmalade, liqueur, and zest. Cover and chill 2 hours or until firm.
2. Use a small scoop to shape the mixture into 3/4-inch balls; roll in the remaining 3/4 cup pecans. Store the candy in airtight containers in a refrigerator up to 3 weeks or freeze up to 12 months. Serve cold.

NOTE: You can substitute 2 tablespoons orange juice for liqueur.

BITTERSWEET TRUFFLES

Sweetened condensed milk gives this truffle a pleasing dense and chewy texture.

MAKES 3 dozen candies • **HANDS-ON** 15 minutes • **TOTAL** 3 hours, 15 minutes, includes chilling

- 1/2 cup butter
- 3/4 cup unsweetened cocoa
- 1 (14-ounce) can sweetened condensed milk
- 1 teaspoon vanilla extract
- Unsweetened cocoa

1. Melt the butter in a heavy 2-quart saucepan over medium; stir in the 3/4 cup cocoa. Gradually add the condensed milk, stirring constantly, until smooth. Cook over medium 3 minutes, stirring constantly, until thickened and smooth. Remove from the heat; stir in the vanilla. Pour the mixture into a lightly greased 8-inch square pan; cover and chill 3 hours or until firm.
2. Use a small scoop to shape the mixture into 1 1/4-inch balls; roll in the additional cocoa. Store in an airtight container in the refrigerator.

RASPBERRY FUDGE TRUFFLES

The double dose of raspberry flavor from the preserves and the liqueur ensures a sweet and slightly tart bite in every ball.

MAKES 6 dozen candies • **HANDS-ON** 40 minutes • **TOTAL** 4 hours, 5 minutes, includes chilling

- 1 (12-ounce) package semisweet chocolate chips
- 2 (8-ounce) packages cream cheese, softened
- 1 cup seedless raspberry preserves
- 2 tablespoons raspberry liqueur
- 45 vanilla wafers, finely crushed (1½ cups)
- 20 ounces chocolate candy coating, chopped
- 3 ounces red candy coating, chopped
- 1 tablespoon shortening

1. Microwave the morsels in a medium-size microwave-safe bowl at HIGH 1 to 1½ minutes or until melted and smooth, stirring at 30-second intervals. Let cool 5 minutes.
2. Beat the cream cheese at medium speed with a mixer until smooth. Add the melted chocolate, preserves, and liqueur, beating until blended. Stir in the vanilla wafer crumbs; cover and chill 2 hours.
3. Shape the mixture into 1-inch balls; cover and freeze 1 hour or until firm.
4. Microwave the chocolate coating in a 4-cup glass measuring cup at MEDIUM 1½ to 2½ minutes or until melted and smooth, stirring at 30-second intervals. Dip the balls in the coating; place on parchment paper-lined baking sheets. Let stand 15 minutes or until set.
5. Place the red candy coating and shortening in a small zip-top plastic freezer bag; seal bag. Submerge in hot water until the chocolate melts; knead until smooth. Snip a tiny hole in 1 corner of bag, and drizzle the mixture over the truffles. Let stand 10 minutes or until set. Store in an airtight container in the refrigerator.

RIPPLE DIVINITY

This treat gets its name from the rippled appearance it takes on when the chocolate chips are folded into the warm sugar and egg white mixture and melt.

MAKES 4 dozen candies • **HANDS-ON** 20 minutes • **TOTAL** 20 minutes

- 3 cups sugar
- ½ cup light corn syrup
- ½ cup water
- 2 large egg whites
- 1 teaspoon vanilla extract
- 1 cup semisweet chocolate chips

1. Combine the sugar, corn syrup, and water in a 2-quart saucepan. Bring to a boil over medium-high; reduce the heat to medium, and cook 3 minutes or until a candy thermometer registers 240°F (soft ball stage).
2. Meanwhile, place the egg whites in the bowl of a heavy-duty stand mixer. Beat on medium-high speed until soft peaks form. Slowly pour one-third of the hot sugar mixture into the egg whites in a thin stream, beating at medium-high speed. Reduce the mixer speed to low.
3. Return the sugar mixture to medium; cook 3 minutes or until a candy thermometer registers 265°F (hard ball stage). Increase the mixer speed to medium-high; slowly pour the remaining sugar mixture into the egg whites in a thin stream. Beat 7 minutes or until the mixture just begins to hold its shape (do not overbeat; the mixture will become more firm as it cools). Beat in the vanilla.
4. Fold in the chocolate chips. Quickly drop by tablespoonfuls onto parchment paper-lined baking sheets.

YEAR-ROUND *Celebrations*

ICONS OF SOUTHERN STYLE

Every great party comes together at an engaging table. From fresh flowers and dinnerware to table linens and more, these inspired settings from some of the South's finest interior designers and style authorities make for party-perfect entertaining. Whether you're planning a cozy autumn dinner, a cottage breakfast, an outdoor Easter lunch, or another special gathering, let the experts here show you the way.

CATHERINE BROWN PATERSON

CATHERINE BROWN PATERSON DESIGN, CHARLESTON, SC

After working in the fashion industry for Ralph Lauren and Hermes of Paris, Inc. and owning a decorative accessory and interiors shop, Catherine Brown Paterson now runs an interior design company to create timeless interiors using texture, color, and pattern.

Continue the celebration of the outdoors post-hunt by dining al fresco. Coral place mats pop off a dark wood table, while sterling silver stirrup cups, themed after Lowcountry game, at each setting summon thoughts of the hunts of lore. Crown the table with an oversized floral arrangement grounded with moss and leaves and highlighted with bright blooms. Finish the look with a few antlers.

① Set up an area where guests can shed unneeded layers. A tall wooden table or a Lowcountry joggling board work best. If guests aren't coming from a hunt, it's still fun to stage clothing to set the mood. Stick to a palette of hunter green, light beige, mud brown, and a touch of "safety" orange. ② Lay woodland patterned china on casual wicker chargers. A monogrammed linen napkin adds a classic touch and elevates the small bundle of pheasant feathers laid neatly on top. ③ A distressed table is the perfect bar for an outdoor affair. An oversized oyster shell makes a chic ice bucket. Heirloom silver and cut-crystal glasses add a sophisticated nod towards old-school tradition, while a tall vase patterned in coastal blues and coral and filled with palm branches lends welcoming, modern flair.

LOWCOUNTRY HUNT LUNCH

This Charleston quail hunt lunch is the definition of high-low style perfection. The more formal notes, such as crystal glasses and antique china and cutlery, are balanced by the natural Lowcountry setting, which keeps the look far from stuffy.

COTTAGE BREAKFAST

Ever a master of seamlessly merging classic elegance with both comforting and modern touches, James Farmer shows how to create a timeless, traditional tablescape that's perfect for special-occasion entertaining or simply for everyday enjoyment.

1

JAMES FARMER

JAMES FARMER DESIGNS,
PERRY, GA

A Jack-of-all-trades including gardening, floral design, cooking, writing, lifestyle consulting, and—not the least of which—interior design, James Farmer is one Southern style icon that every aspiring home decorator should follow.

Skip the tablecloth, opting instead for sophisticated place mats, and let a gorgeous wood surface show, creating a rustic opulence. White roses in simple glass vases keep the look classic and understated.

2

3

1 Small spaces become focal points when filled with artistic touches such as the framed prints of birds here, which brighten an otherwise unnoticed area and subtly up the room's natural vibe. Artfully arranging decor in cabinetry also adds to the ambience. **2** Use your fine china! A formal table can be comfortably enjoyed every day when stately pieces are paired with casual touches. Here, regal china becomes inviting when linen napkins in a casual pattern are nestled into each setting. **3** Instead of the expected vase, use serveware to display blooms. Place a floral frog or floral foam in a serving bowl and spear with flower stems. Tuck moss under the blooms to conceal the stems and steady the arrangement.

DINNER ON THE DOCK

With thoughtfully selected decor and wise style guidance from the experts at J. Banks Design, you can turn a casual seaside supper into a memorable meal displayed with comfort and exotic flair.

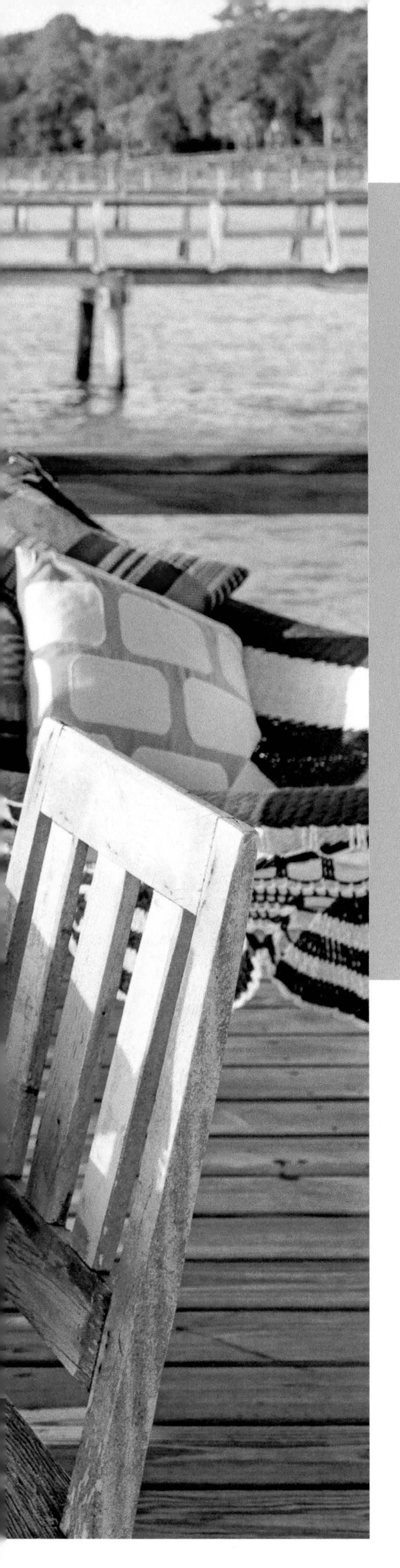

JONI VANDERSLICE

J. BANKS DESIGN,
HILTON HEAD ISLAND, SC

The team at J. Banks Design is enormous, and they have talent and dedication to match. Their talents are wide-ranging as evidenced in resorts, clubs, mountain getaways and coastal cottages. The firm founded by Joni Vanderslice 30 years ago is leading the charge to transform every space into one filled with luxury, inspiration, and a sense of home.

1

2

When eating outdoors, the environment competes for attention as much as the meal does. Bring focus back to your table by incorporating vibrant colors and interesting textures and patterns. To create edgy casualness, layer large cloths in varying colors and patterns and spread them over the table so their corners hang from the table's edges. A wicker holder for cutlery suits the look and makes for easy transporting. Use a large carved-out wooden bowl to display foods in a way that gives a nod to the natural setting.

1 Go the extra step and wrap cutlery in patterned cloth napkins. It's the little details that drive home a well-designed look. When the sun goes down, your outdoor space might need additional lighting. Pillar candles in large nautical-style lanterns are never more apropos. Bright plates with ruffled edges further layer interesting detail as do nontraditional bowls in assorted vibrant colors such as these small strainers that are perfect for this Lowcountry fare. Patterned decorative throw pillows add a special touch to any additional furniture such as a rocker or hammock your outdoor space might afford. 2 For an alternative look: Use ornate bohemian fabrics to cover the table. Their similar color palette—blues and white—keep the look cohesive instead of chaotic. Vibrant chargers with a hand-woven, tribal quality reinforce the foreign feel, while monogrammed seersucker napkins with color-palette tie-ins keep the look polished and upscale.

JULIA REED

NEW ORLEANS, LA

Julia Reed is a Southern author of six books and a contributing editor at Elle Decor *and* Garden & Gun *magazines. She also contributes to* The Wall Street Journal *magazine and shares her entertaining secrets with aspiring hosts through her entertaining column, "Entertaining With Julia," for* Southern Living *magazine.*

1

2

3

4

A screened porch with a ceiling fan makes a comfortable outdoor setting and establishes the tone for this low-key event that celebrates the outdoors in a smart and collected way. The Argus table linen in muted blue and sable adds a soft palette that contrasts against the wood walls and ceiling and bricked floor.

❶ An antique wooden sideboard or chest makes the perfect rustic porch bar and instantly elevates the space beyond patio furniture-appearance. ❷ For this occasion, fresh-cut wildflowers are best. Look for gerbera daisies, lantana, evening primrose, and dusty miller leaves, and gather them into pottery vases of varying sizes. You can also use blue-tinted Mason jars as vases to echo the teal drinking glasses. Tuck in sprigs of rosemary and parsley into each bouquet to complete the look. ❸ There is no better-suited tableware for this occasion than handmade pottery. Stick to two tones of pottery—here, mud brown and green-blue—to keep the look from becoming busy. ❹ No place mats or chargers are needed for this unfussy look. Place earthenware dinner plates directly on the tablecloth. Antique copper or gold cutlery stay true to the elemental tone of the evening. Provide guests with folded linen napkins and drinking glasses in deep teal.

LAKE HOUSE SUPPER

Julia Reed knows how to throw a chic dinner party with easy elegance and simple charm. Here, her casual lake house gathering shows how properly pared down decorating can make the biggest impact.

PORCH PARTY

What could be a better setting for a lively summer bash than a beautiful and comfortable front porch? Take Tara's tips for creating an outdoor space that has all the comforts of an indoor environment plus the energy and refreshment of the outdoors.

1

TARA GUÉRARD

TARA GUÉRARD SOIRÉE, CHARLESTON, SC

Tara Guérard is a long-standing expert in the party design and event planning businesses. Her original focus on styling weddings led her to author two acclaimed books on wedding design. Now, her work also includes customized interior design.

Transform a humble porch into a top entertaining space with functional and inviting furniture. Pad swings and loveseats with thick cushions and throw pillows. A rattan coffee table provides a stylish rest for guests' plates and drinks as do side tables. Bring out a weather-resistant jute rug to create an outdoor lounge.

1 Rather than using plastic, mix and match inexpensive glassware and set them on trays with bottles. Serve large batches of drinks from pretty pitchers, carafes, or dispensers. A large potted hydrangea adds a cozy touch while connecting living spaces with surrounding gardens. 2 Tie appetizer forks to cloth napkins with twine for a pretty presentation that's also easy to pick up. 3 Finger foods can get messy. Soak hand towels in lemon juice and water. Roll and insert them into cored lemons, and chill.

2

3

KIMBERLY SCHLEGEL WHITMAN

DALLAS, TEXAS

As an editor-at-large of Southern Living, a television and radio personality, a book author, and a style entrepreneur, Kimberly Schlegel Whitman has firmly made her mark in the home-entertaining and design world. Over the next several pages, Kimberly shares her tips for creating the perfect look for a cozy fall gathering, Mardi Gras feast, a celebratory dinner, and more.

If you have a gorgeous wooden table, this is the moment to let it shine, allowing its rustic quality to set the foundation for the scene. Use beige linen place mats to complement the table's natural look. Ornate patterned china boasting of autumnal color—purple, gold, and cranberry—stands out against the subtle tones beneath and elevates the look beyond agrarian. A crisp white linen napkin monogrammed in cheerful cranberry makes a chic topper.

1 Take the time to construct (or order) an elaborate floral centerpiece—or a few smaller ones—to properly salute fall's bountiful blooms. This bouquet includes leaves burnished in fall colors, magnolia leaves, purple hydrangea, thistles, cattails, mums, and more. 2 Drape a purple plaid wool cloth across the table to up the cozy vibe. Similarly, small votive candles in warm colors add to the natural ambience. If you'd like, incorporate decorative antlers into the decor to further transport dinner guests to a woodland habitat. A final detail at each place setting makes the meal even more enchanting: Wedge place cards with names inscribed in gold into mini wood rounds cut from tree branches, and nestle it all on top of a bit of decorative moss.

AUTUMN DINNER PARTY

Celebrate the arrival of fall by hosting an intimate dinner for family or friends. This table's look is all about lauding the rich colors and textures of the season.

WORK YOUR SURROUNDINGS

No home is the same. It's important to know how to use your environment effectively when throwing a party. Kimberly Schlegel Whitman shows four ways to work with what you have.

1

2

1 Whether you live at the beach or simply are vacationing there, the sea offers natural decor that can easily be used to create a unique look. Start by gathering found objects from the shore such as seashells, driftwood, and beach grass, and stage it on the table. The key to creating a polished look is to incorporate formal pieces with the earthborn findings. China patterned in a nautical theme, like the coral design shown here, is the perfect blend of stylish and earthy. Not a beachgoer? This concept of harvesting decor from nature can be applied no matter where you reside. 2 Small spaces can make lovely, albeit unexpected, dinner locales when arranged with care. If you have an elegant winding staircase, a showstopping floor, a magnificent piece of artwork or furniture that guests always gravitate toward, why not make it the landscape for your get-together? Be sure to adorn your table with engaging fabrics, shapes, and objects so that the scene looks planned and suits the space. Here, a tablecloth in a large graphic pattern ties in with the flooring, and a mini palm tree shoots up to help fill empty space between the stairs and the table. 3 Any backyard—but particularly a large one—is a space you should utilize for entertaining. If you have significant tree coverage that offers ample shade, you can comfortably use your yard even in the middle of the day. Moreover, take advantage of any beautiful flowerbeds or landscaping to provide an effortless and natural backdrop to your table. Here, a cocktail bar is outlined by a tree and vibrant green bushes, and the tablecloth selected exudes the same garden appeal. 4 A patio or garden is an obvious choice for where to host. Go the extra mile and build a trellis to cover the main entertaining area. You'll be glad you did as planted vines and flowers grow to umbrella the space. You can also hang from it string lights, chandeliers, and other lighting fixtures. Further frame the space with large planters filled with trees or expansive plants.

3

4

MARDI GRAS IN THE GARDEN

Kimberly Schlegel Whitman's open-air dinner bursting with color is a befitting way to celebrate an affair as boisterous as Mardi Gras. One secret to this look: Let the runner of flowers and candles take the spotlight and keep the look otherwise understated.

The more the merrier at this dinner. Invite plenty of guests, and don't skimp on the decor. A white table surface makes this look work, as it provides the needed visual rest for the colors of the candles, flowers, and plates to pop. Under a gorgeous trellis is, of course, a perfect spot to place the table; however, if you don't have one, hang string lights from trees or poles for a similarly magical canopy that will mimick the candles at night.

1 For the flowers, pick the brightest yellow, red, and purple blooms you can find, peppering in white florals. Small, clear glass vases are best as they will let the blooms take centerstage. 2 Place slender carnival-colored taper candles in an assortment of brass candlesticks, and line them down the table's center for a breathtaking centerpiece. This is a perfect example of how small pieces, when styled together, can achieve a stunning unified effect. 3 White place mats and napkins bordered in blue or purple fringe keep the feel festive without dizzying the look, and they will allow more ornately designed plates to shine. With the same logic, using clear drinking glasses won't clutter the table with additional color; however, thin slices of lemon and lime in the glasses will add the right touch of flair.

Move your meal to the most formal eating area of your home. This basic step sets a special tone from the start; however, don't equate a celebratory look with a baroque and stuffy one. A few cheerful and streamlined pieces are all you need to make a jubilant statement. Balance the formality of the dining room and keep the mood friendly by skipping the formal tablecloth.

1 A simple, thin white place mat almost goes unnoticed yet serves the important function of framing the place setting. Layer on a dark-colored charger to match—if possible—the deepest shade found in your table bouquets. 2 Candlesticks fitted with taper candles and placed on both ends of the table balance the look and offer height. Polished pewter or silver vessels are perfect for the occasion. For this polo party, a large centerpiece embellished with a stag's head is a delightful detail. Fill it with tightly packed white, yellow, and deep maroon flowers such as ranunculus, billy balls, and lilies. 3 For a special touch, have a silver victory cup (or a serving bowl or platter for a nonsports celebration) engraved for the man or woman of the hour. It can double as a floral display and be a surprise gift for the victor.

VICTORY BANQUET

Celebrate life's achievements in style, even if the triumph is the simple polo tournament win honored here! Kimberly Schlegel Whitman's classic, polished table will work for other triumphs too, like a new job or marriage proposal.

TEA PARTY

Unexpected details seamlessly combine to create this whimsical tea party look, which is perfect for an all-girls rendezvous or a child's birthday party. It takes a pro to navigate pairing eclectic objects to achieve a unified effect, and Gretchen Black is just the one to show the way.

GRETCHEN BLACK

GREYHOUSE DESIGN, LOUISVILLE, KY

With over 10 years of design experience including designing six of her own homes, Gretchen Black has the know-how and transforming touch to bring her fresh style marked by soft color palettes with pops of color, comfort, and unique finishes to any home.

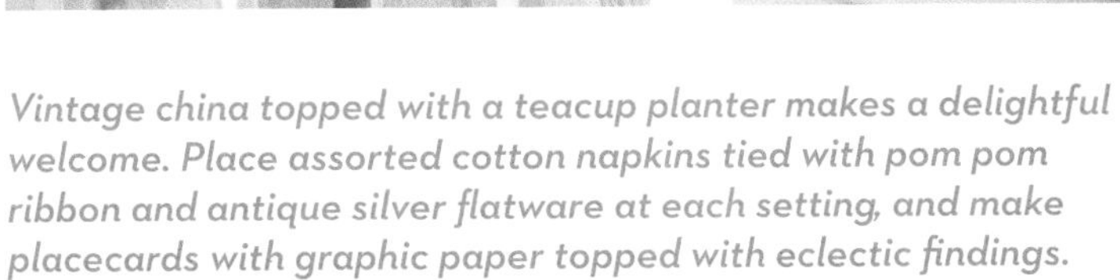

Vintage china topped with a teacup planter makes a delightful welcome. Place assorted cotton napkins tied with pom pom ribbon and antique silver flatware at each setting, and make placecards with graphic paper topped with eclectic findings.

❶ Stacked vintage books give the table interest and playful Alice-in-Wonderland flair. ❷ Get guests in the party mood with fabric flower hair accessories that also make great take-home gifts. ❸ A mobile made with polyester flowers, ribbons, and sewing hoops is a romantic look anyone can achieve. ❹ Arranged creamy pink polyester blooms in a milk glass vase look lifelike, while a decorative birdcage and bright cotton birds make a whimsy statement. When using many decorating elements, containing them is key to a well-planned look. Here, a vintage platter is used to neatly corral diverse decor. ❺ Flea-market finds like a retro typewriter and milk glass pieces provide vintage charm, while a mounted and framed rabbit bust accented with gold antlers creates an interesting and mod focal point.

HEATHER CHADDUCK HILLEGAS

HEATHER CHADDUCK INTERIORS & TEXTILES, BIRMINGHAM, AL

For over 15 years, Heather Chadduck Hillegas has pioneered new frontiers in both casual-chic and Southern styles, holding leading style roles at Coastal Living, Cottage Living, *and* Southern Living *magazines. Not only does Heather decorate and style interiors, she also designs her own artisan textile line.*

1

2

SPRING DINNER PARTY

Heather Chadduck Hillegas shows the right way to kick casual outdoor dining up a notch with her vibrant spring table. This al fresco spread hits notes of both relaxed warmth and festive ceremony, making this fête fit for a fine-weather feast.

3

A long table (or multiple tables pushed together) lined with identically arranged place settings creates dramatic repetition. If you don't have an extra-long tablecloth, layer multiple cloths to cover the full length. Choose antique linens in the same color family—here, Heather uses blues varying from indigo to sky color—yet in various complementary patterns and textiles to create the table's rich, textured look. Furthermore, bamboo chairs are the perfect seating choice as they are chic, outdoor-appropriate, and compact, allowing guests to sit comfortably in close quarters.

❶ Earth-born objects like smooth river rocks placed around pillar candles inside cylinder hurricanes further solidify the natural vibe and tie in with the verdant spring setting. ❷ A collection of Chinese export pottery in blue and white perfectly contain large hydrangeas, roses, and greenery and are, in themselves, a statement piece. ❸ This place setting riffs on the colors of the urns and table linens. The patterned plates contrast pleasingly with the bold striped and solid woven table coverings, while simply textured white plates act as a subtle pause between the patterns. A sterling silver goblet at each setting exudes an opulent tone and is balanced by the vintage bamboo flatware.

OUTDOOR EASTER LUNCH

This dreamy look brought to you by Bear-Hill Interiors will be the rave at your next Easter gathering! The key to this look is to stick to a strict palette of pastel colors.

1

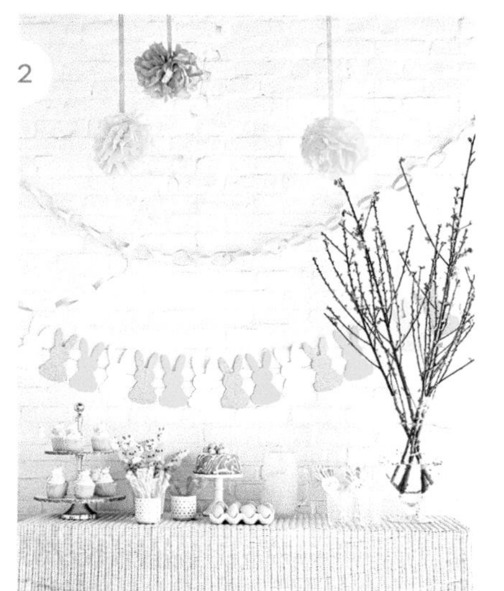

2

3

KEVIN WALSH

BEAR-HILL INTERIORS, LITTLE ROCK, AR

Since its beginning in 2000, Bear-Hill Interiors, founded by designer Kevin Walsh, has been committed to creating spaces marked by classic elegance and the perfect blend of sophistication and comfort. In this party and the next, Kevin gives advice for creating fresh looks for beautiful Easter and Mother's Day celebrations.

4

Set a playful mood this Easter by moving the meal outdoors. A white floor-length tablecloth keeps the look from departing too far from tradition. String paper chains in the palest pink, yellow, green, and purple from the table and any heights your environment offers.

1 This place setting is all about layering to create a nest-like effect. A woven straw charger establishes a natural base for overlaying concentric circles in muted colors. Top the setting with a nest of grass-green straw and pastel-dyed eggs. **2** The neutral-colored tablecloth and wall framing this dessert table allow the understated colors of the decor to dominate. Oversized cherry tree branches in a glass punch bowl further proclaim this ode to spring. **3** A few simple arrangements of soft, fresh blooms in clear vases spaced evenly along the table are the only flowers this spread needs. **4** A reimagined Easter look calls for a nontraditional table runner. Instead of cloth, a swath of mini chocolate eggs and larger dyed eggs will delight guests and offer them a sweet snack. Classic gingham napkins in soft violet add contrast to the circular shapes that dominate this setting. Milk-white goblets accented with colors from the palette complete the look.

The clean, airy look of this room acts as a canvas upon which details like color and texture stand out. Clear your dining room of excess decor and even wall art and furniture, if possible, to achieve the same effect. A glass-shelved bar cart adds the right touch of modernity to this scene. Instead of using it simply for drinks, make it a dessert bar as well. Add flowers, vases, and even desserts in the same palette of varying shades of purple.

❶ A neutral foundational palette for your table spread with strategic pops of color keeps a formal table from looking cluttered and antiquated. For this look, complementary shades of purple—an orchid-purple linen napkin here, a red-purple wine goblet there—pepper the table and create a cohesive scene. ❷ This exquisite bouquet is the focal point of the table. Gather an assortment of blooms—white- and wine-colored chrysanthemums, cream anemones, pink roses, and amethyst hydrangeas to name a few—in a low glass vase so that the flowers fan outwards as much as upwards, creating a bountiful look. ❸ Mix old and new styles—Mom's cherished china with a sleek gold charger and depression glass-like bread plates with evergreen wine glasses. Even embroidery-styled place mats look chic in all-cream coloring. Finally, personalize each setting with a calligraphied place card.

MOTHER'S DAY LUNCH

Let the experts at Bear-Hill Interiors guide you to creating Mother's Day magic with all the traditional touches Mom loves plus plenty of fresh appeal.

VALENTINE'S DAY BREAKFAST

Drawing upon farmhouse inspiration rather than the overdone pink and red decor, Amanda Crowner and Lindsey Foundos, the stylists at Kristin Peake Interiors, show how warm details and charming touches combine to create a fresh look.

KRISTIN PEAKE

KRISTIN PEAKE INTERIORS, ROCKVILLE, MD

Kristin brings almost 20 years of interior design experience, a keen sense of style, and loads of passion to her projects. She and her team of talented designers specialize in decorating high-end homes and in making spaces calm, collected, and comfortably livable.

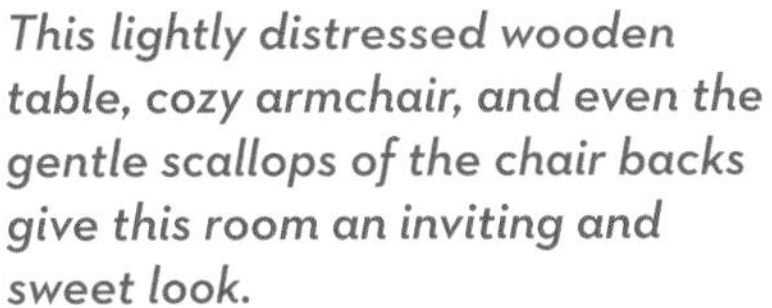

This lightly distressed wooden table, cozy armchair, and even the gentle scallops of the chair backs give this room an inviting and sweet look.

❶ When contained in a singular space, individual objects can make a cohesive statement. Here, an oversized tray confines and highlights plants in varying heights and decorative fruits. ❷ Mix patterns in your place setting—bold stripes, scallops, lace, etc. Top it all with a decorative object like a mini bucket filled with berries. A decorative mailbox makes a fun place for guests to leave notes of appreciation for one another. ❸ A sideboard is a fitting display for food and also brightens a small space, while a tiered stand artfully arranged with apples, donuts, and florals makes a poised and pastoral focal point as well as a functional serving piece.

1

2

3

CELEBRATE YOUR FAVORITE YEAR-ROUND HOLIDAYS

The party doesn't have to end just because the holidays are over. On the following pages, you'll find menus that take the guesswork out of hosting and ensure a showstopping gathering from start to finish.

NEW YEAR'S EVE DINNER

Welcome January with bubbly beverages, a noodle bowl containing black-eyed peas, a fresh salad, comforting sides, and a decadent dessert.

Menu

Sparkling Pear-Brandy Cider
Pomegranate Champagne Cocktail
Asian Pear and Hazelnut Salad
Hoppin' John Noodle Bowls
Lamb Meatballs
Crispy Potato Chips
Banana Brownie Sticky Toffee Puddings

SPARKLING PEAR-BRANDY CIDER

This big-batch beverage is perfect for large gatherings like a New Year's Eve party as you can make the cider before guests arrive and not worry about making individual drinks for guests.

MAKES **14 cups** • HANDS-ON **5 minutes** • TOTAL **5 minutes**

2 cups pear nectar, chilled
¼ cup honey
1 cup brandy (optional)
2 (750-milliliter) bottles sparkling apple cider, chilled
1 (1-liter) bottle club soda, chilled

Stir together the chilled pear nectar, honey, and, if desired, the brandy. Stir in the chilled sparkling apple cider and chilled club soda.

POMEGRANATE CHAMPAGNE COCKTAIL

It's uncouth to have a New Year's Eve celebration without Champagne! Offer guests a flute of this simple, sweet concoction the moment they walk through the door.

SERVES **1** • HANDS-ON **5 minutes** • TOTAL **5 minutes**

1 turbinado sugar cube
2 tablespoons pomegranate juice
½ cup Champagne or sparkling wine, chilled

Place the sugar cube in a Champagne flute; add the pomegranate juice and Champagne. Serve immediately.

NOTE: 1 rock candy stirrer or granulated sugar cube may be substituted for the sugar cube.

ASIAN PEAR AND HAZELNUT SALAD

Winter fruits like Asian pear and pomegranate and rich, fragrant hazelnuts are tossed together with baby greens and a slightly sweet, nutty vinaigrette in this satisfying salad.

SERVES 8 to 10 • **HANDS-ON** 10 minutes • **TOTAL** 10 minutes

3 tablespoons rice vinegar
2 tablespoons fresh orange juice
1 tablespoon honey
½ teaspoon kosher salt
⅛ teaspoon freshly ground black pepper
⅓ cup hazelnut oil
2 (5-ounce) packages spring greens mix
½ cup coarsely chopped hazelnuts, toasted
⅓ cup fresh pomegranate seeds
¼ cup (1-inch) pieces fresh chives
2 Asian pears, cored and sliced

1. Whisk together the rice vinegar, orange juice, honey, salt, and pepper. Slowly whisk in the oil.
2. Place the greens in a large bowl. Add the hazelnuts, pomegranate seeds, chives, and pears. Drizzle with the vinaigrette, and toss gently.

NOTE: Look for pears that are firm to the touch. If you are unable to find Asian pears, Bosc or Bartlett pears make a nice substitute.

HOPPIN' JOHN NOODLE BOWLS

To simplify prep, serve the hot soup straight from the stove, and let guests garnish their own bowls with whatever toppings they desire.

SERVES 12 • **HANDS-ON** 30 minutes • **TOTAL** 45 minutes

1 (16-ounce) package dried black-eyed peas
3 quarts reduced-sodium chicken broth
¼ cup minced fresh ginger
5 teaspoons soy sauce
3 teaspoons fish sauce
Toppings: cooked rice noodles, chopped raw collard greens, sliced scallions, shredded cooked chicken, cilantro leaves, pickled okra, Sriracha chili sauce

SOFT-COOKED EGGS
6 large eggs

SAMBAL PICKLES
1 cup chopped bread-and-butter pickles
2 tablespoons sambal oelek (chile paste)

1. Rinse and sort the peas. Boil the peas in water to cover in a saucepan over high 3 minutes; drain.
2. Bring the broth and ginger to a boil in a large saucepan over high. Add the peas. Reduce the heat to medium, and simmer 10 minutes or until the peas are tender. Reduce the heat to low, and stir in the soy sauce and fish sauce.
3. Make the Soft-Cooked Eggs: Bring the eggs and water to cover to a boil in a saucepan over high; boil 1 minute. Remove from the heat. Cover and let stand 1 minute. Drain; rinse the eggs with cold water until cool. Peel; slice in half.
4. Meanwhile, make the Sambal Pickles: Stir together the bread-and-butter pickles and sambal oelek (chile paste) in a small bowl.
5. Place the Soft-Cooked Eggs, Sambal Pickles, and desired toppings evenly in 12 bowls, and ladle the hot soup over the toppings.

NOTE: Cook the rice noodles according to the package directions, or sub angel hair pasta.

Hoppin' John
Noodle Bowls

LAMB MEATBALLS

This side dish is made in the slow cooker for supereasy prep. Lemon zest adds a nice bright lift to the spicy sauce and complements the Greek-inspired flavors of these meatballs.

SERVES **14** • HANDS-ON **30 minutes** • TOTAL **2 hours, 30 minutes**

1/4 cup grated onion, drained
1/4 cup dried currants
1/2 teaspoon ground cumin
1/4 teaspoon ground allspice
1/4 teaspoon ground cinnamon
1/4 teaspoon crushed red pepper
2 garlic cloves, minced
1 large egg
2 tablespoons chopped fresh mint
1/2 pound ground lamb
1/2 pound ground turkey
3/4 cup fresh breadcrumbs
1 tablespoon olive oil
1 (24-ounce) jar spicy red pepper pasta sauce
1 teaspoon lemon zest

1. Combine the onion, currants, cumin, allspice, cinnamon, red pepper, garlic, egg, and mint in a large bowl. Add the lamb, turkey, and breadcrumbs; stir well. Shape into 28 (1-inch) meatballs.
2. Heat a large skillet over medium-high. Add the oil to pan; swirl to coat. Add the meatballs to the pan. Cook until browned, about 2 minutes on each side. Transfer the meatballs to a 4-quart electric slow cooker coated with cooking spray.
3. While the meatballs cook, combine the pasta sauce and lemon zest in a medium bowl. Pour the sauce over the meatballs. Cover and cook on HIGH until meatballs are done, about 2 hours.

CRISPY POTATO CHIPS

Slice the potatoes as thinly as possible, and choose whatever caviar you desire. Our recommendations are American Bowfin and American Hackleback, both from Caviar Star, Smoked Rainbow Trout from Sunburst Trout, and Paddlefish from Kelley's Katch.

SERVES **12** • HANDS-ON **35 minutes** • TOTAL **1 hour**

4 large russet potatoes (about 4 1/2 pounds)
4 tablespoons white vinegar
12 cups water
Peanut oil
4 tablespoons finely chopped fresh chives
Kosher salt
Toppings: sour cream, caviar (optional)

1. Cut the potatoes into thin slices, using a mandoline or sharp knife; rinse with cold water.
2. Bring the vinegar and water to a boil in a large saucepan over high. Add the sliced potatoes, and cook 3 minutes. Drain the potatoes, and spread on a paper towel-lined baking sheet. Pat dry with the paper towels, and chill 15 minutes.
3. Meanwhile, pour the oil to a depth of 3 inches into a large Dutch oven, and heat to 340°F. Fry the potatoes, in batches, stirring occasionally, 3 to 4 minutes or until golden brown. Drain on paper towels, and immediately sprinkle with the chives and desired amount of kosher salt.
4. Top with sour cream and caviar, if desired.

BANANA BROWNIE STICKY TOFFEE PUDDINGS

If you're lucky enough to have any remaining sauce, use it as a superb topping for ice cream.

SERVES 12 • HANDS-ON 1 hour, 10 minutes • TOTAL 1 hour, 15 minutes

- 1 (18.4-ounce) package fudge brownie mix
- 3 ripe bananas, mashed (about 1¾ cups)
- 1 cup sugar
- ½ cup light corn syrup
- ½ cup butter
- ¼ teaspoon table salt
- 3½ cups heavy cream
- Garnish: chopped chocolate-covered toffee candy bars

1. Make the brownie mix according to the package directions, stirring in the mashed bananas just before transferring the mixture to a 9-inch square pan. Bake according to the package directions.
2. Meanwhile, stir together the sugar, corn syrup, butter, salt, and 1¼ cups of the heavy cream in a medium saucepan. Cook over low, stirring often, 35 to 45 minutes or until dark amber. Stir in 1 cup of the heavy cream, and increase the heat to medium. Cook, stirring constantly, about 5 minutes or until slightly thickened. Remove from the heat, and cool 5 minutes.
3. Cut the cooled banana brownies into ¾-inch cubes. Layer the brownie cubes and the desired amount of the sticky toffee sauce in each of 12 small jars or bowls. Beat the remaining 1¼ cups heavy cream at high speed with a mixer until soft peaks form; spoon the whipped cream over the puddings. Drizzle with more sauce, if desired. Garnish, if desired.

NOTE: Refrigerate the cooled sauce in an airtight container up to 3 days. To soften, microwave at 30 second intervals, stirring until soft.

ASSEMBLE A CHEESE BOARD

A selection of cheeses paired with sweet and salty accompaniments is a satisfying treat at any gathering. Here are simple tips to help you build your own party-worthy display.

THE STAR: Choose the right cheese. The trick to an amazing cheese board is to have a variety of cheeses but not so many that they compete for attention and overwhelm the palate. Choose 3 to 5 cheeses, each distinct in flavor and texture. Here are basic suggestions to point you in the right direction:

AGED	BLUE	FIRM	SOFT
Aged Cheddar, Aged Gouda, Swiss	Danish Blue, Gorgonzola, Roquefort, Stilton	Clothbound Cheddar, Gruyère, Jarlsberg, Monterey Jack, Parmigiana-Reggiano, Provolone, Romano	Brie, Camembert, Chèvre, Humbolt Fog, Muenster

THE SUPPORTS: Like the cheese itself, its accompaniments should boast a variety of flavors and textures. Select grapes still attached to the vine and in different colors as well as figs and small apples, both in sliced and whole forms, for sweetness and pretty presentation. Dried fruits such as apricots or raisins are perfect for munching on as well. Moreover, honey makes an excellent garnish for cheeses, especially strongly flavored ones such as blue cheese, and chocolate also has the same flavor-balancing effect. Toasted baguette slices or crackers ranging from simple to seed-studded wafers make ideal items to be topped with cheese. Incorporate salted peanuts, Marcona almonds, pistachios, and other nuts for crunchiness. Charcuterie, a selection of prepared meats, is also a fantastic pairing for cheese and will make selection heartier and more filling. Finally, a small bowl of olives or cornichon pickles gives the array pleasing acidity.

THE EXTRAS: Don't forget the accesories. Pick a traditional platter, chic serving tray, or rustic cutting board—whatever suits the mood—that's large enough to contain all the foods so that they touch but aren't crushed. Be sure to provide cheese knives and serving tools like wooden picks, tongs, or small spoons and forks. And labels for cheeses are always a good idea. Additionally, place a few small herb sprigs such as rosemary and thyme between foods or along the tray's border for an organic and elegant look. Small fig leaves make helpful and smart linings for cheeses.

THE ARRANGEMENT: When assembling your array of foods, order is important. Start by placing your cheeses in separate areas of the board, placing leaves underneath, if desired. Next, arrange any vessels such as small bowls of nuts or olives. Then, place big pieces of fruit such as grape strands or whole apples, and fill in with smaller pieces and individual items such as figs or crackers. Finally, add the serving utensils, and your gorgeous spread of delicious small bites is complete.

EASTER SUPPER

Gather friends and family around your table, and celebrate the holiday with these dishes that are as beautiful as they are flavorful.

Menu

Herb-Roasted Boneless Leg of Lamb
Roasted Asparagus with Shaved Parmesan
Classic Deviled Eggs
Butter-Dipped Radishes
Green Tea-Honeysuckle Cake

HERB-ROASTED BONELESS LEG OF LAMB

Look for a roughly 5-pound boneless leg of lamb rolled in netting; no need to unroll and retie. Roast in the netting, and then remove it with kitchen shears.

SERVES 6 to 8 · **HANDS-ON** 20 minutes · **TOTAL** 3 hours

- **1 (5-pound) boneless leg of lamb, rolled and tied**
- **3½ teaspoons kosher salt**
- **2 teaspoons freshly ground black pepper**
- **¼ cup loosely packed fresh rosemary leaves**
- **⅔ cup loosely packed fresh flat-leaf parsley leaves**
- **¼ cup loosely packed fresh thyme leaves**
- **2 shallots, coarsely chopped**
- **6 garlic cloves**
- **1 tablespoon fresh lemon juice**
- **10 tablespoons olive oil**
- **2 pounds small new potatoes**

1. Rub the lamb with 2 teaspoons of the salt and 1 teaspoon of the pepper; let stand 1 hour.
2. Pulse the rosemary in a food processor 4 or 5 times or until finely chopped. Add the parsley and next 4 ingredients, and pulse 4 or 5 times or until finely chopped. Add 6 tablespoons of the olive oil, and pulse 7 or 8 times or until smooth, scraping down the sides as needed. Rub the mixture over the lamb; place in a large roasting pan. Let stand 30 minutes.
3. Preheat the oven to 450°F. Toss together the potatoes and the remaining 1½ teaspoons salt, 1 teaspoon pepper, and 4 tablespoons oil; place the potatoes around the lamb in the roasting pan.
4. Bake at 450°F for 50 minutes to 1 hour or until a meat thermometer inserted into thickest portion registers 125°F (rare). Remove the lamb from the pan; cover loosely with the aluminum foil, and let stand 15 minutes before slicing.
5. Serve the lamb with the potatoes and pan juices.

NOTE: Peel the centers of the potatoes for a pretty presentation, if desired.

ROASTED ASPARAGUS WITH SHAVED PARMESAN

With this recipe and a few simple ingredients, delicious asparagus is at your fingertips. (Pictured on page 230)

SERVES 4 • **HANDS-ON** 3 minutes • **TOTAL** 8 minutes

- 1 pound asparagus spears
- 1/2 teaspoon olive oil
- 1 teaspoon lemon juice
- 1/4 teaspoon table salt
- 1/4 teaspoon freshly ground black pepper
- 2 tablespoons shaved fresh Parmesan cheese

1. Preheat the oven to 425°F.
2. Snap off the tough ends of the asparagus. Toss the asparagus with the olive oil, lemon juice, salt, and pepper. Place in a single layer on a nonstick baking sheet.
3. Bake at 425°F for 5 to 7 minutes or until the asparagus is crisp-tender and lightly browned.
4. Place the asparagus on a serving platter; sprinkle evenly with the Parmesan.

CLASSIC DEVILED EGGS

A staple of the Easter table, these deviled eggs are a standby recipe that every Southerner should master.

MAKES 2 dozen • **HANDS-ON** 20 minutes • **TOTAL** 20 minutes

- 12 hard-cooked eggs, peeled
- 1/2 cup mayonnaise
- 1 1/2 teaspoons white wine vinegar
- 1 1/2 teaspoons Dijon mustard
- 1/8 teaspoon kosher salt
- Dash of hot sauce (optional)

1. Slice the eggs in half lengthwise, and carefully remove the yolks, keeping the egg whites intact.
2. Grate the egg yolks using the small holes of a box grater. Mash together the yolks, mayonnaise, and next 3 ingredients. Add more salt or hot sauce, if desired.
3. Spoon or pipe the yolk mixture into the egg whites.

BUTTER-DIPPED RADISHES

The fresh, earthy taste of radishes shines bright when paired with simple butter and salt.

SERVES 10 • **HANDS-ON** 15 minutes • **TOTAL** 40 minutes

- 1 cup salted butter
- 30 radishes, washed and trimmed
- Garnish: sea salt

Melt the butter in a double-boiler over low until thick and creamy. Dip the radishes into the melted butter to coat, and transfer to a parchment paper-lined sheet pan. Chill until the butter sets, about 25 minutes. Garnish, if desired.

Butter-Dipped
Radishes

GREEN TEA-HONEYSUCKLE CAKE

This gorgeous and refreshing cake subtly flavored with matcha and honeysuckle is the perfect showstopping finale to a delightful Easter meal.

SERVES 12 • **HANDS-ON** 30 minutes • **TOTAL** 3 hours, 5 minutes

1 cup butter, softened
1/2 cup shortening
2 1/2 cups sugar
1/4 cup honey
6 large eggs
3 cups all-purpose flour
1 teaspoon baking powder
1/2 teaspoon table salt
3/4 cup milk
2 teaspoons matcha (green tea powder)

HONEYSUCKLE GLAZE
3/4 cup sugar
1/2 cup butter
1/3 cup honey
1/3 cup orange liqueur
3 tablespoons water

1. Preheat the oven to 325°F. Beat the 1 cup butter and shortening with a heavy-duty stand mixer on medium speed until creamy. Gradually add the sugar, beating until light and fluffy. Add the honey, beating until blended. Add the eggs, 1 at a time, beating just until blended after each addition.
2. Stir together the flour, baking powder, and salt. Add to the butter mixture alternately with the milk, beginning and ending with the flour mixture. Beat at low speed just until blended after each addition. Transfer 2 1/2 cups of the batter to a 2-quart bowl, and stir in the matcha until blended.
3. Drop 2 scoops of the plain batter into a greased and floured 10-inch (16-cup) Bundt pan, using a small cookie scoop (about 1 1/2 inches); top with 1 scoop of the matcha batter. Repeat the procedure around the entire pan, covering the bottom completely. Continue layering the batters in the pan as directed until all the batter is used.
4. Bake at 325°F for 1 hour and 5 minutes to 1 hour and 15 minutes or until a long wooden pick inserted in the center comes out clean.
5. During the last 10 minutes of baking, make the Honeysuckle Glaze: Bring the sugar, 1/2 cup butter, honey, liqueur, and water to a boil in a 1-quart saucepan over medium, stirring often; reduce the heat to medium-low, and boil, stirring constantly, 3 minutes.
6. Remove the cake from the oven, and gradually spoon 1 cup of the hot Honeysuckle Glaze over the cake in the pan, allowing the glaze to soak into the cake after each addition. Reserve the remaining glaze. Cool the cake completely in the pan on a wire rack, about 1 hour and 30 minutes.
7. Remove the cake from the pan; spoon the reserved glaze over the cake.

DIY EASTER CENTERPIECE

Creating this vibrant and unique display is easier than you might think. With a few supplies found at the store, you can create an exotic arrangement that will be the talk of the meal.

1-3

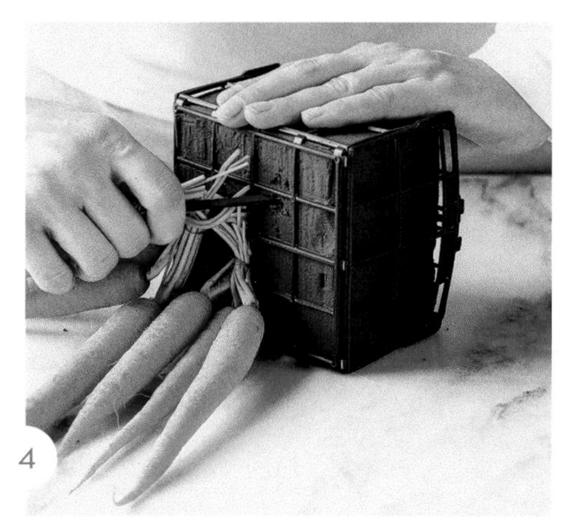

4

5

MATERIALS NEEDED: *caged florist foam; florist snips; carrots, radishes, and Brussels sprouts; thin wire; florist picks; fishbowl; spring flowers and ivy*

❶ Soak florist foam in water until thoroughly saturated. ❷ Cut carrot and radish stems about 2 inches long. ❸ Wire carrot and radish stems to picks. Insert other picks into Brussels sprouts. ❹ Insert florist picks attached to carrots into bottom of florist foam. ❺ Rest florist foam atop fishbowl, allowing carrots to hang inside. ❻ Fill top and sides of foam with flowers, radishes, and Brussels sprouts.

6

GARDEN PARTY

This luncheon with its garden-fresh menu is a beautiful way to welcome spring.

Menu

Spinach-and-Three-Herb Pesto
Cucumbers with Ginger, Rice Vinegar, and Mint
Creamy Basil-Black Pepper Cucumbers
Kale-and-Blueberry Slaw with Buttermilk Dressing
Minty Lemonade
Garden Potato Salad

SPINACH-AND-THREE-HERB PESTO

This versatile pesto is great on grilled bread and hard-cooked eggs. Or toss a spoonful with your favorite pasta.

MAKES about 1½ cups • **HANDS-ON** 10 minutes • **TOTAL** 10 minutes

- **1⅓ cups grated Parmesan cheese**
- **1 cup firmly packed fresh baby spinach**
- **⅔ cup olive oil**
- **½ cup firmly packed fresh basil leaves**
- **¼ cup firmly packed fresh flat-leaf parsley**
- **¼ cup chopped toasted pecans**
- **3 tablespoons cold water**
- **1 tablespoon fresh lemon juice**
- **1 tablespoon fresh tarragon leaves**
- **2 garlic cloves, chopped**
- **¾ teaspoon kosher salt**

Pulse all the ingredients in a food processor until smooth, stopping to scrape down the sides as needed.

CUCUMBERS WITH GINGER, RICE VINEGAR, AND MINT

This menu offers fresh cucumbers dressed up in two ways. Here, the warm-weather veggie takes a tangy-hot twist by being doused with vinegar, ginger, garlic, and red pepper.

SERVES 8 • **HANDS-ON** 15 minutes • **TOTAL** 1 hour, 30 minutes

- 2½ pounds cucumbers, chopped
- 1½ teaspoons kosher salt, plus more to taste
- ½ cup rice vinegar
- 1½ teaspoons fresh ginger, minced
- 2 garlic cloves, minced
- ¼ teaspoon crushed red pepper
- ¼ cup loosely packed fresh mint leaves, chopped
- Freshly ground black pepper

Toss together the cucumbers and salt in a large bowl, and let stand 5 minutes. Whisk together the vinegar, ginger, garlic, and red pepper. Pour over the cucumber mixture; cover and chill 1 to 24 hours. Add the mint, and toss to combine. Let stand 10 minutes before serving. Add salt and pepper to taste.

CREAMY BASIL-BLACK PEPPER CUCUMBERS

The combination of Greek yogurt and cucumbers creates a cool and refreshing taste that gets a pleasing hint of brightness from the lime juice and zest.

SERVES 8 • **HANDS-ON** 15 minutes • **TOTAL** 1 hour, 30 minutes

- 2½ pounds cucumbers, peeled and cut into spears
- 1½ teaspoon kosher salt, plus more to taste
- ½ cup Greek yogurt
- 3 tablespoons extra-virgin olive oil
- 1 teaspoon lime zest
- 2 tablespoons fresh lime juice
- 1 teaspoon freshly ground black pepper
- ½ cup firmly packed fresh basil leaves, chopped
- Garnish: lime zest strips

Toss together the cucumbers and salt in a large bowl, and let stand 5 minutes. Whisk together the yogurt, olive oil, lime zest, lime juice, and black pepper; gently stir into the cucumber mixture. Cover and chill 1 to 24 hours. Add the basil, and toss to combine. Let stand 10 minutes before serving. Add salt to taste. Garnish, if desired.

KALE-AND-BLUEBERRY SLAW WITH BUTTERMILK DRESSING

We like fresh tarragon in this creamy, zippy dressing, but other herbs work just as well.

SERVES 6 • **HANDS-ON** 30 minutes • **TOTAL** 1 hour, 5 minutes

6 tablespoons apple cider vinegar
3 tablespoons grated onion
½ teaspoon Worcestershire sauce
¼ teaspoon hot sauce (such as Tabasco)
1 garlic clove, minced
½ Granny Smith apple, grated
1 cup buttermilk
6 tablespoons mayonnaise
6 tablespoons sour cream
3 tablespoons finely chopped fresh tarragon
½ to 1 teaspoon kosher salt, plus more to taste
¼ to ½ teaspoon freshly ground black pepper, plus more to taste
¼ to ½ teaspoon sugar
6 radishes, thinly sliced
4 medium carrots, cut into thin strips
1 bunch kale, trimmed and thinly sliced
½ small head red cabbage, shredded
1 cup fresh blueberries
1 cup fresh raspberries

1. Stir together the apple cider vinegar, onion, Worcestershire sauce, hot sauce, garlic, and apple in a jar with a tight-fitting lid; let stand 5 minutes. Add the buttermilk, mayonnaise, sour cream, and tarragon. Cover the jar with the lid; shake vigorously until blended and smooth. Add the salt, pepper, and sugar to taste.
2. Toss together the radishes, carrots, kale, red cabbage, blueberries, raspberries, and ½ cup of the dressing in a large bowl; let stand 30 minutes. Add salt and pepper to taste. Serve with the remaining dressing.

MINTY LEMONADE

Transform lemonade in seconds with a handful of fresh mint leaves. Don't chop them—keep the leaves whole to avoid murky lemonade (and bits of green in your teeth). To maximize the mint flavor, cup the leaves in the palm of one hand, and clap your hands together a few times to release the herb's aroma.

MAKES 2½ quarts • HANDS-ON 10 minutes • TOTAL 15 minutes

½ cup water
1 to 1½ cups sugar
1 tablespoon lemon zest (about 2 lemons)
1½ cups fresh lemon juice (about 13 lemons)
7 cups ice water
Whole fresh mint leaves

1. Bring the water to a boil in a medium saucepan. Stir in the sugar and lemon zest, stirring until the sugar is dissolved; remove from the heat. Stir in the lemon juice and ice water.
2. Add the leaves to the lemonade; muddle with a serving spoon.

GARDEN POTATO SALAD

New potatoes are baby spring potatoes with beautifully thin skins. We love how red-skinned potatoes contrast with the vibrant green peas and herbs, but you can use any kind of potato you like.

SERVES 8 • HANDS-ON 15 minutes • TOTAL 1 hour, 25 minutes

3 pounds new potatoes, halved
1½ teaspoons kosher salt, plus more to taste
4 ounces fresh snow peas or sugar snap peas
2 cups water
3 tablespoons coarse-grained Dijon mustard
3 tablespoons fresh lemon juice
1 teaspoon sugar
¼ teaspoon freshly ground black pepper, plus more to taste
⅔ cup olive oil
1 cup loosely packed fresh herbs (such as basil, chives, mint, and dill), coarsely chopped

1. Bring the potatoes, water to cover, and 1 teaspoon of the salt to a boil in a large Dutch oven over medium-high. Reduce the heat to medium-low, and cook 10 to 15 minutes or until tender; drain. Cool 30 minutes.
2. Cook the snow peas in 2 cups boiling water in a medium saucepan over medium-high until crisp-tender, 1 minute; drain, pressing between paper towels. Cut the peas into ½-inch pieces. Cover with plastic wrap; chill until ready to use.
3. Whisk together the mustard, lemon juice, sugar, pepper, and the remaining ½ teaspoon salt in a medium bowl; gradually add the olive oil in a slow, steady stream, whisking until smooth.
4. Gently toss together the potatoes and ½ cup of the dressing in a large bowl, and let stand 30 minutes. Just before serving, gently stir in the peas, herbs, and remaining dressing. Add salt and pepper to taste.

Minty Lemonade

BRIDAL SHOWER

A beautiful table and a menu to match is just what you need to celebrate this happy affair with friends and family.

Menu

White Cheddar-Chive Pimiento Cheese
Muffin Pan Tomato Tarts
Pasta Shells with Spring Vegetables
Buttermilk-Lime Mini Cakes with Vanilla-Mascarpone Buttercream

WHITE CHEDDAR-CHIVE PIMIENTO CHEESE

No Southern wedding shower is complete without a bowl of pimiento cheese. Make it ahead to simplify day-of-party prep. Here's the secret to perfect pimiento-cheese texture: Grate the cheese by hand, half on the large holes of a box grater and half on the small holes.

MAKES **about 2 cups** • HANDS-ON **15 minutes** • TOTAL **30 minutes**

1 (12-ounce) block aged sharp white Cheddar cheese
1/3 cup mayonnaise, plus 2 tablespoons
1 (4-ounce) jar diced pimiento, drained and rinsed
1/3 cup thinly sliced fresh chives
1 tablespoon Dijon mustard
1/2 teaspoon Worcestershire sauce
1/4 teaspoon cayenne pepper
1/4 teaspoon freshly ground black pepper

Grate half of the cheese using the large holes of a box grater; grate the remaining half of the cheese using the small holes of the box grater. Stir together the mayonnaise, pimientos, chives, Dijon mustard, Worcestershire sauce, cayenne pepper, and black pepper. Stir in the Cheddar until well blended. Let stand 15 minutes. Serve immediately, or cover and chill up to 3 days.

THE DETAILS

When hosting a bridal shower, it's thoughtful to include memorable touches for the bride-to-be to cherish. Whether you're an entertaining pro or novice, here are fresh ideas and tips to help you create a special and polished look.

1

2

3

4

1 To create this centerpiece, place a water-soaked block of florist foam in a large, decorative bowl. Next choose a lush filler, like green viburnums, and insert them into the foam. Add garden roses and azalea sprigs (also tucked into the foam). **2** To create this whimsical wreath, cover the surface of a dampened florist foam wreath with natural moss, and secure with floral pins. Place azalea sprigs in florist water picks, and insert along the lower center of the wreath. Loop strands of ribbon around the bottom center. **3** For pretty chairback flourishes, cut a square from medium-weight paper, roll it into a cone shape, and secure with glue or tape. Place two or three azalea sprigs in a florist water pick. Insert the pick into the cone. Punch two holes in the back of the cone about a half inch apart. Thread a ribbon through the holes, and secure to the chairback. **4** Tuck patterned napkins under each place setting to define individual seats. Mix and match tableware in shades of pink and white for a collected, vintage look. Top each with a matching plate.

MUFFIN PAN TOMATO TARTS

This new twist on the classic tomato pie is made with puff pastry sheets and makes adorable individual tartlets for shower guests.

MAKES **18 tarts** • HANDS-ON **20 minutes** • TOTAL **45 minutes**

- **1 (17.3-ounce) package frozen puff pastry sheets, partially thawed**
- **1/2 cup mayonnaise**
- **2 teaspoons kosher salt**
- **1 teaspoon freshly ground black pepper**
- **10 ounces (2 1/2 cups) sharp Cheddar cheese, finely shredded**
- **11 ounces multicolored cherry tomatoes, halved**
- **2 tablespoons torn fresh basil**

1. Preheat the oven to 400°F. Gently unfold both pastry sheets. Spread 1/4 cup of the mayonnaise on each pastry sheet; sprinkle each with 1 teaspoon of the salt and 1/2 teaspoon of the pepper.
2. Cut each pastry sheet into 9 (3-inch) squares. Gently press the squares into 2 lightly greased muffin pans. Divide the cheese and tomatoes among the tarts.
3. Bake in the preheated oven until the pastry is golden brown, about 20 minutes. Let cool in the pans on a wire rack 5 minutes. Top with the torn fresh basil. Serve immediately.

PASTA SHELLS WITH SPRING VEGETABLES

Pea tendrils, the tender tips of pea vines that taste just like the peas, make an unexpected and charming garnish.

SERVES **8** • HANDS-ON **35 minutes** • TOTAL **35 minutes**

- **3/4 pound fresh asparagus**
- **1 (12-ounce) package sugar snap peas**
- **1 1/2 cups ricotta cheese**
- **3 teaspoons lemon zest**
- **6 teaspoons fresh lemon juice**
- **1/4 cup kosher salt, plus 1/3 teaspoon**
- **6 quarts water**
- **3/4 pound large pasta shells**
- **1 1/2 tablespoons olive oil**
- **6 radishes, thinly sliced**
- **1 1/2 tablespoons chopped fresh mint**
- **1/4 teaspoon freshly ground black pepper**
- **Pea tendrils (optional)**

1. Cut the asparagus into 1-inch pieces, discarding the tough ends. Cut the snap peas in half.
2. Stir the together ricotta, 1 teaspoon of the zest, lemon juice, and 1/3 teaspoon of the salt in a medium bowl.
3. Bring the water to a boil in a stockpot over high. Add the remaining 1/4 cup salt; return to a boil. Add the pasta; boil, stirring occasionally, until al dente, 11 minutes. Add the asparagus and sugar snap peas, and cook until tender, 2 to 3 minutes. Drain the pasta mixture, reserving 1/4 cup of the pasta water. Return the pasta to the pot. Stir in the olive oil, radishes, and the reserved pasta water.
4. Spread half of the ricotta mixture in a serving dish; top with the pasta mixture. Dollop with the remaining ricotta mixture. Sprinkle with the mint, remaining zest, and pepper. Garnish with the pea tendrils, if desired. Serve immediately.

BUTTERMILK-LIME MINI CAKES WITH VANILLA-MASCARPONE BUTTERCREAM

These party-perfect cakes are brushed twice with a tangy lime syrup (easily made with melted frozen limeade concentrate), once when the sheet cake comes out of the oven and again after the cake has been cut into rounds with a biscuit cutter.

SERVES 8 · **HANDS-ON** 1 hour · **TOTAL** 2 hours, 10 minutes

CAKE

- 3 cups cake flour
- 3 teaspoons baking powder
- 1 teaspoon table salt
- 1/2 cup unsalted butter
- 1/2 cup canola or vegetable oil
- 2 cups granulated sugar
- 4 large eggs
- 1 tablespoon vanilla extract
- 1 1/3 cups whole buttermilk
- 1/2 (12-ounce) container frozen limeade concentrate, thawed

BUTTERCREAM

- 1 pound powdered sugar
- 1 cup unsalted butter, softened
- 1 teaspoon vanilla extract
- 8 ounces mascarpone cheese, softened

GARNISHES

White chocolate curls, white nonpareils, edible flowers, fresh raspberries, fresh strawberries

1. Make the Cake: Preheat the oven to 350°F. Coat a 17- x 12-inch half-sheet pan with cooking spray, and line the bottom of the pan with parchment paper. Sift the cake flour, baking powder, and salt together in a medium bowl. Set aside.
2. Beat the butter and oil in a large bowl with a mixer on medium-high speed until smooth and creamy. Add the sugar, and beat until light and fluffy, 4 to 5 minutes. Add the eggs, 1 at a time, and beat on medium-low speed until well blended after each addition. Beat in the vanilla. Add the flour mixture, one-third at a time, to the butter mixture alternately with the buttermilk, beginning and ending with the flour mixture. Beat on low just until smooth after each addition. (Do not overbeat or the cake will be tough.) Spread the batter evenly in the prepared sheet pan. Gently tap the pan on the countertop to release air bubbles.
3. Bake in the center of the preheated oven until a wooden pick or cake tester inserted in the center of the cake comes out clean, 18 to 22 minutes. Place the pan on a wire rack.
4. Heat the thawed limeade concentrate in a small saucepan over medium just until warmed through, about 3 minutes. Brush the cake lightly with about half of the limeade syrup. (Reserve the remaining limeade syrup for later use.) Cool the cake completely in the pan, about 45 minutes. Freeze the cooled cake, uncovered, until very cold and very firm, about 30 minutes.
5. Meanwhile, make the Buttercream: Beat the powdered sugar and butter in a large bowl with a mixer on medium-high speed until thick and creamy, 4 to 5 minutes. Beat in the vanilla. Add the mascarpone cheese, and beat on low speed just until combined, stopping to scrape down the sides of the bowl as needed. (Do not overmix or the mascarpone will start to break down and the frosting will become too thin.)
6. Fit a large disposable piping bag with a large star tip. Fill the piping bag with 3 cups of the Buttercream. Remove the cake from the freezer. Using a 2 3/4-inch round cutter, carefully cut 16 circles from sheet cake. Use an offset spatula to transfer the cake circles to another sheet pan. Discard the cake scraps or reserve for another use.
7. Brush the top and sides of each cake circle with the reserved remaining limeade syrup. Pipe a tight spiral of icing on 8 of the cake layers. Top each frosted layer with an unfrosted cake layer to make 8 miniature 2-layer cakes. Hold 1 cake on your fingertips, and, using an offset spatula, carefully swipe the sides of the cake with a thin layer of the buttercream, barely covering the cake. Repeat with the remaining cakes. Pipe a rosette of buttercream on top of each cake. Garnish, if desired.

FATHER'S DAY BRUNCH

Dad will love this spread of morning-time dishes from flavorful chicken-and-waffle sandwiches to Breakfast Enchiladas to sugary cake and beyond.

Menu

Hot Chicken-and-Waffle Sandwiches with Chive Cream
Coffee Milk Punch
Creamy Baked Eggs with Herbs and Bacon
Breakfast Enchiladas
Golden Potato-and-Smoked Sausage Hash
Streusel Coffee Cake

HOT CHICKEN-AND-WAFFLE SANDWICHES WITH CHIVE CREAM

Show Dad you love him by waking him up to a savory sandwich made with two of his favorite foods—spicy fried chicken and fluffy buttermilk waffles.

SERVES 6 • HANDS-ON 40 minutes • TOTAL 40 minutes

HOT CHICKEN
9 fried chicken breast tenders
1 tablespoon cayenne pepper
1 teaspoon paprika
½ teaspoon garlic powder
2 tablespoons sugar
½ cup peanut oil

WAFFLES
2 cups all-purpose flour
1½ teaspoons baking powder
¾ teaspoon baking soda
¾ teaspoon table salt
1½ cups buttermilk
¼ cup salted butter, melted
2 large eggs

CHIVE CREAM
½ cup sour cream
2 tablespoons thinly sliced chives
1 teaspoon water

1. Make the Hot Chicken: Preheat the oven to 200°F. Place the chicken tenders in a single layer on a baking sheet, and keep warm in the oven until ready to use.
2. Stir together the cayenne pepper, paprika, garlic powder, and 1 tablespoon of the sugar in a small saucepan. Whisk in the peanut oil, and cook over low, whisking constantly, until well combined, about 5 minutes. Set aside.
3. Make the Waffles: Whisk together the flour, next 3 ingredients, and remaining 1 tablespoon sugar in a medium bowl. Whisk together the buttermilk, butter, and eggs in a small bowl. Stir the buttermilk mixture into the flour mixture until combined. Cook the batter, in batches, in a preheated, lightly greased waffle iron until golden brown, 4 to 5 minutes.
4. Make the Chive Cream: Stir together the sour cream, chives, and 1 teaspoon water in a small bowl.
5. Assemble the Sandwiches: Toss the tenders and cayenne mixture in a large bowl. Place 1½ tenders on each of 6 waffles; top each with 2 tablespoons of the chive cream and 1 waffle. Serve immediately.

COFFEE MILK PUNCH

Whether you serve it hot or cold, this punch has just the right amount of kick to jump-start your Father's Day celebration.

MAKES 9 cups • **HANDS-ON** 15 minutes • **TOTAL** 15 minutes

- 6 cups strong brewed hot coffee
- 1/2 cup hot fudge topping
- 1/4 cup sugar
- 2 cups half-and-half
- 1 cup coffee liqueur
- 1 tablespoon vanilla extract

Whisk together the hot coffee, fudge topping, and sugar in a large Dutch oven until smooth. Add the half-and-half and remaining ingredients, stirring until blended. Bring the mixture to a simmer over medium-high. Serve immediately, or let cool. Cover and chill 1 to 24 hours, and serve over ice.

CREAMY BAKED EGGS WITH HERBS AND BACON

This flavor-loaded dish is quick to make and easy enough for the kids to help with.

SERVES 4 • **HANDS-ON** 15 minutes • **TOTAL** 21 minutes

- 1/2 cup heavy whipping cream
- 2 tablespoons thinly sliced chives
- 2 tablespoons chopped fresh flat-leaf parsley
- 2 teaspoons chopped fresh dill
- 1/2 teaspoon kosher salt
- 1/4 teaspoon freshly ground black pepper
- 8 large eggs
- 4 cooked bacon slices, crumbled (about 1/2 cup)

1. Preheat the oven to 425°F. Stir together the whipping cream, chives, parsley, dill, salt, and pepper in a large ovenproof skillet. Bring to a simmer over medium-low. Break the eggs into the cream mixture; do not stir.
2. Bake at 425°F until the whites are set and the yolks are at the desired degree of doneness, 6 to 8 minutes. Sprinkle with the bacon, and serve immediately.

Creamy Baked Eggs
with Herbs and Bacon

BREAKFAST ENCHILADAS

Remove the eggs from the stove-top while they're still a bit wet; they'll finish cooking in the oven.

SERVES 6 • HANDS-ON 20 minutes • TOTAL 1 hour

2 tablespoons unsalted butter
3/4 cup chopped red bell pepper
1/2 cup chopped sweet onion
12 large eggs
1/2 teaspoon table salt
1/4 teaspoon freshly ground black pepper
2 tablespoons water
1 (16-ounce) jar salsa verde
12 (6-inch) flour tortillas
2 1/2 cups (10 ounces) shredded Colby Jack cheese
2 tablespoons chopped fresh cilantro
Halved grape tomatoes, chopped fresh cilantro, chopped avocado (optional)

CHEESE SAUCE
1/4 cup salted butter
1/4 cup all-purpose flour
2 cups milk
1 1/2 cups (6 ounces) shredded Colby Jack cheese
1 (4.5-ounce) can chopped green chiles
1/2 teaspoon table salt

1. Preheat the oven to 350°F. Melt the butter in large nonstick skillet over medium. Add the bell peppers and onions; sauté until tender, 4 to 5 minutes. Stir together the eggs, salt, pepper, and water in a medium bowl. Add the egg mixture to the bell pepper mixture, and cook, without stirring, until the eggs begin to set on the bottom, about 1 to 2 minutes. Draw a spatula across the pan to form large curds. Cook, stirring occasionally, until the eggs are thickened, about 6 to 7 minutes. (Do not overstir.)
2. Spread 2 tablespoons of the salsa verde in the center of each tortilla. Spoon about 1/4 cup of the egg mixture over the salsa; sprinkle with 2 tablespoons of the cheese and 1/2 teaspoon of the cilantro. Roll up, and place, seam side down, in a lightly greased 13- x 9-inch baking dish.
3. Make the Cheese Sauce: Melt the butter in a heavy saucepan over medium-low; whisk in the flour until smooth. Cook, whisking constantly, 1 minute. Increase the heat to medium. Gradually whisk in the milk; cook, whisking constantly, until thickened, 5 minutes. Remove from the heat; whisk in the cheese, chiles, and salt.
4. Add the Cheese Sauce and remaining cheese immediately. Bake at 350°F until the sauce is bubbly, 30 minutes. Serve with the tomatoes, cilantro, and avocado, if desired.

GOLDEN POTATO-AND-SMOKED SAUSAGE HASH

Make this hash even heartier by adding a fried egg on top.

SERVES 6 • **HANDS-ON** 55 minutes • **TOTAL** 1 hour, 5 minutes

- 1 pound baby golden potatoes, each cut into 8 pieces
- 1/4 cup kosher salt
- 1 pound smoked sausage, sliced
- 1 medium-size sweet onion, thinly sliced
- 2 tablespoons red wine vinegar
- 3 cups arugula
- 1/4 cup shaved Parmesan cheese

1. Place the potatoes, salt, and water to cover in a medium saucepan. Bring to a boil over high; reduce the heat to medium-low, and simmer until tender when pierced, 10 minutes. Drain, and place in a single layer on a baking sheet. Cool completely, 15 minutes.
2. Meanwhile, cook the sausage in a large skillet over medium-high, stirring often, until browned, 10 minutes. Remove with a slotted spoon, and drain on paper towels, reserving the drippings in the skillet.
3. Cook the potatoes in the hot drippings over medium, stirring occasionally, until the potatoes are browned and crisp, 10 minutes. Add the onions, and cook, stirring occasionally, until tender, 10 minutes. Add the vinegar, and cook 30 seconds.
4. Stir in the sausage and arugula, and cook, stirring until the arugula is wilted, about 5 minutes. Transfer to a serving platter. Top with the Parmesan.

STREUSEL COFFEE CAKE

Finish the feast with something sweet and crumbly. To make this cake one day ahead, just bake, cool completely, and wrap in aluminum foil.

SERVES 8 to 10 • **HANDS-ON** 30 minutes • **TOTAL** 1 hour, 25 minutes

CRUMB TOPPING

- 1/2 cup all-purpose flour
- 1/2 cup sugar
- 1/2 cup coarsely chopped pecans
- 1/4 cup butter, cut into pieces

- 1/2 cup butter, softened
- 1 (8-ounce) package cream cheese, softened
- 1 1/4 cups sugar
- 2 large eggs
- 2 cups all-purpose flour
- 2 teaspoons baking powder
- 1/2 teaspoon baking soda
- 1/2 teaspoon table salt
- 1/2 cup milk
- 1 teaspoon vanilla extract
- 1/2 teaspoon almond extract

1. Preheat the oven to 350°F.
2. Make the Crumb Topping: Stir together the flour, sugar, and coarsely chopped pecans in a bowl. Cut in the 1/4 cup butter with a pastry blender or fork until the mixture resembles small peas.
3. Beat the 1/2 cup butter and cream cheese at medium speed with a mixer until creamy. Gradually add the sugar, beating at medium speed until light and fluffy. Add the eggs, 1 at a time, beating just until the yellow disappears.
4. Sift together the flour, baking powder, baking soda, and salt; add to the butter mixture alternately with the milk, beginning and ending with the flour mixture. Beat at low speed just until blended after each addition. Stir in the vanilla and almond extracts. Pour the batter into a greased 13- x 9-inch pan; sprinkle with the Crumb Topping.
5. Bake at 350°F until a wooden pick inserted in the center comes out clean, 35 to 40 minutes. Let cool 20 minutes before serving.

Golden Potato-and-Smoked Sausage Hash

BACKYARD COOKOUT

Nothing beats a good old-fashioned cookout! This menu takes out the guesswork of meal prep, allowing you more time to kick back with friends.

Menu

Buttermilk Hot Sauce-Brined Chicken
Grilled Tomatoes on the Vine
Street Corn Salad
Rum-Baked Beans
Colorful Collard Slaw
Sour Cream Potato Salad
Corn-off-the-Cobb Bread

BUTTERMILK HOT SAUCE-BRINED CHICKEN

The secret to extra moist grilled chicken is an overnight soak in a hot sauce-laced buttermilk marinade.

SERVES 6 • **HANDS-ON** 25 minutes • **TOTAL** 25 hours, 45 minutes, includes chilling

2 cups buttermilk
2 cups cold water
1/4 cup kosher salt
1 tablespoon freshly ground black pepper
1/2 cup hot sauce, plus 3 tablespoons
1/4 cup packed light brown sugar, plus 2 teaspoons
1 lime, thinly sliced
4 garlic cloves, smashed
4 to 5 pounds skin-on, bone-in chicken breasts and leg quarters
1/4 cup ketchup
2 tablespoons melted salted butter
1 tablespoon apple cider vinegar

1. Whisk together the buttermilk, water, salt, pepper, 1/2 cup of the hot sauce, and 1/4 cup of the brown sugar in a large bowl until the sugar is dissolved; stir in the lime slices and garlic.
2. Place the buttermilk mixture and chicken in a large ziplock plastic freezer bag; seal the bag, and chill 24 hours. Remove the chicken from the marinade, discarding the marinade; pat dry with paper towels.
3. Heat the grill to medium (350°F to 450°F) with an area cleared of coals (for charcoal grill) or a burner turned off (for gas) to make an indirect heat area. Place the chicken, skin side up, over indirect heat, and grill, covered, until a meat thermometer inserted in the thickest portion registers 165°F, about 1 hour and 15 minutes.
4. Whisk together the ketchup, butter, vinegar, and the remaining 3 tablespoons hot sauce and 2 teaspoons brown sugar.
5. Brush the ketchup mixture onto both sides of the chicken; transfer, skin side down, to the direct heat side of the grill, and grill, uncovered, 1 to 2 minutes or until the skin is browned and crispy; turn and grill, uncovered, 1 to 2 more minutes. Let stand 5 minutes before serving.

GRILLED TOMATOES ON THE VINE

From vine to grill to table, a heap of fresh tomatoes makes the perfect summer tag along to any summer cookout menu. You can use heirloom tomatoes on the grill, if you prefer. To do this, be sure to use a grill basket or fine grill grate. It will make it much easier to work with the tomatoes.

SERVES 8 • **HANDS-ON** 5 minutes • **TOTAL** 20 minutes

2 pounds cherry tomatoes on the vine
2 teaspoons olive oil
1 teaspoon kosher salt
½ teaspoon freshly ground black pepper
1 tablespoon torn basil, thyme, or oregano leaves or 1 rosemary sprig
Coarse sea salt

1. Heat the grill to medium (350°F to 450°F). Place the tomatoes (attached to the vine) in the center of an 18- x 18-inch piece of heavy-duty aluminum foil. Drizzle with the olive oil, and sprinkle with the salt and pepper. Sprinkle with the desired herb. Seal the foil to make a packet.
2. Grill the tomatoes, covered, 10 minutes; open the packet slightly, and grill until the tomatoes soften and are heated through, 5 to 10 minutes. Sprinkle with the sea salt, and serve.

STREET CORN SALAD

Easy Street Corn Salad comes together in a snap. Simply combine the ingredients with a dash of olive oil and sprinkle with cheese. Now that's summer siding made simple!

SERVES 8 • **HANDS-ON** 20 minutes • **TOTAL** 20 minutes

½ cup chopped fresh cilantro
3 tablespoons fresh lime juice
1 teaspoon kosher salt
½ teaspoon freshly ground black pepper
2 tablespoons olive oil
4 cups fresh corn kernels
1 cup thinly sliced radishes
1 cup cherry tomato halves
⅓ to ½ cup crumbled Cotija cheese (or feta cheese)

1. Combine the cilantro, lime juice, salt, and pepper; whisk in the olive oil.
2. Stir together the corn, radishes, and tomatoes in a medium bowl. Gently stir in the dressing. Spoon the mixture onto a serving platter; sprinkle with the cheese.

RUM-BAKED BEANS

The secret to this tender baked bean medley? Rum. Make it ahead of time by preparing Steps 1 and 2. Cover with foil and refrigerate up to two days until ready to bake.

SERVES 10 • **HANDS-ON** 20 minutes • **TOTAL** 1 hour, 50 minutes

6 thick-cut bacon slices, chopped
1 cup chopped sweet onion
2 garlic cloves, minced
1 (28-ounce) can baked beans with bacon and brown sugar
1 (16-ounce) can navy beans, drained and rinsed
1 (16-ounce) can dark red kidney beans, drained and rinsed
1 (16-ounce) can light red kidney beans, drained and rinsed
1 (15-ounce) can black beans, drained and rinsed
½ cup packed dark brown sugar
½ cup ketchup
½ cup gold rum
¼ cup apple cider vinegar

1. Preheat the oven to 350°F. Cook the bacon in a large skillet over medium until crisp; remove, reserving 2 tablespoons of the drippings in the skillet. Add the onion, and cook, stirring often, until tender, about 5 minutes; add the garlic, and cook 1 minute.
2. Stir together the bacon, onion mixture, baked beans, navy beans, dark red kidney beans, light red kidney beans, black beans, brown sugar, ketchup, rum, and apple cider vinegar in a large bowl. Spoon into a lightly greased 13- x 9-inch baking dish.
3. Bake, covered with aluminum foil, 30 minutes; uncover and bake 30 more minutes.

COLORFUL COLLARD SLAW

Our cruncy coleslaw, made with apples, thinly sliced collards, and carrots, can be prepared a day ahead; toss with dressing right before serving.

SERVES 10 • **HANDS-ON** 20 minutes • **TOTAL** 20 minutes

½ cup white wine vinegar
5 tablespoons granulated sugar
2 tablespoons fresh lime juice
2 teaspoons prepared horseradish
¼ teaspoon crushed red pepper
2 teaspoons kosher salt
½ cup olive oil
1 bunch collard greens
2 cups matchstick carrots
1 sweet apple (such as Braeburn, Pink Lady, or Honey Crisp), diced

1. Whisk together the white wine vinegar, sugar, lime juice, horseradish, red pepper, and 1½ teaspoons of the salt in a small bowl until the sugar is completely dissolved; slowly whisk in the olive oil until completely incorporated.
2. Trim and discard the tough stems from the collard greens; thinly slice the leaves, and place in a large bowl. Sprinkle with remaining ½ teaspoon salt, and gently massage into the greens 1 to 2 minutes. (This helps tenderize them and remove any bitterness.) Pour off any liquid.
3. Add the carrots, apple, and 2 tablespoons of the dressing to the collards; stir gently to combine, and let stand 30 minutes. Add ¼ cup of the dressing to the slaw, and toss. Serve the remaining dressing on the side.

SOUR CREAM POTATO SALAD

Everyone needs an easy potato salad recipe in their summer sides rotation. We used sour cream to lighten up this mayo-based potato salad. To lighten it up even more, substitute Greek yogurt for the sour cream.

SERVES 8 • **HANDS-ON** 20 minutes • **TOTAL** 1 hour, 20 minutes

- 3 pounds small russet potatoes thinly sliced (about 1/4 inch thick)
- 6 thick-cut bacon slices, cooked crisp and crumbled
- 3/4 cup sour cream
- 1/2 cup mayonnaise
- 1 tablespoon chopped fresh flat-leaf parsley
- 1 tablespoon finely chopped fresh chives
- 1 tablespoon white vinegar
- 1 1/2 teaspoons table salt
- 1 teaspoon granulated sugar
- 1/4 teaspoon garlic powder
- 1/8 teaspoon white pepper
- 1 scallion, finely chopped

1. Place the potato slices in a Dutch oven, and cover with cold water; bring to a boil over medium-high. Reduce the heat to medium-low, and simmer until tender, about 15 minutes. Drain and cool. Place the potatoes in a large bowl; gently stir in the bacon.

2. Whisk together the next 10 ingredients in a small bowl. Add the sour cream mixture to the potato mixture, and stir gently to incorporate.

CORN-OFF-THE-COB BREAD

This cornbread skillet incorporates fresh corn kernels, as well as cornmeal for an easy, go-to side dish.

SERVES 8 • **HANDS-ON** 15 minutes • **TOTAL** 45 minutes

- 1/2 cup salted butter
- 1 1/2 cups self-rising white cornmeal mix
- 1/2 cup all-purpose flour
- 1 1/2 cups buttermilk
- 1 cup fresh corn kernels
- 2 large eggs

1. Preheat the oven to 425°F. Place the butter in a 10-inch cast-iron skillet, and heat in the oven until the butter has melted and the skillet is hot, about 5 minutes.

2. Meanwhile, whisk together the cornmeal and flour in a large bowl. Whisk together the buttermilk, corn kernels, and eggs in a medium bowl. Stir the buttermilk mixture into cornmeal mixture. Add the melted butter from the skillet to the cornmeal mixture, and stir just until blended. Pour into the hot skillet.

3. Bake until golden brown, 25 to 30 minutes. Remove from the oven, and immediately turn out onto a platter.

Sour Cream
Potato Salad

LOWCOUNTRY LUNCH

This menu offers the best of coastal South Carolina fare: crab cakes, crawfish, Hoppin' John, gumbo, and étouffée.

Menu

Crab Cake Hush Puppies with Rémoulade Sauce
Crawfish Dip
Hoppin' John Rice Bowl
Gumbo Gravy over Grits
"Crawdogs"
Crawfish Étouffée

CRAB CAKE HUSH PUPPIES WITH RÉMOULADE SAUCE

Hush puppies, a Southern classic made by deep-frying a cornmeal batter, get a seafood makeover. These salty critters are a great option for a potluck meal or an appetizer. Freeze any leftovers and defrost up to three months later.

SERVES 8 • **HANDS-ON** 30 minutes • **TOTAL** 40 minutes

8 ounces fresh lump crabmeat
1 cup self-rising white cornmeal mix
1/2 cup self-rising flour
3 scallions, thinly sliced
1/2 cup finely chopped red bell pepper
1 tablespoon sugar
1/4 teaspoon kosher salt
1 large egg
3/4 cup beer
Vegetable oil

RÉMOULADE SAUCE
1 cup mayonnaise
1/4 cup sliced scallions
2 tablespoons Creole mustard
1 tablespoon chopped fresh parsley
1 tablespoon minced fresh garlic
1 teaspoon prepared horseradish

1. Pick crabmeat, removing any bits of shell.
2. Stir together the cornmeal mix, flour, scallions, bell pepper, sugar, and salt in a large bowl. Stir in the crabmeat, egg, and beer until just moistened. Let stand 10 minutes. Pour the oil to depth of 2 inches into a Dutch oven; heat to 360°F. Drop the batter by tablespoonfuls into the hot oil, and fry, in batches, until golden brown, 2 to 3 minutes, turning once.
3. Make the Rémoulade Sauce: Stir together the mayonnaise, scallions, Creole mustard, parsley, garlic, and horseradish; cover and chill until ready to serve. Serve with the hush puppies.

CRAWFISH DIP

Cook and serve this appetizer dip in a slow cooker to keep it warm.

SERVES 10 • **HANDS-ON** 15 minutes • **TOTAL** 1 hour

- 2 tablespoons salted butter
- 1/2 cup diced green bell pepper
- 1 small yellow onion, diced
- 1/2 cup diced celery
- 3 garlic cloves, chopped
- 1 jalapeño chile, diced
- 1 teaspoon kosher salt
- 1/2 teaspoon freshly ground black pepper
- 2 teaspoons paprika
- 1/2 teaspoon cayenne pepper
- 1 pound frozen peeled crawfish tails, thawed according to package directions
- 8 ounces cream cheese, softened
- 8 ounces grated extra-sharp Cheddar cheese (about 2 cups)
- 1/4 cup heavy whipping cream
- 2 tablespoons Creole mustard
- 1 tablespoon Worcestershire sauce
- 2 teaspoons hot sauce
- 2 tablespoons fresh lemon juice
- 2 tablespoons chopped fresh flat-leaf parsley
- Crackers, toasted baguette slices

1. Melt the butter in a large sauté pan or skillet over medium. Add the bell pepper, onion, celery, garlic, jalapeño, salt, and black pepper, and cook 6 minutes. Add the paprika and cayenne pepper, and cook 1 more minute.

2. Place the crawfish, cream cheese, Cheddar, and cream in a 6-quart slow cooker. Stir in the bell pepper mixture, Creole mustard, Worcestershire sauce, and hot sauce. Cover and cook on HIGH 45 minutes. Reduce the heat to WARM. Stir in the lemon juice and parsley; serve with crackers or toasted baguette slices.

HOPPIN' JOHN RICE BOWL

You can also serve this dish in eight individual parfait glasses. Make sure the glasses are clear so that dinner guests can see the layers.

SERVES 8 • **HANDS-ON** 20 minutes • **TOTAL** 30 minutes

4 (3.5-ounce) boil-in-bags rice, uncooked
2 tablespoons butter
2 (8-ounce) packages diced smoked ham
1 medium onion, diced
2 teaspoons minced garlic
4 (15½-ounce) cans seasoned black-eyed peas
1 cup water
2 tablespoons apple cider vinegar
6 scallions, chopped
⅔ cup chopped fresh parsley
2 large tomatoes, chopped

1. Prepare the rice according to the package directions.
2. Melt the butter in a large sauce pan over medium-high; add the ham, onion, and garlic, and sauté until the onion is tender, 8 to 10 minutes. Stir in the black-eyed peas and water. Bring to a boil; reduce the heat, and simmer about 10 minutes. Stir in the vinegar.
3. Place the hot cooked rice in a serving dish; spoon the ham mixture over the rice. Sprinkle with the scallions, parsley, and tomato.

GUMBO GRAVY OVER GRITS

Indulge in a gumbo of andouille sausage, Cajun shrimp, and okra served over creamy slow-cooked stone-ground grits.

SERVES 8 • **HANDS-ON** 25 minutes • **TOTAL** 4 hours, 15 minutes

2 cups all-purpose flour
1¼ pounds large raw shrimp, peeled and deveined
2 teaspoons Cajun seasoning
8 ounces andouille sausage, diced
2½ teaspoons vegetable oil
2½ cups diced sweet onion
¾ cup diced green bell pepper
2½ garlic cloves, minced
1¼ cups reduced-sodium, fat-free chicken broth
1¼ cups sliced fresh okra
2½ large plum tomatoes, peeled, seeded, and diced
Scallions, sliced (optional)

SLOW-COOKER STONE-GROUND GRITS

2 cups uncooked stone-ground yellow grits
5¾ cups water
Table salt
Black pepper

1. Preheat the oven to 400°F. Spread the flour in a 12-inch cast-iron skillet. Bake 20 to 25 minutes or until the flour is the color of pecan shells, stirring with a wooden spoon every 7 minutes. Remove from the skillet, and cool completely, about 30 minutes. Refrigerate the browned flour in an airtight container up to 2 months.
2. Make the Slow-Cooker Stone-Ground Grits: Stir together the grits and water in a 3-quart slow cooker. Let stand 2 minutes, allowing the grits to settle to the bottom; tilt the slow cooker slightly, and skim off the solids using a fine wire-mesh strainer. Cover and cook on HIGH 2½ to 3 hours or until the grits are creamy and tender, stirring every 45 minutes. Season with salt and pepper to taste.
3. Toss the shrimp in the Cajun seasoning in a medium bowl.
4. Cook the sausage in a large skillet coated with cooking spray over medium 6 minutes or until lightly browned. Add the oil, onion, bell pepper, and garlic; sauté 5 minutes or until tender. Sprinkle 4 tablespoons of the browned flour over the sausage mixture; stir until blended. Stir in the chicken broth, and increase the heat to medium-high. Bring to a boil, stirring often, and boil, stirring occasionally until thickened, about 4 minutes. Add the shrimp, okra, and tomatoes. Cook just until the shrimp turn pink, about 6 minutes.
5. Serve the gumbo gravy over the cooked grits. Sprinkle with scallion slices, if desired.

Allegations Of "Fish
Stories" Par For The
Course At Local Events
Fish Pirate's Daughter
Caught Up In Crowd

"CRAWDOGS"

If you serve our étouffée (see below) and have leftovers, slather it on top of grilled 'dogs.

SERVES 8 • **HANDS-ON** 15 minutes • **TOTAL** 15 minutes

8 hot dogs
¼ cup Creole mustard
8 hot dog buns
2 tablespoons salted butter, melted
2 cups Crawfish Étouffeé (see below)
Fresh jalapeño slices, diced red onion, and diced plum tomato (optional)

1. Coat the cold cooking grate of a grill with cooking spray, and place on the grill. Preheat the grill to medium (350°F to 450°F). Brush the hot dogs with the Creole mustard. Split the hot dog buns (if necessary), and brush inside with the melted butter. Place the hot dogs on the cooking grate, and grill, turning occasionally, until slightly charred, 3 to 4 minutes. Transfer the hot dogs to the side of the grate, away from the heat, and place the buns, buttered side down, over the heat. Grill the buns until golden brown, about 30 seconds.
2. Heat the Crawfish Étouffée in a saucepan over medium-low just until warm. Place the hot dogs in the buns, and spoon ¼ cup of the étouffée over each hot dog. Serve with jalapeño, red onion, and plum tomato, if desired.

CRAWFISH ÉTOUFFÉE

Étouffée is French for "smothered," so don't scrimp when pouring this thick Cajun stew over rice.

SERVES 8 • **HANDS-ON** 40 minutes • **TOTAL** 55 minutes

1 tablespoon paprika
2 teaspoons kosher salt
1 teaspoon freshly ground black pepper
1 teaspoon dried thyme
½ teaspoon cayenne pepper
½ cup vegetable oil
1 cup all-purpose flour
1 poblano chile, seeds removed, diced
3 celery stalks, diced
1 medium-size yellow onion, diced
3 garlic cloves, chopped
1 jalapeño chile, seeds removed (if desired), diced
2 cups seafood stock
2 pounds frozen peeled crawfish tails, thawed and rinsed
¼ cup chopped fresh parsley
2 tablespoons fresh lemon juice
1 tablespoon Worcestershire sauce
2 teaspoons hot sauce, plus more for serving
8 cups hot cooked long-grain white rice
½ cup sliced scallions, white and light green parts only

Stir together the paprika, salt, pepper, thyme, and cayenne pepper in a small bowl. Heat the oil in a large stockpot over medium-high. Add the flour, and stir well to combine. Reduce the heat to medium-low, and cook, stirring, until the roux is the color of caramel sauce, about 20 minutes. Add the poblano, celery, and onion. Cook, stirring, until the vegetables are tender, about 10 minutes. Add the garlic, jalapeño, and paprika mixture. Cook 2 minutes. Gradually whisk in the stock. Return to a simmer over medium-high. Stir in the crawfish, parsley, lemon juice, Worcestershire sauce, and 2 teaspoons hot sauce. Cook until warm, 2 to 3 minutes. Serve with the hot rice, scallions, and hot sauce.

THANKSGIVING DINNER

From a stunning and juicy turkey and savory wild rice dressing to tender rolls and flavor-loaded veggies, there's plenty to be thankful for this year.

Menu

Sweet-and-Spicy Roast Turkey
Honey-Glazed Spiced Carrots
Slow-Cooker Green Beans
Yeast Rolls
Herbed Wild Rice Dressing
German Chocolate-Pecan Pie

SWEET-AND-SPICY ROAST TURKEY

This bird prepared with our sweet-and-spicy dry rub will be a magnificent centerpiece for your table.

SERVES 8 • **HANDS-ON** 20 minutes • **TOTAL** 3 hours, 25 minutes

3 tablespoons kosher salt
2 tablespoons light brown sugar
1 tablespoon onion powder
1 tablespoon paprika
2 teaspoons ground ginger
2 teaspoons dry mustard
3/4 teaspoon cayenne pepper
1 (12-pound) fresh whole turkey
3 tablespoons canola oil
Kitchen string
2 tablespoons honey
1 tablespoon hot sauce (such as Tabasco)
3 cups water

1. Stir together the salt, brown sugar, onion powder, paprika, ginger, dry mustard, and cayenne pepper in a small bowl. Reserve 2 tablespoons of salt mixture.
2. Remove the giblets and neck from the turkey; reserve for another use. Pat the turkey dry, and remove the excess skin. Starting from the neck, loosen and lift the skin from the turkey without completely detaching it. Spread the remaining salt mixture evenly under the skin. Carefully replace the skin. Drizzle the skin with 2 tablespoons of the oil, and rub with the reserved 2 tablespoons salt mixture. Tie the ends of the legs together with kitchen string; tuck the wing tips under. Let stand at room temperature 1 hour, or refrigerate 12 to 24 hours. (If refrigerated, let the turkey stand at room temperature for 1 hour before cooking.)
3. Stir together the honey, hot sauce, and remaining 1 tablespoon oil in a small bowl until well blended.
4. Preheat the oven to 375°F. Place the rack in a roasting pan; coat the rack with cooking spray. Place the turkey on rack, and transfer to the oven. Add the water to the pan. Bake at 375°F for 1 hour and 10 minutes. Rotate the pan halfway (on the same rack), brush with half of the honey mixture, and continue baking until a meat thermometer inserted in the thickest portion of the thigh registers 165°F, about 25 more minutes. Remove the turkey from the oven, and brush with the remaining honey mixture. Let stand at least 30 minutes.

NOTE: You may skip brushing the turkey with the honey mixture when you rotate it if the turkey is already dark. Just brush the mixture on at the end.

HONEY-GLAZED SPICED CARROTS

Spiced carrots will soon be your family's most requested Thanksgiving side.

SERVES 8 • **HANDS-ON** 5 minutes • **TOTAL** 35 minutes

- **4 tablespoons unsalted butter, melted**
- **3 tablespoons honey**
- **1 tablespoon light brown sugar**
- **1½ teaspoons kosher salt**
- **½ teaspoon ground cinnamon**
- **¼ teaspoon ground nutmeg**
- **¼ teaspoon freshly ground black pepper**
- **2 pounds small carrots, peeled and trimmed**
- **1 tablespoon thinly sliced fresh chives**

1. Preheat the oven to 400°F. Stir together the melted butter, honey, brown sugar, salt, cinnamon, nutmeg, and pepper in a small bowl; reserve 2 tablespoons of mixture. Pour the remaining butter mixture over the carrots; toss to combine. Spread in a single layer on 2 baking sheets; bake at 400°F for 30 minutes.
2. Toss the roasted carrots with the reserved 2 tablespoons butter mixture; transfer to a serving platter. Sprinkle with the chives.

SLOW-COOKER GREEN BEANS

This recipe frees up precious stove-top space and reminds us of the traditional green beans our grandmothers used to make.

SERVES 8 • **HANDS-ON** 20 minutes • **TOTAL** 3 hours, 20 minutes

- **8 thick-cut bacon slices**
- **1 large yellow onion, sliced**
- **2 pounds fresh green beans, trimmed**
- **¼ cup reduced-sodium chicken broth**
- **2½ teaspoons kosher salt**
- **1 teaspoon freshly ground black pepper**
- **4 fresh thyme sprigs**

1. Cut 6 of the bacon slices into ½-inch pieces. Cook, stirring often, in a large skillet over medium-high until crispy, about 8 minutes. Transfer to a plate lined with paper towels to drain; reserve the drippings in the skillet. Crumble the cooked bacon, and set aside. Add the onion to the skillet; cook, stirring occasionally, until just tender, about 3 minutes. Stir in the green beans; cook, stirring often, 2 minutes.
2. Transfer the green bean mixture to a 5-quart slow cooker. Stir in the broth, salt, pepper, thyme sprigs, and 2 uncooked bacon slices. Cover and cook on HIGH until the beans are tender, about 3 hours. Discard the bacon and thyme; top with the crumbled cooked bacon.

Yeast Rolls

YEAST ROLLS

You can make the dough for these tender, buttery rolls the night before.

MAKES 16 rolls • **HANDS-ON** 20 minutes • **TOTAL** 9 hours, 20 minutes, includes chilling

- 1/2 cup warm water
- 1 (1/4-ounce) envelope active dry yeast
- 1/4 teaspoon granulated sugar
- 1 cup warm (110°F) milk
- 1/4 cup honey
- 1 large egg, beaten
- 1/2 cup melted salted butter, plus 3 tablespoons
- 1 1/2 teaspoons kosher salt
- 4 cups all-purpose flour

1. Combine the warm water, yeast, and sugar in a small bowl; let stand until the mixture bubbles, about 5 minutes.
2. Beat the warm milk, honey, egg, and 1/2 cup of the melted butter with a heavy-duty stand mixer on medium speed until well blended. Add the yeast mixture and salt; beat until combined. With the mixer running, gradually add the flour until well combined.
3. Transfer the dough to a bowl coated with cooking spray. Cover with plastic wrap, and chill 8 hours or overnight.
4. Lightly grease 2 (12-cup) muffin pans. Place the chilled dough on a lightly floured surface; punch the down dough into an 8-inch circle. Cut the dough into quarters. Cut each quarter into 4 wedges; roll each wedge into an 8-inch-long rope. Starting at the end, roll each rope into a spiral shape, and place in a prepared muffin cup. Cover the pans with plastic wrap; let rise in a warm place (80°F to 85°F), free from drafts, 45 minutes.
5. Preheat the oven to 400°F. Brush the rolls with 2 tablespoons of the melted butter; bake at 400°F until golden brown, 15 to 18 minutes. Cool on a wire rack. Brush with the remaining 1 tablespoon melted butter.

HERBED WILD RICE DRESSING

Wild rice, apples, and walnuts combine to make a dressing full of flavor and crunch.

SERVES 10 • **HANDS-ON** 15 minutes • **TOTAL** 40 minutes

- 5 sourdough or white bread slices, cut into 1/2-inch cubes
- 2 tablespoons unsalted butter, melted
- 2 tablespoons extra-virgin olive oil
- 1 cup chopped celery
- 1 medium-size red onion, diced
- 2 Honeycrisp or Fuji apples, diced
- 4 cups cooked wild rice
- 1 cup toasted walnuts, roughly chopped
- 2 tablespoons chopped fresh flat-leaf parsley
- 1 tablespoon chopped fresh sage
- 1 tablespoon fresh lemon juice
- 2 teaspoons kosher salt
- 1/2 teaspoon freshly ground black pepper
- 1/4 cup firmly packed fresh flat-leaf parsley leaves

1. Preheat the oven to 400°F. Toss the bread cubes with the melted butter in a medium bowl. Spread on a baking sheet, and bake until crispy and lightly browned, 5 to 8 minutes.
2. Heat the oil in a skillet over medium-high. Add the celery and onion; cook, stirring occasionally, until tender, about 8 minutes. Add the apples; cook, stirring occasionally, until the apples are crisp-tender and browned, 5 to 7 minutes. Stir in the toasted bread cubes, rice, walnuts, chopped parsley, chopped sage, lemon juice, salt, and pepper. Cook until heated through, about 3 minutes. Spoon onto a serving platter. Top with the parsley leaves.

GERMAN CHOCOLATE-PECAN PIE

If choosing between beloved German chocolate and gooey pecan pie is too difficult, then don't! You can have it all with this pie.

SERVES 8 • **HANDS-ON** 25 minutes • **TOTAL** 6 hours, 50 minutes, includes chilling

CRUST

1½ cups all-purpose flour
½ tablespoon granulated sugar
½ teaspoon table salt
¼ cup cold salted butter, cubed
¼ cup cold shortening, cubed
4 to 5 tablespoons ice water

CHOCOLATE FILLING

1 (4-ounce) German's sweet chocolate baking bar, coarsely chopped
½ cup salted butter
¾ cup granulated sugar
3 tablespoons all-purpose flour
⅛ teaspoon table salt
2 large eggs
1 (5-ounce) can evaporated milk
1 teaspoon vanilla extract

COCONUT-PECAN FILLING

½ cup packed light brown sugar
½ cup dark corn syrup
¼ cup salted butter, melted
2 large eggs
1 teaspoon vanilla extract
2 cups pecan halves and pieces, lightly toasted
⅔ cup sweetened flaked coconut

CHOCOLATE-COVERED PECANS

¾ cup milk chocolate chips
35 toasted pecan halves

1. Make the Crust: Stir together the flour, granulated sugar, and salt in a large bowl. Using a pastry blender, cut the butter and shortening cubes into the flour mixture until the mixture resembles small peas. Using a fork, gradually stir in 4 tablespoons of the ice water, stirring until the dry ingredients are moistened and the dough begins to form a ball and pulls away from the sides of the bowl, adding up to 1 more tablespoon of water, if necessary. Turn the dough out onto a work surface; shape and flatten into a disk. Wrap in plastic wrap, and chill 1 to 24 hours.
2. Preheat the oven to 425°F. Unwrap the chilled dough disk, and place on a lightly floured surface. Let the dough stand at room temperature until slightly softened, about 5 minutes. Sprinkle the dough with flour, and roll into a 13-inch circle. Fit the dough into a 9-inch glass pie plate. Trim the dough, leaving ½-inch overhang; fold the edges under, and crimp. Prick the bottom and sides 8 to 10 times with a fork. Freeze 20 minutes. Line the piecrust with parchment paper, and fill with pie weights or dried beans. Bake in the preheated oven 14 minutes. Remove the weights and parchment paper, and bake until the crust has lost its raw dough sheen, 5 to 7 minutes. Transfer to a wire rack, and cool completely, about 30 minutes. Reduce the oven temperature to 350°F.
3. Make the Chocolate Filling: Microwave the German's sweet chocolate and butter in a microwave-safe bowl at HIGH 1 to 1½ minutes, until melted and smooth, stirring at 30-second intervals. Whisk in the granulated sugar, flour, and salt. Add the eggs, 1 at a time, whisking just until blended after each addition. Whisk in the evaporated milk and vanilla until blended. Pour the chocolate filling into the prepared piecrust. Shield the edges with aluminum foil to prevent excessive browning, and place on a rimmed baking sheet. Bake at 350°F for 30 minutes. (Pie will be partially baked.)
4. Make the Coconut-Pecan Filling: Whisk together the brown sugar, corn syrup, melted butter, eggs, and vanilla until blended. Stir in the pecans and coconut. Beginning at the outer edges of the partially baked chocolate filling, carefully spoon the Coconut-Pecan Filling over chocolate filling, and immediately return the pie to the oven. Bake until the crust is golden and the center is set, 35 to 40 minutes, shielding the edges with aluminum foil to prevent excessive browning, if necessary. Cool the pie completely on a wire rack, about 3 hours.
5. Make the Chocolate-Covered Pecans: Microwave the chocolate chips in a small microwave-safe bowl at HIGH, 30 to 45 seconds or until melted and smooth. Dip the lower half of each pecan into the melted chocolate, allowing the excess chocolate to drip back into the bowl, and place on a parchment paper-lined baking sheet. Chill until the chocolate is firm, about 30 minutes. Arrange the Chocolate-Covered Pecans decoratively around the outer edge of the pie. (You may have some left over.)

TABLESCAPES 3 WAYS

No matter the size or shape of your dining table, an inspired Thanksgiving scape is within reach. Take our tips for designing an elegant look that will suit your needs.

❶ Setting a long, rectangular table is a balancing act. The arrangement should run the length of the surface. For this twist on the traditional cornucopia, choose fresh fall veggies, fruits, flowers, and foliage. Accentuate an attractive wood surface with layers. Make your own runner using fabric from a crafts store. Be sure to buy enough fabric so the runner will extend about 12 inches beyond both ends of your table. ❷ At a round table, all eyes are drawn to the center. The goal is to create a pretty, low-profile arrangement that encourages dinner conversation. For Thanksgiving, skip the everyday white tablecloth and pick a rich autumnal hue. Layering linens in contrasting colors, such as teal and marigold, gives this table a warm and inviting appeal. ❸ For an oval table, rather than using a typical vase, choose a conversation piece such as a family heirloom. This silver bowl was filled with flowers in varying heights and placed diagonally for an unexpected touch. Place mats can feel casual, so if your undressed table is beautiful, build around the au naturel vibe. Small, vibrant accents—such as these lavender napkins—provide sophisticated bursts of color.

2

3

INDEX

ACKNOWLEDGMENTS

LOWCOUNTRY HUNT LUNCH

DESIGNER: Catherine Brown Paterson/Catherine Brown Paterson Design www.catherinebrownpaterson.com

PHOTOGRAPHER: Upwind Studios/ Rich King, Mt. Pleasant, SC www.upwindstudios.com

PROPS: Leontine Linens placemats and napkins, www.leontinelinens.com

Croghan's Jewel Box, Charleston, SC, www.croghansjewelbox.com: Glass vase with pewter stag's head; Pewter hunt stirrup cups made for Croghan's with Lowcountry alligator embellishment; Antique silver place card holders; Silver ice bucket; Croghan's Goldbug Collection on cocktail napkins

Vieuxtemps, Charleston, SC, www.vieuxtemps.net: Gien china place setting (Sologne Pattern); Pewter oyster salt cellar and spoon set; Horn salt and pepper shaker, Waterford wine hocks, Lucite barware wine glasses, Portugal vase on the bar was commissioned by Vieuxtemps to commemorate the city of Charleston, SC, with the cotton motif at bottom made with local Sega Palms, Staghorn embroidered linen cocktail napkins on the bar

The Original Old Charleston Joggling Board Co., Charleston, SC, www.jogglingboard.com

HOMEOWNERS: Jill and Billy Ford, Sullivan's Island, SC

COTTAGE BREAKFAST

DESIGNER: James Farmer/James Farmer Designs www.jamesfarmer.com

PHOTOGRAPHER: Emily Followill

DINNER ON THE DOCK

DESIGNER: Joni Vanderslice/J. Banks Design, www.jbanksdesign.com

PHOTOGRAPHER: Ingalls Photo/ Southern Coastal Living for Gibbs Smith

LAKE HOUSE SUPPER

DESIGNER: Julia Reed

PHOTOGRAPHER: Hector Manuel Sanchez

PORCH PARTY

DESIGNER: Tara Guérard/Tara Guérard Soirée, www.taraguerard.com, www.taraguerardsoiree.com

PHOTOGRAPHER: Laurey W. Glenn

AUTUMN DINNER PARTY

DESIGNER: Kimberly Schlegel Whitman, www.kimberlywhitman.com

PHOTOGRAPHER: John Cain Photography/John Cain Sargent

WORK YOUR SURROUNDINGS

PHOTOGRAPHERS: Dan Arnold (patio), Scott Womack (beach), Scott Womack (small space), Kelsey Foster Wilson (backyard)

MARDI GRAS IN THE GARDEN

PHOTOGRAPHER: Dan Arnold

PROPS: Halo Home linens www.halohomebyksw.com

FLORAL ARRANGEMENT: Carly Cylinder, www.flourla.com

VICTORY BANQUET

PHOTOGRAPHER: John Cain Photography/John Cain Sargent

TEA PARTY

DESIGNER: Gretchen Black/ Greyhouse Design www.greyhousedesign.com

PHOTOGRAPHER: Gretchen Black

SPRING DINNER PARTY

DESIGNER: Heather Chadduck Hillegas/Heather Chadduck Interiors & Textiles, www.heatherchadduck.com, www.heatherchadducktextiles.com

PHOTOGRAPHER: Hector Manuel Sanchez

OUTDOOR EASTER LUNCH, MOTHER'S DAY LUNCH

DESIGNER: Kevin Walsh/Bear-Hill Interiors, www.bearhillinteriors.com

PHOTOGRAPHER: Rett Peek

VALENTINE'S DAY BREAKFAST

DESIGNER: Kristin Peake/Kristen Peake Interiors www.kristinpeakeinteriors.com

STYLISTS: Amanda Crowner, Lindsey Foundos

PHOTOGRAPHER: Tracy Marshall Photography